Amelia Holowaty Krales

KAITLYN TIFFANY

Everything I Need I Get from You

Kaitlyn Tiffany is a staff writer at *The Atlantic*, where she covers technology and internet culture. She was previously on the same beat at *Vox*'s consumer vertical, The Goods, after starting her career writing about pop culture, fandom, and online community at *The Verge*. She lives in Brooklyn.

For Sophie

EVERYTHING I NEED

I GET FROM YOU

MCD × FSG Originals
Farrar, Straus and Giroux
New York

EVERYTHING I NEED I GET FROM YOU

How Fangirls Created the Internet as We Know It

Kaitlyn Tiffany

MCD × FSG Originals
Farrar, Straus and Giroux
120 Broadway, New York 10271

Printed in the United States of America
First edition, 2022

Half-title-page image by TopRated / Shutterstock.com.
Dedication page images by Turkan Rahimli / Shutterstock.com.

Library of Congress Cataloging-in-Publication Data
Names: Tiffany, Kaitlyn, 1993– author.
Title: Everything I need I get from you : how fangirls created the Internet as we know it / Kaitlyn Tiffany.
Description: First edition. | New York : MCD × FSG Originals, Farrar, Straus and Giroux, [2022] | Includes bibliographical references.
Identifiers: LCCN 2021061246 | ISBN 9780374539184 (paperback)
Subjects: LCSH: Internet and women. | Internet—Social aspects. | Fans (Persons) | Women and mass media.
Classification: LCC HQ1178 .T54 2022 | DDC 004.67/8082—dc23/eng/20220107
LC record available at https://lccn.loc.gov/2021061246

Designed by Janet Evans-Scanlon

10 9 8 7 6 5 4 3 2 1

Life will be happier for the on-line individual because the people with whom one interacts most strongly will be selected more by commonality of interests and goals than by accidents of proximity.

—J.C.R. LICKLIDER AND ROBERT W. TAYLOR,
"The Computer as a Communication Device," 1968

if i die tonight tell one direction I'll see them in hell

—LISETTE HERNANDEZ, Twitter, 2014

Contents

EVERYTHING I NEED

I GET FROM YOU

Introduction

IF YOU CAN STAND IT, I'M GOING TO DESCRIBE A SIX-SECOND video.

It goes like this: the British boy band One Direction is onstage, on tour, in the summer of 2015. You can't actually see them—the camera is too far back in the crowd. You can only *kind of* see one of them, the then twenty-one-year-old Irish singer and sometime guitar player Niall Horan, bottle-blond in a black T-shirt, blown up on a stadium monitor and washed out into a bright white mess owing to a crappy cell phone camera attempting to record another screen. You can hear a downbeat in a sweet if unremarkable ballad about young love from the band's fourth album, *Four*, and then you see Horan wringing his hands as he steps to the mic to sing the line "We took a chance." It comes out wrong and we'll never know why. The *a* is an *o*. He does not usually do this. He usually sings "chance." Odd, but you wouldn't necessarily notice or care if it weren't for the fact that—in the tiny space between this phrase and the next—you then hear another voice, coming from at least several yards behind the camera and begging, credulously, in a molar-crunching scream: "What the fuck is a chonce?" She must know. She won't. The end.

This video was posted originally on the Twitter-owned short-form video app Vine shortly after the concert, and was adopted as the One Direction fandom's latest and greatest in-joke. It was reblogged and retweeted, the footage was downloaded and reposted. Within a few weeks of the first upload, Harry Styles acknowledged the moment onstage, singing his line of the song as usual, then tossing to Horan for his part, and muttering into the mic, "But don't say 'chonce.'" At that, the crowd screams as if they have just found out they're alive. On Tumblr, fans shared this clip—with all-caps "ASDFGHJKL" and similar expressions—and from then on, there were clips of Horan at subsequent shows, nodding and laughing as tens of thousands of people sing at him, in unison, "chonce." Though Vine has since been shuttered, "WTF is a chonce" persists on YouTube, where the comments years later are one-note: "Why do I still find this funny even though I've seen it millions of times?" The joke is *not* funny, but it is for insiders, and it has a special bittersweetness to it because the original footage was taken just a few months before One Direction's final public performance.

The internet's ephemera is often better left unexamined, not just because so much of it ends up having a disgusting or depressing backstory, but because so much more of it is impossible to explain at all. One Direction was known for its onstage mishaps and physical accidents, made funnier by their contrast with the band's otherwise meticulously managed and physically grueling stadium tours. There are entire supercuts of Harry Styles falling over in catastrophic fashion, and of sophomoric pranks that involve two or three of the band members ganging up on another. Yet "chonce" became the single-syllable talisman, clung to even after everything was all over.

Four years after the first clip went viral, I scrolled past a tweet from an account with the handle @isasdfghjkls:

> me: :(
> niall: we took a chonce
> me: :)

I retweeted it, even though the majority of the people who follow my Twitter account would have no idea what it was referring to.[1] It was a plain statement of fact—they could edify themselves if they wanted to live better. "We took a chonce" is so dumb—so pure a joke at the expense of someone who can take one and would love to—the weight of life lifts off of my shoulders when I'm reminded of it. Watching this video smacks me with a lingering hit of dopamine, like a gumball-machine-sticky-hand landing on a windowpane. When I need to, I can watch "We took a chonce" and experience what some people feel when they put their faces in front of a seasonal affective disorder lamp. What a different sort of person feels when they jog. If it so happens that we arrive at a dystopian future in which always-on screens are embedded directly into our retinas, I'll spend every crowded train ride and mandatory all-hands meeting and one-year-old's birthday party washing my eyes with "We took a chonce." That's the only way I can describe what One Direction does for me without saying something as useless as "I love them."

Even now, the serendipity of the Tumblr feed leads me to treasures: a watercolor painting of "WTF is a chonce?" in curling bridesmaid script; a flyer with tear-off strips at the bottom that read "Chonce"—get it? Take one!—supposedly hung up by a pair of friends in their local bowling alley. "The only problematic thing about my fav is he can't pronounce 'chance,'" reads another post reblogged into my feed. "Other than that he's a chill little sun drop that loves sports."[2] A commemorative T-shirt cost me a mere $19 plus shipping on Etsy—"WTF is a chonce?" printed in white bubble letters, on pale blue. If you're the type of person who still peruses Urban Dictionary, you might notice that "chonce" is defined there: "An alternative for the word 'chance.' Commonly used by One Direction's Niall Horan."

• • •

A COLDLY ASSEMBLED CONSUMER PRODUCT, ONE DIRECTION was an idea that Simon Cowell takes credit for having while serving as a judge on the British reality competition TV show *The X Factor* in 2010. The five individual boys he met on the show were too bland and young and poorly dressed to make sense on their own, so he pushed them together and made them into a litter of commercially viable puppies. They released their first single in 2011, in the moment that social media was revealing itself as our new shared reality. It was the year teenagers started getting Twitter accounts, which happened just as Tumblr started selling advertising, which was around the same time that Instagram launched and exploded and was acquired by Facebook, while YouTube was cleaning up its design so that young people would have an easier time falling into algorithmic wormholes. One Direction fans—who seemed mostly to be young women—were mocked for embracing a boy band, an inauthentic thing pieced together for money. They also used, as the means of their expression, a collection of websites that profited off them yet again.

"Women are the internet, and the internet is women," the editors of *n+1* announced to start their winter issue in 2013.[3] "Supposing the internet was a woman—what then?" the writer Moira Weigel asked in *Logic* in the spring of 2018. The loose, woven structure of the internet, which enables things like whisper networks, reflexive personal sharing, and complex storytelling, has been more useful to women and marginalized groups than it has been to men, Weigel suggested. Men have always had easy access to other, more streamlined types of communication. But she cautioned readers not to romanticize the internet. It's home to bad actors and misinformation, both given reach they would not have otherwise. It's also where women are expected to perform tasks they've always been expected to perform, she noted: posing, preening, affirming, doing things for other people in exchange for the feeling of being loved. Women are the ones fueling the engine "for the accumulation of vast piles of capital," Weigel wrote, and they are not the ones generally benefiting from it. "Yet the internet also provides tools that can be used as alternatives," she pivoted. "In this sense, the internet is ambivalent. Fortunately, inhabiting ambivalence is something that women are good at, having had to practice it for so long."[4]

Any examination of online fandom has to be approached with the same ambivalence. The cultural phenomena of fandom and the internet are braided together—one can't be fully understood without the other. Both, in providing structure, have also produced chaos. Both, in providing meaning, have sometimes oversupplied it. Yet fans' role in shaping our present culture, politics, and social life is often overlooked, and the roots of this oversight go back decades. When listing off pivotal subcultural movements, hardly anyone would think of fangirls. The midcentury sociologists who invented subcultural studies even literally considered rebellion the province of middle- and working-class young men, spending their postwar discretionary income on weird outfits and aggressive haircuts; girls—who at the time were screaming over the Beatles or sitting at home watching soap operas with their mothers—didn't jump out as a compelling subject for study. Or, these activities did not seem subcultural. They looked generic.

Yet a fangirl still exists in contradiction to the dominant culture. She's not considered normal or sane; her refusal to accept things the way they are is one of her defining characteristics. She is dropping out of the mainstream even while she embraces a thing that is as mainstream as a thing can get. Publicly, the fangirl wastes money and refuses to make her time useful. With the advent of social media, she started publishing thousands of messages to idols who would never read them. The constant, ambient disapproval of the general population can sequester fangirls joyfully, in semiprivate spaces with like-minded and creative groups of fast friends; or dismally, in semiprivate spaces that are still open to scorn, and therefore lean on self-policing or outward-facing aggression to protect the boundaries of a sensitive community. All of this happens on platforms with a financial incentive to produce more and more of it, but not necessarily to foster its best and most inspiring characteristics.

The labor of fans, which makes no sense because it is performed for free, can confuse even friendly onlookers. In 2011, Maciej Cegłowski, founder of the bookmarking site Pinboard, was one of the first technologists to notice the business opportunity fans represented.[5] He saw that fans of various TV shows and film franchises and musical groups had created elaborate tagging systems on rival site Delicious, and he saw that Yahoo's corporate takeover of Delicious, and YouTube's subsequent takeover of the shell of *that* Delicious, had ended in the destruction of many of the tagging features that were so important to them. Fans lost the ability to build up vast collections of tags, sort them, and search them, which had been critical to the project of keeping open records of a fandom's history as it developed. So, in a stroke of genius, Cegłowski offered them the opportunity to do that somewhere else. He published a mass-editable Google Doc and asked all kinds of people, who wouldn't typically have any say or hand in the construction of the platforms they would later be expected to use and generate profit for, to come in and tell him what features they would need if they were to make Pinboard their new bookmarking home. The Google Doc "ended up being fifty-two pages long," he recounted breathlessly on his blog. "At times, there were so many people editing the document that it tucked its tail between its legs and went into a panicked 'read only' mode. Even the mighty engineers at Google couldn't cope with the sustained attention of fandom." The Google Doc had rules, color codes, a full index, and a promise not to write any fanfiction about Cegłowski unless he gave the okay. "The editors of this document were anonymous, but they somehow seemed to know each other," Cegłowski wrote. He titled his account of the whole affair "Fan Is a Tool-Using Animal," and concluded it with praise for what he saw as a DIY, punk-y energy: "Fans transgress. Fans never sold out, man!"[6]

Cegłowski's praise of fandom as a practice became a more common perspective throughout the 2010s in part because of pro-pop trends in music criticism and pro-girl trends in marketing, but also significantly because of the way highly visible online pop music fandoms played to and existed within the media's imagination of liberal politics, as well as its fascination with the overt goodness of youth. The everywhereness of fans was remarkable; they seemed to accomplish anything they wanted. But fans are not magical, nor are they a unified group. They are people. Online fandom can be progressive, and it can also be reactionary; it can foster creativity, and it can also smooth away individuality; it can create new tools and compel fascinating action just as easily as it can provide the dull, repetitive skills required for activities like media manipulation and harassment. The One

Direction fandom has done all of this, and it has meant all sorts of things to all kinds of people who share one particular affinity but might not necessarily share much else.

OFTEN DESCRIBED AS THE THIRD BRITISH INVASION—POST- Spice Girls and post-Beatles—or part of a new 1990s-like boy band boom, One Direction was unlike either of those phenomena. The closest thing One Direction has to a predecessor is not any transatlantic act from a previous century or the tightly choreographed boy bands of the generation prior, but Justin Bieber—discovered on YouTube in 2007, made famous by young women on MySpace, elevated to stardom by the relentless tweeting of millions of people who had boundless affection and plenty of free time. Bieber's first album, *My World*, released in 2009, debuted at number six on the *Billboard* charts. One Direction released their first single in September 2011 and arrived in the United States in February 2012. A few weeks later, *Up All Night* made them the first British group to enter the U.S. charts at number one with a debut album. (It took four years for Beatlemania to hit the United States, and even longer for it to spread globally.) Their next three albums did the same, which had never been done by any group at all. "We all sat and watched the film of the Beatles arriving in America, and to be honest, that was really like us," Harry Styles said in 2014. "None of us think we're in the same league as them music-wise. We'd be fools if we did . . . Fame-wise, it's probably even bigger."[7]

Five boys: for the time being, they all dress approximately the same, like mall kids who have only ever seen zip-up hoodies and loose khaki pants. Harry Styles is the youngest, with a baby face and the liveliest hair; he is the focus of tabloids and gossip accounts because he is often publicly dating. Liam Payne has the second-floppiest hairdo and a sweet obsession with rules, as well as an expressed fear that nobody will ever love him separately from his fame. Niall Horan is the Irish and fake-blond one, with the most boyish sense of humor—a love of farting and pulling down pants. Nominally, he knows how to play the guitar. Zayn Malik is the most interested in asserting that this is not a regular boy band, it's a "cool" boy band, and he is regarded as *the mysterious one*, possibly because he is quiet and possibly because the media is inclined to cast the band's sole Muslim member as the odd one out. Louis Tomlinson is the oldest, the least often spotlighted singer, the one with a longtime unfamous girlfriend, and the class clown, pulling pranks and shouting swear words.

Before One Direction, becoming a pop star took time, sacrifice, restriction, discipline. The boys of NSYNC lived on $35 per diems under the thumb of a notoriously manipulative and coercive manager who also stole tens of millions of dollars from the Backstreet Boys and wound up in prison.[8] The Jonas Brothers, the next iteration of the boy band idyll, were the Disney-approved version, expected to give moving testimonials about their commitment to remaining chaste and drug-free.[9] One Direction had a punishing touring schedule and a strict album a year as contracted deliverables, but they were never beholden to the traditions of the genre in quite the same way—they were always permitted to eschew choreography and matching outfits and conversations about purity rings. They were "anarchic," Cowell said in their 2013 documentary.[10] They had tattoos. They had sex. They even smoked! Niall Horan, unfamiliar as he was with the way Irish slang would translate in an American cultural context, was filmed shouting at some photographers at an airport that they were a "shower of cunts," which became another fandom catchphrase.[11] This was all allowed, it seemed, mostly because it was what the fans wanted.

By the time One Direction reached the United States, they were the biggest subculture on Tumblr, a platform designed to let affections snowball through a dizzying system of additive reblogs and visual stockpiling. Each member of the band had well over 1 million followers on Twitter. Within a few years the platform was defined by the rivalry between Justin Bieber and One Direction fans, and the passions of fandom were impossible for regular users not to notice. In 2015, a four-year-old tweet from Louis Tomlinson—"Always in my heart @Harry_Styles. Yours sincerely, Louis"—was retweeted enough times for it to become the second-most retweeted message in the site's history—edging out Barack Obama's 2012 reelection victory tweet but falling short of Ellen DeGeneres's Oscar selfie.[12] At that point, it had been retweeted over 700,000 times. A number that's now more than 2.8 million. (More on that never-ending story later.) This was a habit of the mythmaking One Direction fandom, which enjoyed selecting and recirculating key moments of its own history even as it was still unfolding. Another was from Niall Horan, in January 2010: "applied for xfactorhope it all wrks out," he tweeted six months before he'd even heard the words "One Direction" himself. The fans dug it up *after* they'd made him famous, and by the time I started going to One Direction concerts, it had become common—maybe even played out—to print poster-size enlargements of the tweet and wave them at Horan if he looked your way in the crowd.

In public, fangirls were a joke: a ball of hysteria, so noisy! On the internet, the joke was on everybody else. The Rihanna Navy moved over from a small co-run blog to a Twitter account called @RihannaDaily in 2009, the same year that the biggest fan accounts for Beyoncé and Lady Gaga appeared. At the time, Twitter had not yet decided what to be. These early Twitter-using fans often came from the cultural powerhouse of Black Twitter, or from insular fandom spaces like LiveJournal and Yahoo Groups, and initially found themselves in small, tightly knit clusters, discussing the movements of their heroes in circular conversations. They came up with the internet-age semantic convention of using an abstract plural pronoun even when speaking alone. As in, "We have no choice but to stan." As their circles grew, they realized they could disrupt conversation and funnel attention at will, taking over the Trending Topics sidebar whenever they had a whim to. Eventually, they settled into a rhythm—Tumblr was the confusing and therefore secluded site for longer-form conversations and strategy sessions, while Twitter was the faster-paced site for a public-facing display, where they showed off their numbers and their no-limit capacity for posting.

When One Direction *lost* in the finals of *The X Factor*, its nascent fandom mimicked what previous fan groups had done but made it bigger and faster. "They lost *The X Factor* but won the world," fans repeated to themselves like a mantra, willing the dream to life. From the beginning, their efforts hinged on direct participation from the stars they were centered on, which the One Direction boys provided in the form of intimacies, inside jokes, and regular online conversation—they disclosed how many hours they'd slept, the type of cereal they'd eaten and at what time, the game shows and cheesy film franchises they watched to turn off their brains. They spent so much time talking to their fans in blurry behind-the-scenes livestreams and casual, crackling Twitter threads that some fans were genuinely shocked when they were unwelcome at Niall Horan's nephew's baptism.[13] They'd never been uninvited before.

FOR ME, ONE DIRECTION ARRIVED JUST IN TIME—LIKE BEING yanked out of the crosswalk a second before the bus plows through. Or like waking up from a stress dream and realizing that your teeth have not fallen out: *Thank goodness, and why was I so scared?*

I was nineteen, home for the summer, working in the mall food court. I loved school, but I hated the event of *college*, and couldn't find a place to insert myself in a fraternity-dominated social landscape. Most Saturday nights, I would put on something ugly, drink two beers in a fraternity annex and wait for someone to say something I could throw a fit about, then leave. I watched so much television my freshman year, I received a warning email about exceeding my limit for campus internet usage. I hadn't kissed anyone, and I'd made only a handful of friends I wasn't sure I even liked. At the same time, I was obsessed with a coworker at the mall who was older and generally cruel. I'd driven home most weekends just to make minimum wage elbow to elbow with him, pulling weak espresso shots and drizzling caramel syrup over whipped cream. When I wasn't doing that, I was stewing on Tumblr, scrolling through moody imagery and photos of feminist-lite prose tattooed into rib cages. The year was a bad one for me in general, and I didn't have any idea why I—the gleaming try-hard of suburbia!—was suddenly failing at essentially everything.

But I still liked the feeling of being taken care of by my parents, sinking back into the arrangement of being one of four children, all girls, taken on outings and lectured for this or that. I still wanted to be a child, and to enjoy childish things. It was August, and the heat was insane. We weren't a summer activities family, apart from the travel soccer leagues we played in every year, but we were a movie theater family. So my mom's minivan took us to a matinee showing of the One Direction documentary *This Is Us*. My younger sisters were already fans, but I wasn't. I didn't care about anything except the air-conditioning and the snacks and the fact that I wouldn't be paying, driving the car, or trying to be charming. I could just slump, maybe sleep, and occasionally wake up to ask someone to dump some more popcorn into the paper napkin on my lap.

Here's what I saw at first: five boys, impossible to differentiate. Boring. The songs blend together. There's too much shiny brown hair. But then, for whatever reason, One Direction decides to go camping. This is a physical comedy sequence—why would these boys know how to set up tents? (Liam does know, because competence is his signature.) When it gets dark, they sit around a fire and talk about how they'll "always be a part of each other's growing up," and will *probably* stay friends forever. Then Louis says something incredible, which is that he anticipates someday being forgotten by most of the world, but that he hopes to be remembered, by "a mom telling her daughter" about the band she loved when she was young. "They just had fun, they were just normal guys, but terrible, terrible dancers." At that, I felt a jolt. My covetousness of approval from men my age, maybe, or my sort of saccharine interest in intimate lifelong friendship, or my deepest desire, which was for nothing to fundamentally change—some combination of these things produced an outsized reaction to a twenty-one-year-old boy describing what he wants as the legacy of his time on earth: to stay in touch with his boys, for women to recall him sometimes as they age. It's not any easier to explain than other kinds of infatuation. In fact, it's harder, because it wasn't as if I'd developed a crush—in fact, I generally found Louis the least charming of the five. I'd only been enchanted by this one little idea of his, tossed off so casually.

It took a while for it to sink in. But a few months later, I sat in a high school friend's car in a parking lot outside of a Red Robin in Ohio, near the small art college where she was studying graphic design. We were dehydrated and exhausted, depleted from a night of celebrating both Halloween and her twenty-first birthday. It was a weekend together that was about to end—I was going to get on a Greyhound bus back to a college campus where I still loved no one and was making no progress toward building an identity for myself that wasn't tied to sitting in cars in parking lots of chain restaurants with people I'd known all my life. On the radio, One Direction was singing about their mothers and sisters. My friend was already a big-time fan, so she knew whose vocal part was which. She picked them out quietly, forehead on the steering wheel. "The story of my life, I take her home, I drive all night to keep her warm," Harry Styles shouted—as she informed me. "The story of my life, I give her hope," he said next. If I focus, I can put myself back in that car and feel the hot rush of gratitude and surprise. I can see my oldest friend's hand on the dial, turning it up without comment while our waves of nausea passed.

ONE OF THE MORE EVOCATIVE PIECES OF MODERN ART I have seen in my life was posted to Tumblr shortly after One Direction's final performance together.[14] It started as an illustration from a 1967 issue of the DC comic *Young Romance*, the one showing a woman in a purple turtleneck with a close-cropped auburn bob, holding red manicured nails up to her lips while two long tears stretch down her face, out from under a pair of sunglasses. Reflected in her shades, usually, are two images of a couple kissing—she's torn up about it. Romantic jealousy, captioned "Can any man *really* be trusted?" But in this Photoshopped version, the image that bounces off the plastic is a GIF of Louis Tomlinson and Harry Styles hugging.

This was an act of public affection the two had abstained from for several years at that point, hoping to discourage the popular fandom theory that they were secretly in love ("Larry Stylinson" in shorthand). But apparently moved by the significance of the night and the moment, they gave in to feeling and embraced. In this remix, the woman's tears are of surprised joy rather than romantic betrayal. "I remember the whole fandom feeling so happy," the artist, Maëlys Wandelst, told me when I emailed her years after she posted the image.[15] She'd made it in Photoshop in under an hour while sitting in bed. It was just a hug, but now it is *the* hug. The hug, the hug, the hug. Scroll through Tumblr long enough and you'll see—there's only one hug that needs no further identification. (Even the day *before* the hug's anniversary is celebrated every year on Tumblr, with well wishes of a happy Hug Eve.) The darker elements of the story are missing from the meme. You can't see how the Louis and Harry fanfiction community was subsumed by the Louis and Harry *truther* community, or how a conspiracy theory unfurled over the course of several years, incorporating new villains at random. At one level, looking at this image is a pure and singular sensory experience, like carbonation. It reminds me of having a crush. But looking closer, as part of the subculture that would really understand it, it reminds me of years of conflict and paranoia—it reminds me that something as beautiful as One Direction, brought to the internet, can somehow produce *years* of conflict and paranoia.

This is not actually a book about One Direction, for a couple of reasons: I don't think they'd appreciate it, and, as much as I love them, they are not so interesting. (They are boys, and we are the same age.) It's not a book about Twitter or Tumblr or the hundreds of years of technological innovation that brought us to free GIF-making software either. What I would like it to be is a book that explains why I and millions of others needed something like One Direction as badly as we did, and how the things we did in response to that need changed the online world for just about everybody who spends their time in it. The people, many of them young women, who catapulted One Direction from reality show failure to international pop stars did so with methods that had never been seen on such a scale before, and with a dedication and single-mindedness that defied easy understanding. They catalogued every wince and wink for years on end. They sent threats of violence to girlfriends and to journalists. They were warm and witty and generous, sharing in-jokes and spare dollars for iTunes downloads. They were cruel and stupid; they schismed and broke down. Like many of us, they had a habit of needing more than they could get, and of giving too much of themselves in spaces where they were unlikely to be rewarded.

One Direction fans, locked in a never-ending death match with Justin Bieber fans, pioneered the idea of a Twitter stan war. On Tumblr, they created new language, spoke in code, and popularized the core phraseology of our time, including "I want [X] to run me over with their car." The artifacts of their elaborate conspiracy theories published daily to Tumblr read stranger than a Pynchon novel. They invented new methods for getting what they wanted, which included such methodical and bureaucratic techniques as teaching international acquaintances how to fake American IP addresses and thereby accrue Spotify and YouTube streams that would count on the *Billboard* charts.[16] They were driven by passion, but also by a desire for control. Because of their role in promoting and financially supporting the artists they love, these fans have maintained a creator's hand throughout those artists' careers, treating them as collaborative projects. They take responsibility for every setback and share in the thrill of every success.

When I sat down in front of my Tumblr dashboard as an adult, looking at it for the first time as a reporter rather than a participant, I wrote two questions: *How did fans use the internet to create and accrue a new kind of power?* And then, *What are the characteristics and limitations of that power?* These questions cut at multiple levels; the way individuals experience fandom in their personal lives is much different from the way fans experience a community together, which is different from the way we *all* experience fandom, in its collective version, at its most visible and insistent. One Direction arrived at the same time as commercial social media, and they rose at the same time as a new wave of anxiety, isolation, and fractured attention. Their success in that context doesn't strike me as a coincidence, but the mystery of how so many people were able to find happiness through watching them and talking about them deserves documentation. So, too, does the unfortunate side effect of that joy, which is its commodification—fanfiction websites cut deals with major film studios, brands trade merch for tweets from major fan accounts, "fan" is at this point an industry term for "consumer." If fangirls seem powerful, that power still comes from taciturn platforms that want them almost solely for the ease of selling ads that align with their interests—it can be taken away at any time. See Tumblr's acquisition by Verizon, which led to mass purges of "NSFW" fan content and is only a recent example in a long history of censorship in fan spaces.[17] Or the way moderation systems on Twitter and YouTube implicitly and explicitly favor rich copyright holders over those who might appeal to principles of fair use, placing strict boundaries around the way fans are permitted to communicate.[18] As one-dimensional "girl power" rhetoric and corporate feminism have once again succeeded in leeching real meaning from the women's movement, pop stars have also appropriated it for their own use, to charm greater allegiance from fans by embracing an extremely narrow idea of what it means to support women: supporting the beautiful women they've turned into stars, defending them on the internet by lashing out against anybody who would criticize them.

What can we expect under these conditions? Within the current arrangement, with full command of the tools now available, with the best possible understanding of the promise and limitations of the platforms that presently exist, years ahead of everyone else, fans wield a specific and fragile kind of power. What do we all stand to lose if it slips out of their grasp? And if they manage to hold on to it—well, what then?

MY FAVORITE ONE DIRECTION SONG IS FROM THE BAND'S fifth album, *Made in the A.M.*, released in November 2015, shortly before the start of their indefinite hiatus. It's called "I Want to Write You a Song," and it is earnest to the point of being nearly unpleasant. It really teeters on the edge. It's the discomfort of an adult writing a love letter in crayon, and I like it mostly because of the way it explains to me, in clear terms, my most enduring and childish hopes. "I want to write you a song," Niall Horan informs me matter-of-factly. "One to make your heart remember me." This is sort of the classic definition of a lullaby. "Any time I'm gone, you can listen to my voice and sing along." Harry Styles and Louis Tomlinson would like to write me a song as well—and lend me their coats, or so they say. "So when the world is cold, you'll have a hiding place you can go." Liam Payne is going to build me a boat—it's so my heart won't sink. This is all so generous, it's hard to believe I deserve it. The twist, as revealed in the song's chorus, is that I might. "Everything I need I get from you," the four of them say to me in turn. (Zayn Malik left the group with a farewell Facebook post, eight months prior to this song's release.)

Of course, this is too much. This is not a normal thing to say. This would not be a very mature thing to feel. It's pretty twisted, actually, playing as it does on the existence of an uncountable number of parasocial relationships, and each time I hear it, I think about the teenage fear I was swimming in when I went to see that documentary. But I also think about how much fun I've had, and how many times I've been surprised by what I've seen. For every disappointment or flare-up of viciousness, there have been days and days and years on end when most people who love One Direction feel only that, and it leads them to a desire to create things:

art, writing, music, community, funny videos of people screaming. "One Direction reminds me that love, joy, giddiness, even hysteria are crucibles of intelligence," the novelist Samantha Hunt wrote on *The Cut* the year that song came out. "There's a darkness in this light music that stirs thoughts of life."[19] If I'm really honest, I like One Direction because their music reminds me of myself. I'm nineteen and I'm not nineteen; I get to hold the two images side by side and think about the ways in which I'm changing and the ways in which I will always be the same.

"I Want to Write You a Song" is a promise and an apology. Dripping with proactive nostalgia, it seems to admit that this is the last time we will be written a song, even though members of the band have always publicly insisted that they are only taking a break, embracing an opportunity to nurture their individual strengths and pursue divergent artistic interests. It's the coded language of the end of a romance—keenly felt but ultimately untrue. *I'll care about you forever. This will always matter as much as it does now.* It can't and won't! It's fitting because One Direction is just a band: special to the people who love it, ordinary to everyone else. The song, sweet as it is, has a cool remove to it that inclines me to believe that the performers agree. This music will not be remembered as particularly innovative. These stadium tours will be eclipsed; these chart records will inevitably be broken.

The legacy is something else: the people who took the paragon of a commercial product and made it the foundational text of a new kind of culture. Their indefatigable belief that the dull, senseless pain of modern life could be undone—the world remade in the likeness of a pop song.

Screaming

ON THE MORNING OF AUGUST 25, 2014, A SIXTEEN-YEAR-OLD girl arrived at the University of Texas Southwestern Medical Center in baffling condition. She was short of breath but had no chest pain. She had no history of any lung condition, and there were no abnormal sounds in her breathing. But when the emergency room doctor on duty pressed on her neck and chest, he heard noises like Rice Krispies crackling in a bowl of milk—spaces behind her throat, around her heart, and between her lungs and the walls of her chest were studded with pockets of air, an X-ray confirmed, and her lungs were very slightly collapsed. Somehow, the upper half of her body had become bubble wrap.

The doctors were confused until she said that she'd been screaming for hours the night before at the Dallas stop on One Direction's Where We Are tour. The exertion, they hypothesized, had forced open a small hole in her respiratory tract. It wasn't really a big deal—she was given extra oxygen and kept for observation overnight, requiring no follow-up treatment. But the incident was described in all its absurd, gory detail in a paper published in the *Journal of Emergency Medicine* three years later—titled "'Screaming Your Lungs Out!' A Case of Boy Band–Induced Pneumothorax, Pneumomediastinum, and Pneumoretropharyngeum." The lead physician wrote that such a case had "yet to be described in the medical literature." Doctors were familiar with military pilots, scuba divers, and weightlifters straining their respiratory tracts, but this case presented the first evidence that "forceful screaming during pop concerts" could have the same physical toll.[1]

This was a novelty news item: an easy headline and a culturally salient joke about the overzealousness of teenage girls. It was parody made real, and recorded with the deepest of seriousness, for all time, in a medical journal. I stumbled across that article while idly combing Google Scholar for stuff that would be personally interesting to me, a habit I developed in order to waste time at work while describing what I was doing as "research." I probably typed in "One Direction" and "screaming." It *is* kind of funny. When I tweeted about it, a woman I had already interviewed for this book replied immediately, "That's worse than when I got so excited during 'One Thing' and bit down on a glow stick by accident, pouring viscous glow poison into my mouth."[2] I don't know precisely when that happened to her, but she was thirty-four years old when she wrote the tweet, which I only bring up because loving One Direction enough to cause oneself physical harm is not unique to the teenage years. It's just teenagers we picture when we talk about it.

I know nothing else about the girl who loved One Direction so much that she collapsed her lungs over it. Her doctor wrote to me that he'd asked, at the time, for her permission to tweet about the incident to Jimmy Fallon—he'd argued that maybe she would get to meet One Direction. "But she was too bashful!!!! Classic teenager," he said, adding a laugh-crying emoji.[3] I'll never know who she is or hear her personal explanation of what made her scream so much. In this specific circumstance, that's because of medical privacy laws, which are good. But it's also emblematic of a bigger lack: we have had so many screaming girls. Every time we see them, we're like, "They're screaming." And that's it. It's not that the image of the screaming fan isn't *true*—we can all see it; it's in the medical literature; many of us have embodied it. It's that the screaming fan doesn't scream for nothing, and screaming isn't all the fan is doing. It never has been.

• • •

"BEATLEMANIA STRUCK WITH THE FORCE, IF NOT THE CON-viction, of a social movement," Barbara Ehrenreich wrote in 1992.[4]

We've all seen the famous photos of girls open-mouthed and crying, arms draped over police barricades. Beatlemania was an on-the-ground occupation of Europe's and America's major cities. When the Beatles visited Dublin for the first time in 1963, *The New York Times* reported that "young limbs snapped like twigs in a tremendous free-for-all."[5] When they arrived in New York City in February 1964—a little over a month into the U.S. radio chart reign of "I Want to Hold Your Hand"—there were four thousand fans (and one hundred cops) waiting at the airport and reports of a "wild-eyed mob" in front of the Plaza Hotel.[6] "The Beatles Are Coming" posters and stickers were distributed all over the country before that first 1964 visit, with Capitol Records sales managers instructed to put them up on "literally" any surface, "anywhere and everywhere they can be seen," and to enlist unpaid high school students in the effort. (The sales managers were also asked to wear Beatles wigs to work "until further notice.")[7] On the night of the band's historic *Ed Sullivan Show* performance, 73 million people tuned in—more than a third of the country's entire population.[8]

"All day long some local disc jockeys [have] been encouraging truancy with repeated announcements of the Beatles' travel plans, flight number, and estimated time of arrival," the NBC news anchor Chet Huntley reported the evening the Beatles arrived. "Like a good little news organization, we sent three camera crews to stand among the shrieking youngsters and record the sights and sounds for posterity."[9] Ultimately that footage didn't air—it was deemed too frivolous for the nightly news.

At the time, the media couldn't figure Beatlemania out. They didn't see a reason for so many girls to be so obviously disturbed. For *The New York Times*, the former war correspondent David Dempsey attempted a "psychological, logical, anthropological" explanation of Beatlemania.[10] In it, he used German cultural theorist Theodor Adorno's famous words on the conformity and brainlessness of "jitterbugs"—which was originally a racist excoriation of the dancers in Harlem's jazz clubs. "They call themselves jitterbugs," Adorno had written, explaining one of the ideas of his that has held up least well over time, "as if they simultaneously wanted to affirm and mock their loss of individuality, their transformation into beetles whirring around in fascination."[11] Dempsey was misquoting him really, playing superficially off the available beetle pun. He was defending the teenage girls by calling their passions stupid and harmless, and he either didn't know or didn't remember that Adorno found jitterbugs dangerous, and had also described their movements as resembling "the reflexes of mutilated animals."[12] (In their racism, however, the two were ultimately on the same page: Dempsey chided Black rock 'n' roll artists for encouraging young white girls to act as vulgarly as "aboriginals," and compared the Beatles to "witch doctors who put their spells on hundreds of shuffling and stamping natives.")[13]

Nearly all the writing about the Beatles in mainstream American publications was done by established white male journalists—many of whom, at the most important papers, were not even music writers. One exception was Al Aronowitz, the rock critic best known for introducing the Beatles to Bob Dylan and to marijuana (simultaneously) in a New York City hotel room in the summer of 1964. That year, he reported that two thousand fans "mobbed the locked metal gates of Union Station" when the Beatles performed in Washington, D.C. Then, when the Beatles came to Miami, seven thousand teenagers created a four-mile-long traffic jam at the airport, and fans "shattered twenty-three windows and a plate-glass door."[14] A plate-glass door! These are compelling images, but I found it challenging to sort through the details in some of the reports of Beatlemania, many of which read to me as improbable or at least difficult to prove. There was the actual hysteria of the fans, and then, it seemed, there was the mythmaking of that hysteria. According to unsourced early reports, some cities tried to ban the Beatles from their airports because of the cost of securing them; legend has it that carpets and bedsheets from their hotel rooms were sometimes stolen by the entrepreneurial, cut up into thousands of pieces to be sold with certificates of authenticity.[15] Supposedly, an entire swimming pool in Miami was bottled up and auctioned off after the Beatles swam in it.[16]

The media, having little to say about the Beatles' music, had a lot to say about the women who went "ape" for it. After the *Ed Sullivan Show* debut, the New York *Daily News* reporter Anthony Burton recapped the event, describing a "wild screaming as if Dracula had appeared on stage."[17] The Simon & Schuster editor Alan Rinzler reviewed the Beatles' equally famous Carnegie Hall performance for *The Nation* a few days later with a devastating description of what would become the popular image of a boy band audience:

> *The full house was made up largely of upper-middle class young ladies, stylishly dressed, carefully made up, brought into town by private cars or suburban buses for their night to howl, to let go, scream, bump, twist, and clutch themselves ecstatically out there in flood lights for everyone to see and with the full blessing of all authority; indulgent parents, profiteering businessmen, gleeful national media, even the police . . . Later they can all go home and grow up like their mommies, but this was their chance to attempt a very safe and very private kind of rapture.*[18]

It's all there: the disdain, the condescension, the awe, the panic, of course the screaming. There's even, amid the mocking, maybe a little sympathy: "this was their chance." The media's bewildered contempt congealed into reflexive disdain and flat dismissal. In *The New York Times*, a cartoon showed a young woman coyly crossing her legs and explaining to an older man, flat-faced, "But naturally they make you want to scream, daddy-o; that's the whole idea of the Beatles' sound."[19] *Was* the screaming the "whole idea"?

The conditions for the Beatles' arrival in America could not have been more ideal—meaning they were bleak. In November 1963, the band played "Twist and Shout" at the Prince of Wales Theatre with the queen and Princess Margaret in the audience—the concert, and the hysterics of its attendees, were rebroadcast on British television a week later, to widespread concern about the level of emotion on display, but American TV reports about the event were scrapped in the wake of the assassination of President John F. Kennedy. There was a pall of anxiety hanging over the entire country, and it was caused not only by the president's death. Barbara Ehrenreich, in her accounting of what made Beatlemania take hold in the United States, quotes Betty Friedan's *The Feminine Mystique*, published in February 1963. Friedan had noticed "a new vacant, sleepwalking, playing-a-part quality of youngsters who do what they are supposed to do, what the other kids do, but do not seem to feel alive or real in doing it." She described speaking to many such teenagers, including a thirteen-year-old girl from a Westchester suburb, who seemed "not quite awake, like a puppet with someone else pulling the strings."[20] The Beatles, Ehrenreich argued many years later, had presented an opportunity.

Ehrenreich interviewed women who had been young at the peak of Beatlemania. While they had found the Beatles "sexy," and that was certainly part of the allure, many of them had also remembered a feeling of identification: they wanted to be, like the Beatles, *free.* They'd wanted to go on adventures and provoke feelings—"the louder you screamed, the less likely anyone would forget the power of fans," Ehrenreich summarized.[21] The band played into this explicitly: Paul McCartney reminisced about the group's first American tour in a 1966 interview, saying, "There they were in America, all getting house-trained for adulthood."[22] He relished relieving the girls of that imperative, even if he was more general rabble-rouser than sincere feminist. But his intentions are largely beside the point. Every generation's boy band serves a slightly different purpose, but if there is one unifying characteristic I can see, it's that a boy band opens up space. Infatuation is irrational but it can be a precursor to introspection. The experience of bodily joy is an invitation to reconsider the conditions that hold you away from it most of the time. Screaming at pop music is not direct action, and screaming does not make a person a revolutionary, or even resistant, but what screaming can and does do is punctuate prolonged periods of silence.

I WANTED TO KNOW HOW THE SCREAMING FANGIRL BECAME a trope.

"Being a fan is very much associated with feminine excess, with working-class people, people of color, people whose emotions are seen as being out of control," says Allison McCracken, an associate professor and director of the American studies program at DePaul University. "Everything is set up against this idea of white straight masculinity, where the emotions are in control and the body is in control."[23]

McCracken is an expert on the history of the "crooner" in American culture, and her 2015 book *Real Men Don't Sing* credits Rudy Vallée and Bing Crosby for making the blueprint for a pop sensation in the late 1920s and early 1930s.[24] (Vallée was the first, and became a star on NBC's national radio network. Crosby was positioned as his rival when he rose to fame on CBS's competing network a few years later.) The two were, she argued, gender blurrers, who performed emotion-filled and romantic music appreciated by women and feared by many men, who were threatened by this alternative mode of what masculinity could be. The kind of ardor they inspired in the early days of music radio was seen as a problem by psychologists, by educators, by the Catholic church, and by just about every major institutional power at the time—not least because of concern over whether the crooners' massive success meant that women had somehow wrested control of American popular culture. (McCracken emphasized that the idea that only women were fans of the crooners was a media invention—their style had long been popular with working-class white male ethnic groups, especially immigrant and first- or second-generation audiences who were "almost completely erased by the press and critics," but who were similarly subjected to shame over their aesthetic taste.)[25]

As part of her research, McCracken visited the American Radio Archives in Thousand Oaks, California, to see Vallée's personal archive of fan letters, dating back to 1928.[26] She was fascinated by them because they were so full of questions—the women who were writing to Vallée were surprised by their own emotional reactions to his music and were confused by the idea of falling in love with a voice they'd heard only over the radio. "They were responding to his voice and saying, *I don't understand why I'm so happy and joyous and why you're moving me so much*," she told me.[27] "They were writing to him and saying, *Can you explain what's happening to me?*"

They were also writing to journalists, in ways that may sound familiar to anyone who has witnessed a Twitter altercation between a blogger and a fan army. In 1929, the New York *Daily News* columnist Mark

Hellinger wrote a story about Rudy Vallée, calling him obnoxious and crossing his fingers that women would soon get over him and move on to someone else. ("He has women of 50 bouncing around as though they were 15," he complained.) "You are jealous. You are stupid. You must be insane," one woman countered. Fans wrote to him by the thousands. Some threatened violence or told him to hang himself. When Ben Gross of the *Sunday News* then wrote a negative column about Vallée, a fan reportedly wrote to him: "The sweetest music to my ears would be to hear Rudy play a march at your and Hellinger's funeral."[28]

"They didn't have the word *teen* yet," McCracken told me, so that wasn't how journalists mocked the largely female audience that adored these stars. "They used *moronic* at that time. Women were seen to have the minds of children." (She clarified that this was originally a clinical term coming out of the eugenics movement, used to indicate that a person's IQ had peaked when they were about twelve years old, and that they were "primarily emotionally rather than intellectually responsive.") The shift from "moron" to "bobby-soxer"—the term used in the 1940s, when Sinatra was king—didn't have anything to do with a rising estimation of women, but rather with the premise of Sinatra's marketing and publicity. It was a purely financial decision based on the even earlier age at which fandom was starting, with younger girls who were starting to receive some of their own spending money, and one that cemented the association between crooner idols and supposedly immature audiences.

Though psychologists had started describing adolescence as a unique stage of life in the early 1900s, the word "teenager" itself wasn't widely used until the late 1940s, McCracken explained, and the most eager speakers of the term were also marketers. They realized in the postwar boom years that far fewer kids were dropping out of school to earn money for their families, and that far more were being given allowances and plenty of leisure time. The 1950s and 1960s saw more and more products marketed explicitly to teenagers, often reinforcing the idea that they were a distinct group of people with a separate identity from their parents, and with the rise of teen-marketed products came teen-oriented TV shows during which they could be advertised. The most popular of all was Dick Clark's *American Bandstand*, the after-school music and dance hour widely credited with bringing rock 'n' roll into the white mainstream and, according to Ehrenreich, making it "the organizing principle and premier theme of teen consumer culture."[29] In 1958, a review in the *Pittsburgh Courier* described the show: "The kids screamed and chomped gum. Dick Clark giggled and sold more gum."[30]

So long as teens existed as a lucrative market category, the industry would supply them with a "teeny-bopper" idol. When these idols were written about by journalists and critics, it was often with full acquiescence to their marketing, tinged with disdain. This was the case as recently as the 2010s, when the idol was Justin Bieber. When he performed his first sold-out show at Madison Square Garden that September, the *New York Times* music critic Jon Caramanica titled his review "Send in the Heartthrobs, Cue the Shrieks" and wrote that Bieber "teased the crowd with flashes of direct emotional manipulation."[31] Two years later, another *Times* reporter covered the release of Bieber's latest fragrance, Girlfriend, and the girls who camped outside Macy's overnight to be the first to purchase it. "Justin Bieber's Girlfriend" was "not only the name of the flowery fragrance," he observed, "but also the fervent wish of many of those who bought it."[32]

By that time, One Direction was battling Bieber for the number one spot on the U.S. charts, and in the hearts of American teenagers, and Caramanica started reviewing their output with equal attentiveness. He called their 2012 sophomore album, *Take Me Home*, "a reliable shriek inducer in girls who have not yet decided that shrieking doesn't become them."[33] He panned their 2013 album, *Midnight Memories*, writing, "They play the part almost resentfully, with the mien of people who know better . . . Whether this is transparent to the squealers who make up their fanbase is tough to tell."[34] Aware of the machinations of the pop industry, he situates himself in alignment with the put-upon boys, and implicitly blames the girls who love them for the fact of their presumably beleaguered existence. Caramanica invokes history to make his point without having to make it; he understands that we all know what the shrieking girls look like. It's easy to find photos of young Beatles fans with their hands out and their faces drawn into tearful shock. It's also easy to find nearly identical photos of Backstreet Boys fans and Justin Bieber fans and One Direction fans and BTS fans—but placing them side by side to highlight their similarity does not feel satisfying to me. Visually, it's a neat trick, but the timelessness of a scream isn't much of an observation.

DANIELA MARINO WAS NOT IMPRESSED BY ONE DIRECTION when she initially learned about their existence. They were too popular.

"I didn't like them at first because they were all over my timeline on Twitter and Tumblr," she said.[35] She was eighteen at the time. But then she watched the music video for "What Makes You Beautiful" once or twice, and then she started tweeting a little bit, and a decade later she waves the rest of that history away, saying, "Now I'm here, it's been, what, almost ten years I've been here with One Direction?" As a teenager in Colombia, she became one of the organizers of a major One Direction fan club, which hosted meet-ups, birthday parties in honor of each of the band members, and anniversary parties every July commemorating the day One Direction was formed. She was on Twitter all the time, and the president of the fan club became one of her best friends. She had no real expectation that she would ever interact with any of the band members directly, but she felt a powerful connection to them because they were the same age. "We grew up together in a way," she told me. "They're just this amazing part of my history and biography."

Daniela was twenty years old in 2013, when she moved to the United States with her mother and brother so that her mother could marry a man who lived in a large suburb of Atlanta. The transition was much worse than any of them expected. "We had a lot of moments where we just wanted to go back, and we questioned if we made the right choice," she told me. She and her mother were unfamiliar with American culture, shaky on the language, and struggled to bond with a new stepfamily. "My mom was depressed for a while," she said. "I was basically the only person she could rely on and she was the only person I could rely on. But I couldn't tell my mom how I was feeling or cry because that would make it worse for her." That was when she would go back to One Direction—the music, the videos, but also the online community she had built and the responsibilities she had assigned herself. She stayed in touch with the president of the Colombian fan club, whom she by then regarded as a sister. "They helped me stay put," she said. "Their music was always there." When she went to her first and only One Direction concert in 2014, in Atlanta, she went alone and screamed.

"As soon as I set foot in that stadium, I lost it," she said. "I was by myself; nobody went with me. That was the best moment for me, in my life, to be honest."

Every scream has a personal context, but we rarely hear about it. The trope of the screaming fan also ignores the possibility that some fans know they're being looked at, and that they don't care. "My own family kind of judge me for still liking One Direction, but I'm obviously never going to not like them," Freya Whitfield, a fan from London, told me breezily.[36] Jacob Gaspar, a fan from Ohio, told me everyone thinks it's a joke when he says he's a One Direction fan. "I'm a straight male, and that's not a big demographic for One Direction fans," he said. "But I'm like, listen, I could play you like five songs and change your mind right now." "A lot of people think I'm putting it on but it's a genuine thing I really enjoy," he insisted. "They ask me stuff and I prove my knowledge."[37]

This style of self-aware acquiescence to an irrational passion may always have been part of the screaming fangirl experience. In 1964, a group of girls in Encino, California, founded an organization they called Beatlesaniacs, Ltd. It was advertised as "group therapy" and offered "withdrawal literature" for fans of the Beatles who felt that their emotions had gotten out of hand. In a 1964 issue of *Life* magazine, the group is covered credulously. (The spread on Beatlemania features a full-page image of a girl kneeling on the ground, grass clenched in her hand, tears streaming down her face—whether or not she was actually thinking, "Ringo! Ringo walked on this grass!" that is how the photo is captioned.) The club is mentioned in a small sidebar, titled "How to Kick the Beatle Habit." "What Beatlesaniacs Ltd. offers is group therapy for those living near active chapters, and withdrawal literature for those going it alone at far-flung outposts," it read. "Its membership card immediately identifies the bearer as someone who needs help."[38]

The club was *obviously* a joke. Its rules included such items as "Do not mention the word Beatles (or beetles)," "Do not mention the word England," "Do not speak with an English accent," and "Do not speak English." So not only was it a joke, it was a pretty funny one! But nobody is primed to see self-critique or sarcasm in fans. Seeing them toy with their own image, recognize their own condition, or mess with anyone's heads contradicts the popular image that has circulated for the last one hundred or so years. The Beatlesaniacs president Cheryl Tuso was later compelled to write a letter to the editor of *Life* clarifying that her group was *not* in fact attempting to stop loving the Beatles.[39] They were only "campaigning against any form of behavior which might endanger the Beatles or their fans (i.e., mob riots, throwing of objects onto the stage, attacking the Beatles, etc.)." Also, they were just kidding.

• • •

WHEN I WAS IN COLLEGE, I HAD A SMALL FIGHT WITH MY BOY-friend because I wore a "Mrs. Horan" T-shirt to a One Direction concert in Toronto. My then twelve-year-old sister made it for me in advance, and she was joking. The zebra-print letters ironed onto the back were crooked and crumbling by the time the shirt made it to Canada. It was gauche on purpose, the tackiness of "wearing the merch to the show" taken to higher heights to make for a good bit. Wearing it, I was joking. I couldn't believe this wasn't obvious. I was impatient texting an explanation, mostly because I was furious that I'd been made to feel embarrassed. I hadn't really thought Niall Horan might like to *marry me* or that I would like to marry him—an Irish teenager whose tweets indicated that he could barely spell. In fact, at twenty years old, I didn't think much of myself at all, so it felt like being called out for having an overly aspirational crush on the star of a sports team, or the president. I wriggled out of it by saying "Sorry" and turning off my phone. As my mom drove our minivan through the streets of Toronto, Sophie peered out the windows with my dad's military-grade binoculars, saying it was just in case she could catch a glimpse of Niall in traffic six lanes over. Or Harry in a hotel-room window twenty stories above. She was not seriously hopeful—she was twelve, and she was kidding. She hammed it up, hunting. I laughed so hard I activated the child safety lock on my seat belt.

At the time, it wouldn't have occurred to me to

situate myself in a lineage of screaming fangirls, but it's fun to try it now. Beatlemania was "the first mass outburst of the 1960s to feature women," Ehrenreich wrote the year before I was born. They weren't rioting *for* anything, "but they did have plenty to riot against."[40] To see or hear me and my sisters at the One Direction concert that night, early August, you would say we were hysterical. We were screaming. I can't speak for everyone in the crowd—the Rogers Centre holds more than fifty-three thousand—but for me, it wasn't the sight of five famous boys that made me feel like something uncommon was happening. It wasn't the sound of their voices, which I couldn't even hear. It was the fifty-thousand-person shouting match disguised as a sing-along, and the thunderclap of sneakers hitting concrete on every downbeat, eliminating the need to speak or catch any individual eye. Outside, the strange things we were capable of feeling were sneered at or smiled off or commercially packaged as "girl power," but here they were rough and loud. The sounds were ugly. Our hairlines were damp and the tendons in the backs of our knees were screaming. One pair of hands looked just like every other, outstretched in the dark, lining the bottom of other people's camera frames. We knew that our lives would not be fantasies, except for the fact that they were right now. When we shrieked, it was at the knowledge that the moment would end.

Deep-Frying

A GIRL YOU RUN INTO SCREAMING AT A CONCERT MAY GO HOME afterward and cut up the footage she recorded to make GIFs and memes that will pass through many other hands, becoming something entirely different and totally bizarre. Unsatisfied by One Direction's constriction in time and place and situation, screaming girls who are also fanfiction writers will cast them as employees of suburban coffee shops, or plop them into the 1960s to operate alongside that other famous British band, or go behind the scenes with totally imagined detail, drawing out what they imagine to be the emotional consequences of fame or the more universal pangs of secret love. The writer Zan Romanoff has interviewed women who dress themselves up in the spirit of Harry Styles—indulging in elaborate cosplay—as an expression of devotion that is also a prolonged creative exercise.[1]

The image of the screaming fangirl is so familiar and dramatic, it precludes curiosity. But for decades, fans have not just passively enjoyed or loudly desired the objects of their fandom. They've also edited them and recirculated them and used them as the inspiration for a range of creative works so enormous—and largely uncatalogued—that it can't even be grasped. The art, the stories, and the in-jokes are as much a part of what it means to be a fan as staking out an airport or memorizing dozens of songs. I would never, ever, *ever* want to meet a member of One Direction, and I actively evaded the opportunity one afternoon when a coworker messaged me on Slack to announce that Harry Styles was just sitting around in the coffee shop on the ground floor of our office building. But I would like to spend every day online talking about them, and I've spent years now tinkering with my ideas about what they might signify.

The term "transformational fandom" comes from Dreamwidth—an iteration of LiveJournal, built using the same code in 2008, after LiveJournal's new ownership implemented draconian content guidelines. It was coined by a pseudonymous fanfiction writer who was trying to explain the origin of an ongoing conflict between copyright holders and the amateurs who were appropriating from their work to make new stories. It's "all about laying hands upon the source and twisting it to the fans' own purposes," they wrote in 2009. "It tends to spin outward into nutty chaos at the least provocation, and while there are majority opinions [and] minority opinions, it's largely a democracy of taste; everyone has their own shot at declaring what the source material means, and at radically reinterpreting it."[2]

Transformational fandom separates itself from "affirmational" or "mimetic" fandom that celebrates the "canon" exactly as it is, copying it with exact replicas or precise cosplaying. It sometimes takes the form of playful disrespect, and you can't always understand it by taking it at face value. Its practice takes many forms, some of which could reasonably be described as mutilation, and from the outside, it might not even look like love at all. The One Direction fandom, as I experienced it on Tumblr in the early 2010s, was playfully vicious and much grosser than you might expect. The images I remember best were surrealist—sometimes creepy or disgusting. There's Niall Horan, somehow flying through the air in maroon skinny jeans, doing a split, upper body completely rigid, face frozen with eyes dead ahead, a blurry still from a long-lost video. There he is hovering in the dark corner of a concrete structure, foregrounded by twin bundles of sticks, never explained. Or there are his teeth in close-up before he had braces, or the weird toe on his left foot that's shaped like a lima bean. Girls on Tumblr made use of these images as naturally as if they were words.

To take things to another level: one method for making a meme totally indecipherable to the uninitiated is "deep-frying" it. Though "deep-fried memes" originated on Tumblr and were popularized by Black Twitter, they're most often associated now with the boys of Reddit. The subreddit r/DeepFriedMemes had 1 million members and self-described as a living archive for "memes that imitate and exaggerate the degradation of an image," before the moderators made the forum private in 2020. (In a farewell letter published via a public Google Doc, one mod wrote that the popularity of the subreddit had doomed it; "people began frying more lazily.")[3] It's a category of form, not content, and the original meme can be almost anything, but in practice the jokes skew toward the "bruh" and "too lit," sex and weed and guns and Yoda. These images, crackling with yellow-white noise and blurred like the edges of a CGI ghost, evoke the distance between writer and reader on social platforms. Posts are refracted through filter after filter and pixels lost through screenshot after screenshot, singeing off the fingerprints. If a human face goes through this process, it never fails to come out the other side demonic. If this startles you, it seems to say, you haven't spent enough time online. The deep-fried One Direction memes on Tumblr are "deep-fried" not just because of the way they look—like magazine pages forgotten in the pocket of a pair of jeans that have then gone through a washing machine—but because they announce the absurdity of knowing enough about One Direction to appreciate them.

While many of the biggest subreddits for niche interests in gaming and internet culture explicitly prohibit "normies," to my knowledge no one on Tumblr has ever bothered to do anything like that. You simply wouldn't wind your way to the center of a Tumblr subcommunity without effort—drive-by spectatorship is unlikely, and when it happens, it's immediately checked by the indecipherability of the conversations and images it witnesses. One of my favorite deep-fried One Direction memes—which looks as though it might have been, at one point, several lives ago, a screenshot of a tweet—was posted to Tumblr with a fuzzy background, the color of an eyeball in close-up, and bold Times New Roman text that is chopped off on one side and decapitated all along the top. "Friend: i don't like 1D Because there not bad boy" is wedged into the upper left corner. "Me: oh really!" is squished up against the edge of a photo of a boy who is barely recognizable as Niall Horan in a cardigan—he has holes for eyes—sitting with his legs stretched out across a staircase, which has a red-and-white sticker on it reading "Do not sit on stairs."[4]

Whoever made this image may or may not have had any fidelity to the stereotype of a screaming fangirl. All I know about them is that they were infatuated with or intrigued by One Direction enough to make something funny and weird using an image that most people would have considered pretty uninspiring. The resulting meme makes fun of One Direction and it makes fun of the people who love them—it may read in other ways to other fans, but to me it looks like a sardonic wink or a playful jab at fans' ridiculous fervor for defending something that doesn't really need defending. (Nobody was going to change their minds about One Direction just because we insisted they were "bad boys" worth loving; One Direction was not at risk of being viewed as unpopular even if various people in each of our lives were unimpressed.) Though the criticism of fangirls is that they become tragically selfless and one-track-minded, the evidence available everywhere I look is that they become self-aware and creatively free.

THEODOR ADORNO, THE MOST FAMOUS CULTURAL THEORIST associated with the mid-century Marxists of the Frankfurt School, did not find "music for entertainment" very entertaining. This is probably the opinion he's cited on most often, and it's become a useful straw man (he's dead!) in contemporary essays in defense of popular things. Pop music "seems to complement the reduction of people to silence, the dying out of speech as expression, the inability to communicate at all," he wrote in his 1938 essay "On the Fetish Character in Music and the Regression of Listening."[5]

Though critics often deride him as a snob, this isn't

exactly true. He was disdainful of high art as well, which could be created only through patronage made possible by wealth accumulation. His issue was not exactly the quality of the music, though he sometimes undermined himself with blanket statements about that too, but the cold, systematized manner in which it was produced and sold. To him, the culture industry—a term he coined so that he would not have to use the term "mass culture," which implied too much agency on the part of said masses—was the exact opposite of possibility. It secured the status quo. It offered only a brief respite from work, providing the worker with energy to work more. It offered the "pretense" of individual identity and choice, but was really a force for making everyone agree that they thought and felt the same. He found this devastating and predicted a dark future in which love would be imagined only as it is described in the pop songs, happiness would be the car that the pop song advertised, and songs would eventually serve only as billboards for themselves and their industry. (The lyrics of the One Direction song "Better Than Words" are almost entirely made up of the titles of eighteen famous love songs . . .) Of the fans he saw losing their cool at live music performances, he wrote, "Their ecstasy is without content." And of the type of person who could fall for all of this, he wrote with a tinge of sympathy that they must have "free time and little freedom."

Adorno's work has been the starting point for the

last seventy years of pop culture analysis. When I read it now, I obviously see things I didn't see as a college freshman, flipping through it to pull essentially random quotations for an English paper, before One Direction came so forcefully into my life. I feel an embarrassing knee-jerk defensiveness, and I also feel resistant to the central claim that culture is something that happens to almost everyone the same way, or that it is strictly possible for "ecstasy" to be "without content." I can't skim over what I recognize: One Direction fans, or Beatles fans, the screaming girls who went home and holed up in their bedrooms to make whatever they were going to make in response to their outsized emotions, did have plenty of free time and "little freedom." That's the default condition of a teenager, and it's also the way I felt about my life when I was a friendless undergrad on a two-thousand-acre campus, confined to a narrow range of activities that didn't make me happy. (This is obviously not exactly what he meant.) But the world opened up for me online in unexpected form; wanting to understand what I loved so much about One Direction, I started asking rhetorical questions and observing my own reactions. At eighteen, I was ashamed to be exactly what everyone imagines when they think of a boy band fan, and I didn't think I was dreaming of making out with any pop stars, but what if I did? I didn't feel trapped or manipulated. I felt like I'd been given a jigsaw puzzle, and if I could put it together, I would understand something about myself, maybe even see the whole picture.

When I read fanfiction, I see others taking on this same task. This is a tradition of fandom that precedes the internet, and some of the earliest fanfiction involving real people—rather than fictional TV, film, or literary characters—was about the Beatles. It was circulated only in small batches, through letters, likely because of a powerful taboo applied to real person fiction (RPF) that lasted until the social media age. ("I've talked to one or two old fans who used to do that, and who would still hang out on fandom websites when I found the fandom back in 2010," a popular Beatles fic writer who goes by ChutJeDors told me, but that was as close I got to any of them.)[6] Basically none of that writing has survived, and the Fanlore wiki notes that "not much is known about the players, fanworks, or fan activities of the community," particularly in contrast to the well-documented *Star Trek* fanfiction community that emerged around the same time, largely among men.[7] Whatever might have been saved and posted to FanFiction.net at the dawn of online fandom would have been lost in 2001, when the website banned fiction featuring "non-historical and non-fictional characters."

But decades later, the most popular category of Beatles fanfiction being disseminated through the proto–social network Yahoo Groups was slashfic—stories that focus on same-sex romantic pairings—

that imagined a relationship between Paul McCartney and John Lennon. This kind of hypothetical romance is called a "ship," a noun that doubles as a verb, as in "I ship Paul and John." Today, the Groups service is impossible to access—the service was shut down by the parent company Verizon in 2020—and even the most famous fics are difficult to find. Some smaller fic sites are partially archived via the Wayback Machine, but stories are often viewable only as snippets, and collections that were hosted on the fannish platforms Dreamwidth and LiveJournal are largely inactive now. Most *new* "McLennon" stories are posted on Archive of Our Own or Tumblr.

I am not a Beatles fan, but I enjoy clicking through the tags that bring me to stories as long as books, following the unlikely adventures of McLennon. Many of them are written based off of prompts, or requests, as is a common practice in fic-writing communities. A fan who enjoys the ship will ask a talented writer to craft them a story with a premise they have in mind, like "What about a fanfiction where Paul starts feeling ill but doesn't tell anybody until he gets really sick and then John . . . has to take care [of] him? That would be so cute!"[8] Or "Can you do a fic where paul is pregnant and going into labor?"[9] There are alternative universe—"AU"—stories in which the members of the Beatles are a bunch of college students or young wizards at Hogwarts, or in which Paul McCartney is a woman named Mary and the Beatles are a co-ed band.

I found and could only skim a forty-nine-thousand-word story about Paul McCartney coming out in 1966—the same for a forty-three-thousand-word story about McCartney and Lennon living together in New York City from the mid-1970s to the present. There are Tumblr pages dedicated to curating and aggregating the best McLennon fiction from Archive of Our Own, LiveJournal, and Wattpad, and that specialize in finding "lost fics"—stories you have a vague memory of reading once and loving. The fic writer ChutJeDors describes her blog, called *Your Quality John/Paul-Library*, as a lost and found, as well as a place for recommendations and for fic-writing resources.[10] (She plans to add research materials about Liverpool and a dictionary of Scouse, its local dialect, to help writers who are interested in using authentic details.) *Your Quality John/Paul-Library* recommends a super-short story about John touching Paul's butt, as well as a thirty-thousand-word story about John agreeing to serve as a fake boyfriend at Paul's family Christmas party. The light is mixed in with the dark, and there are also stories about death and illness. There are even stories about nothing, as is the case with one Chut published in January 2021: "No plot—just boring, perfect everyday life on Thomas Lane, Liverpool," the description of an eighty-six-thousand-word story about Lennon and McCartney as "an old married couple" reads.[11]

There are thousands of pieces of long-form slashfic

about each possible pairing of One Direction members as well, but there are also novel forms of transformation enabled by newer internet platforms. On Tumblr, which is primarily an image-based platform, micro fanfics called "imagines" overlay tiny point-of-view scenarios on top of photos of the boys, inviting the reader to "imagine" themselves in some specific situation or another. They can be boring, asking the viewer to imagine such obvious things as kissing Harry Styles or marrying Zayn Malik. They can be fun, as when they goofily sketch out a situation the viewer might really be curious about experiencing. They can also be horrifying and surprising, for any number of reasons—the most surrealist of them seem to be written by people who are reaching to find something that has not already been proposed, or people who just have uncontrollable imaginations, or people who are making fun of the form. One that I think about often goes like this: "Imagine: You and Harry are on a date and you're playing chubby bunny." This text is positioned at the top of a photo of Harry Styles eating a bunch of large marshmallows. "On your first try you accidentally swallow the whole marshmallow and run to the bathroom and poop it out. You and Harry look at it in the toilet and laught [*sic*] and he hugs you."[12] You and Harry look into the toilet and laugh and he hugs you!

The most inexplicable entries are archived on a Tumblr called "bad1dimagines." It can be difficult to tell which scenarios were dreamed up sincerely, which were jokes about the practice of fandom in general, and which were concocted as imitations of a person's own morbid longings—satire that would be ineffective were it not for the commentary of the account's anonymous twentysomething curator. She has been providing this service for years now, after starting it on a whim in 2015, and her captions often receive tens of thousands of likes and reblogs, indicating that a sizable chunk of the fandom is in on the joke. A probably sincere post asks the reader to imagine: "Zayn just moved to your neighborhood and one day when you're walking to school he tells you to come and get on his scooter so you agree and when you two get to the school everyone's staring at you and the strange, exotic boy besides you and eventually rumors go around that you two are dating and then you two fall in love." Underneath, the bad1dimagines curator added, "I wonder if they're staring at you bc you're with zayn or if, and just hear me out here, if it's because you're two people riding one scooter."[13] Though the captions can sometimes be a little mean, their author accepts every premise as it's presented to her. Never does she suggest that it's unrealistic to dream of personal interactions with the extremely famous members of a boy band.

Bad1dimagines is structured around a much more coherent tagging system than your average Tumblr, which makes it easy to find the scary stuff. There's a whole section of the blog dedicated to "Dark Harry" imagines—stories about Harry Styles being violent or controlling or murderous.[14] These strike some of the same notes as the wealth of fanfiction about Justin Bieber dying in hideous ways, seeming to reach for the only higher-pitched and more confusing emotional reaction imaginable for someone who already feels as strongly as they think is possible.[15] Liam stabs you in the abdomen. Niall pushes you off a bridge. Harry runs you over with his car, laughing, or cuts your collarbones out of your chest "because he loved them so much."[16] These violent images are culled from other forms of popular culture, remixed to star a group of boys whose commercial proposition is that they would never hurt you. How scary—and why do it? If there's a joke, what is it? (One post, seared into my brain, is a collection of images plotting "the outfit you wear to jump in front of niall's car." It includes a blue gown covered in Swarovski crystals and a microwavable Kid Cuisine meal with *Shrek*-branded packaging.)[17] I didn't think I knew, until I'd scrolled through so many "bad" imagines that I no longer understood what any common nouns directly signified and could not remember how to put together a sentence. That's when I really started laughing.

The joke is that we have talked so much about these people that we no longer have anything left to say that isn't totally absurd. "Imagine: niall horan crawling inside your ear" goes one of my favorite Tumblr posts. "you tell him to stop, but he is in there."[18] I don't have any idea who made this, or why, or how it became so well known among girls who were on the internet in 2013 that references to it persist to this day. What I like about it is its senselessness and the creator's evident delight in her own unusual mind; it invokes the nightmarish nonsense of love for a stranger and the hilarity of losing control, and when I see it, I remember what I wanted more than anything when I was nineteen years old. I wanted something to happen to me that couldn't be described.

Shrines

I'M LOOKING FOR THE SHRINE TO HARRY STYLES'S VOMIT. I know it was on Tumblr—I remember seeing it there. In the fall of 2014, at the beginning of my last year of college, I also remember a GIF set of Harry Styles, answering an interview question about the shrine to his own vomit, nodding diplomatically and saying, first in one frame, "It's interesting. For sure," and in a second, "A little niche, maybe."[1]

Those are my memories. These are the facts. That October, Harry Styles went to a party at the British pop singer Lily Allen's house in Los Angeles.[2] The next morning, riding in a chauffeured Audi, in his gym clothes, on the way back from "a very long hike," he requested that the driver pull over. On the side of the 101 freeway just outside Calabasas, he threw up near a metal barrier, looked up, and locked eyes with a camera. He is sweaty, peaked; his hair is dirty, pulled up in a messy bun. Yet dehydrated in gym shorts and athletic socks, hands-on-knees by the side of the road, he still exudes the elegance of Harry Styles. His cheekbones find the direction of the light, thanks to reflex or a gift from God.

The day they were taken, the photos circulated in tabloids and on Tumblr and Twitter, and a few hours later, a Los Angeles–based eighteen-year-old named Gabrielle Kopera set out to find the spot and label it for posterity. She drove there alone, then taped a piece of poster board to the barrier: HARRY STYLES THREW-UP HERE 10-12-14, she wrote in big block letters. The grainy photo she posted first to her own Instagram circulated later on Tumblr, Twitter, Pinterest, YouTube, and all those junky-looking celebrity blogs that are actually just search engine scams. Even more than the photos of Harry Styles, I remember that I loved the photo of this sign. Harry Styles threw up here! That's all he did—but given that we've seen him throw up only once before (gross story), and we've never seen him do it on *this* strip of gravel, the sign suggested that the event was worth recording for posterity. Harry Styles threw up here! Six months prior, the *Los Angeles Times* reported that the then twenty-year-old Styles had dropped $4 million on a five-bedroom house in Beverly Hills (a photo gallery of the home's interior was removed from the story shortly after publishing).[3] Yet he descended from the Hills, jumped out of the car in fancy suburbia, and threw up in the street. Why stop at a piece of poster board? Why not a plaque?

The idea of Harry Styles throwing up on the side of a highway and the idea of a girl I don't know erecting a shrine to it is the most precise possible representation of what I find interesting. Imagining what could make me feel most myself, I thought it would be standing on that ground. No, I would not touch it—I would just look at it, photograph it, and delight in executing the dramatic act of Photoshopping myself into a meme in the physical world. So, in December 2019, I flew to Los Angeles for two days and drove around in a rented minivan, stopping only at places where I knew Harry Styles had been.

I had no other curiosities about the city in which I had spent fewer than forty-eight hours in my entire life. My first move upon arriving was to hop confidently onto the wrong shuttle bus, then walk two miles in the sun to pick up my rental car. I wanted to take photos of the Christmas decorations in the Budget office—piles of tinsel and glimmering metallic mini trees made every surface look like an imminent fire hazard and the set of a music video. But I was too embarrassed to take out my phone, so I just absorbed what I could, accepted my keys, and headed for a donut shop. Harry Styles wore a crewneck sweatshirt with the donut shop's logo on it while out for a jog in the summer of 2016, according to a Styles-specific fashion blog that blocked me on Twitter sometime after. I spent my time waiting in line in the parking lot of Randy's Donuts deliberating over what sort of donut Harry would be most likely to eat. I didn't think it would be anything too elaborate—something classic, not *too* rich to sit well with black coffee. (For a while, Harry Styles had a habit of drinking black coffee with a spoonful of butter and a spoonful of coconut oil in it, part of one of those terrifying new diets for men.) I settled on a classic glazed donut and a jelly-filled one, because this was vacation. Then I drove around Los Angeles with gobs of strawberry dripping down my arm, memorizing the words to the new Harry Styles album, singing with my mouth full and the windows down. I spent the whole trip chasing him around the city in a dogged pursuit that I certainly felt was nearly cinematic. There were costume changes! Mishaps! A long montage of scribbling in a notebook in public! I put on my nicest New Year's Eve dress to go to the Nice Guy on La Cienega Boulevard, a restaurant to which both Harry Styles and Zayn Malik have taken dates, and where cameras are forbidden, and I also paid $15 to park my car above a gentlemen's club. My reservation was so early that there was nobody else in the entire restaurant. I stayed for ten minutes, drinking one $18 glass of wine, then swiped a handful of souvenir matchbooks and went back to the hotel.

The next morning, wearing a baseball cap low over my face as if I were myself a celebrity, I went to the Beachwood Cafe on the edge of Griffith Park. I was afraid that the workers might see something in my eyes or the tilt of my phone camera that would indicate I was there only because Harry Styles had referenced the place in a new song—a ballad about his ex-girlfriend Camille Rowe, with whom he apparently used to eat brunch there. The lyric goes, "The coffee's out / At the Beachwood Cafe / And it kills me 'cause I know we've / Run out of things we can say." Sad! The coffee was not out, for the record, just a little watery. I tucked the receipt into my wallet, in the spot where some people might carry their business cards or photos of their children. I sat and drank the coffee and snuck photos of my surroundings, thinking not about the possibility of breathing in a speck of dust made from Harry Styles's dead skin, but of how many girls just like me would do this very thing. I was early; the album had come out only the night before. But now, if I click through the tagged photos for the Beachwood Cafe on Instagram, I see them. One after the other—hundreds. "The coffee actually WAS out" on one afternoon, around 1:00 p.m. Pacific time, though it "WAS NOT out" just two hours before, when a different Styles fan got there. Many of the pictures tagged with Beachwood Cafe are not actually of the Beachwood Cafe, but just of girls in their rooms, wherever they may be, listening to the same song. On Tumblr, there are mood boards for an afternoon at the Beachwood Cafe with Harry Styles, and blogs with URLs like out-of-coffee-beachwood-cafe.tumblr.com, and, of course, speculation about whether Styles has ever been to the Beachwood Cafe with Louis Tomlinson, to whom many still believe he is secretly married. I came back an hour later and ate pancakes—why not! This time I snuck photos of the royal-blue-and-yellow-triangle-checkered flooring, as well as my dirty plate.

And of course, I drove thirty miles from my hotel, taking the interstate to the 101 freeway and following it through Calabasas, toggling between watching where I was going, sipping hot coffee—black!—and scanning the shoulder for a familiar patch of gravel. I'd billed this trip as a pilgrimage, and I felt a feverish dedication to securing a moment of spiritual bliss. Without Harry Styles, Los Angeles to me was just an American city like any other I had seen mostly on TV. A freeway was just a freeway. A shoulder of the road was something I would never risk life and limb to stare at while steering a borrowed vehicle with one hand. I drove ten miles one way and then ten miles back down the other side. In the original photo, you can't see anything except the edge of a guardrail, some pebbles, and the direction of traffic, which was toward the camera. I'm not sure why I thought the exact spot it was taken would be so obvious—I guess I grossly overestimated my ability to differentiate one piece of roadside from any other—but I convinced myself I'd gotten close enough. The sound of crunching gravel was familiar and significant; the air was heavy, not with humidity but with history. Here we were! This contact, while glancing and totally imaginary, was more intimate than the time I'd spent in stadiums and arenas with Harry Styles, and funnier to me than life itself.

It's one of these patches of dirt here, I imagined telling a double-decker tour bus. *It's very important to remember.* Then I imagined a Los Angeles ghost tour one hundred years in the future: *This is where that journalist was decapitated by a tractor trailer as she knelt at the side of the road looking for the spot where a pop star threw up. She hovers over the 101 to this day, searching, but not unhappily. See, there she is now, she's eating a donut.* I got everything I wanted, really, because what I wanted was an opportunity to make my own digital shrine—just some photos of the highway, just some tweets about how good it felt to go in search of it. Just a little joke about how I'm getting older, and how I'm allowed to rent a car. Just something to report back to the girls on the internet.

THE EARLIEST EXPERIMENTS IN ONLINE COMMUNITY HAD AN odd gravitational pull, for whatever reason, for Grateful Dead fans. Community Memory, the first digital bulletin board, was installed in a Berkeley record store in 1973 and was tightly intertwined with the California counterculture—it was dedicated to the sharing of art and literature, and full of Deadheads.[4] The same year, the Stanford University artificial intelligence researcher Paul Martin created the distribute command "dead.dis@sail" to collate his lab's email conversation about the Grateful Dead into a proto listserv. In early 1975, he made the mailing list semipublic by putting it on ARPANET—the U.S. Department of Defense's experiment in communication protocols that would eventually lead to the invention of the internet as we know it—and researchers from other universities started joining.[5] Martin programmed automatic news updates that crawled for information about the Grateful Dead and sent them out immediately to all subscribers, and they, in turn, crowdsourced information from other fans in a manner and with a purpose strikingly similar to those of pop stans today. In 1975, for example, based on group intel, several members of the dead.dis@sail mailing list crashed a wedding at a country club outside Palo Alto after learning that the Dead guitarist Bob Weir had been hired to play with his side band Kingfish.[6] (They were allowed to stay.)

According to the internet researcher and historian Nancy K. Baym, "hundreds, perhaps thousands" of dial-up computer bulletin board systems were launched throughout the 1970s and 1980s, and many were specifically set aside as forums for Grateful Dead fans.[7]

Here, early adopters innovated the idea that the internet might be organized by affinity. Though early internet fandom was invite-only and near exclusive to well-paid white men, it was also the first evidence of a pattern. Fans became, almost as a rule, the first to adopt new platforms and to invent new features of the internet—a habit molded by the fact that they were the people with the most obvious incentive to do so.

The WELL, the most influential early virtual community—the story of which is chronicled in Howard Rheingold's 1993 history *The Virtual Community*—was founded by Stewart Brand and Larry Brilliant in 1985 as a general interest dial-up bulletin board system for the Bay Area in California. (Later, in the early 1990s, it morphed into a broad-use internet service provider.) Though many of the other early users of the WELL were technologists, scientists, journalists, and academics to whom computers were already familiar, Deadheads invested hours of free time to learn about the technology that would make it possible to practice their fandom together in cyberspace.[8] Their "conference" on the WELL was known only as "GD," and it was always busy with chatty fans—dissecting lyrics, discussing concerts, sometimes swapping memorabilia or tapes. It could be joined only by emailing an administrator or "host" personally, and was founded by the Deadhead historian David Gans, with the help of the tech journalist Mary Eisenhart and the programmer

Bennett Falk, who came up with the idea at a Grateful Dead concert. In *The Virtual Community*, Matthew McClure, the WELL's first director, identifies two major growth spurts for the board: the first was word of mouth among Bay Area computer professionals and journalists; the second was the Deadheads. "Suddenly, we had an onslaught of new users," he tells Rheingold. "The Deadheads came online and seemed to know instinctively how to use the system to create a community around themselves."[9] At the time, individual internet users had to pay à la carte for the hours they spent online, and being a member of the WELL—if you used it fanatically—could run up a bill of hundreds of dollars a month. These funds were necessary to keep the service operational, and the Deadheads were therefore crucial to its survival. According to Rheingold, the Grateful Dead conference on the WELL was "so phenomenally successful that for the first several years, Deadheads were by far the single largest source of income for the enterprise."[10]

By the 1990s, people building alternate lives through online fandom were also imagining the future of the internet. Fan sites with rudimentary features like guestbooks and photo collections were some of the most heavily trafficked pages on the internet once the World Wide Web opened up to a broad recreational-users base, and in 1995, Yahoo's free web hosting service, GeoCities, took off, filling up with thousands of fan sites that had something for everyone. The full range of these pages is difficult to see today, but amateur archivists have put substantial effort into preserving it: you can still browse partially salvaged pages for *The X-Files* (with names like "24 Hour News X" and "The Hall of X"), *Buffy the Vampire Slayer* ("Buffyology—The Academic Study of Buffy"), *Sailor Moon* ("The Moon Palace Archive"), the boy band Hanson ("Grown Up Hanson Fans Unite"), Harry Potter ("Perfect?," a Percy Weasley fanfiction archive), Sherlock Holmes ("The Sexiest Lines in Sherlockian Canon"), *CSI* ("Naked Truth," a site dedicated to an imagined relationship between investigators Catherine Willows and Sara Sidle), Britney Spears ("Jen's Britney Spears Page," "Jerry's Britney Spears Page," "Matt's Britney Spears Page," "Britney People," "Britney Space"), and almost any other media property or personality you can think of.[11] Backstreet.net, "the MOST famous/best BSB page on the Net," was created in 1997, and though its guestbook is now littered with phone-sex spam, it is still browsable. A faux-LED "I <3 BSB!" GIF still spins around on the front page, above links to 25,000 photos, 12 discussion boards, and an RSS news bulletin that sent out 1,691 updates about the Backstreet Boys before it ceased publication in 2012.

These pages were social networks in their own right, bound by limitations that meant conversation could happen only clunkily in guestbooks or by linking and cross-posting, but richly interconnected nonetheless. Some of the more elaborate sites had discussion boards; Murmurs, an R.E.M. fan site built using Microsoft's FrontPage HTML editor by then sixteen-year-old Ethan Kaplan, debuted in 1996 and had ten thousand users and five thousand new posts per day during its peak. When Kaplan shut the site down after eighteen years, he reflected on it as "a great example of an emergent community around fanaticism."[12] In August 1998, David Bowie announced that he would be launching the "first artist-created Internet Service Provider." BowieNet, as it was called, was a fully functioning ISP for eight years. Fans paid $19.95 a month for a "davidbowie.com" email address, Bowie chat rooms, exclusive Bowie content (including concert "cybercasts"), 5 MB of storage space on their Bowie fan pages, and "full uncensored" internet access. "I wanted to create an environment where not just my fans, but all music lovers could be a part of the same community," Bowie said in a press release, "a single place where the vast archives of music information could be accessed, views stated and ideas exchanged."[13]

THE IDEA OF MAILING A MONTHLY WIRELESS BILL TO TAYLOR Swift or sending your professional correspondence from an "@justinbieber.com" email address would be ridiculous now, but that kind of participation was, for a time, a logical way for music fans to experiment with the possibilities of the internet. Before most people were using the internet for anything, fans were using it for everything. Still, for much of the 1990s, these fans were mostly men—well-educated, affluent, and white. The World Wide Web was born in 1994, and though millions of people came online throughout the mid-1990s, the gender gap in the United States didn't close until 2000. (In a study of women's internet adoption from 1997 to 2001, the economists Hiroshi Ono and Madeline Zavodny argued that the delay could be attributed to men and women's differences "on average, in socioeconomic status, which influences computer and internet access and use.")[14]

To see the women of the early internet, and of early online fandom, you have to look for them. Women were expressly unwelcome on the web in its early days. "There are no girls on the internet," a catchphrase that originated in Usenet gaming communities in the early 1990s, was in wide use on 4chan and Reddit and other forums well into the aughts. It was codified in "The Rules of the Internet," a digital document that has fluctuated in length and form as it's been passed around message boards for the past fifteen years but still contains several phrases that are instantly recognizable to anybody who has spent time online.[15] (Rule 34—"if it exists, there is porn of it"—is so well known that it's regularly quoted by people who probably can't name the source or a single other "rule." Same for Rule 32, "pics or it didn't happen.") Rule 30 is "there are no girls on the internet," and it's followed by a correlated rule, number 31, "tits or GTFO," a common refrain from the days in which any internet user claiming to be a woman was demanded to prove it with a photo of her body.

Before TikTok, Instagram, Facebook, YouTube, MySpace, Friendster, and all the other Web 2.0 platforms that incentivized the hoarding of attention and the cultivation of a personal brand, pseudonymity was the online norm. Though the lack of real names or bodies made it a difficult task, men in these spaces were still fixated on identifying the sex of the users they interacted with—and driving women off the web by insisting they weren't there to begin with. "The discourse of male-by-default is pervasive across pseudonymous spaces," the internet researcher Siân Brooke observed in a retrospective.[16] But there were, of course, girls on the internet; they were just hidden. Nancy Kaplan and Eva Farrell's 1994 ethnography of "young women on the net" staged a direct challenge to earlier studies that had dwelled on the negative experiences of adult women who'd tried to participate in internet culture, and instead emphasized the importance of speaking to teenage girls. Teen girls, Kaplan and Farrell pointed out, had no professional reason to be online, and so it was only their "desires" that brought them there. This made them an ideal subject for study of what anyone might be seeking on the internet, and whether they were finding it. "We have been so busy noticing what hinders and repels us that we have failed to ask what draws some of us," Kaplan and Farrell wrote, introducing a deep dive into the public messages on a handful of popular online bulletin boards—all owned and operated and populated predominantly by men, and all used, also, by teenage girls. These girls were going to boards for thoughtful, long-form correspondence that differed from the conversations men were having in both style and intent. Girls were writing "to maintain connection rather than to convey information," Kaplan and Farrell observed. Their sketch was self-admittedly simplistic, using anecdotal accounts to point at behavioral stereotypes, but it was pivotal in demonstrating the reality that girls, in fact, had not been uniformly dissuaded from computers or from life online. Farrell watched the conversations of others and kept her own diaries. "I noticed that even as I was inducted into this world, I invoked changes in it," she wrote. "You create the net in the act of accessing it."[17]

In the late 1990s, women contributed disproportionately to the boom of fan websites—a boom that was energized by the creation of thousands of GeoCities pages in honor of boy bands like NSYNC, Boyz II Men, and the Backstreet Boys in the United States, as well as Take That, Westlife, and Boyzone in Europe, all of which grew in parallel to the wealth of pages created by the enormous, women-led fandoms for TV shows like *The X-Files* and *Buffy the Vampire Slayer.* "Girls and women are a substantial presence on the World Wide Web," the researcher Pamela Takayoshi wrote in 1999, bucking the general assumption—it was just that the sites they were building occupied "a non-mainstream, nondefault position" and were going unnoticed.[18] Even as men continued to argue that women did not exist online, women were outpacing them: most new users of the internet in 2000 were young women, according to a Pew Research Center study conducted at the time, and most of them were young women who were "more enthusiastic" about the internet than their male counterparts. The report referred to these energetic new users as "Instant Acolytes" and credited them with a projected societal shift of enormous consequence:

> *With Instant Acolytes' inclination to go online from home and for fun, the Internet may be evolving much like the telephone into a domestic tool for sociability used more heavily by women. Rather than a mysterious technology that is the province of men, the Internet is on the cusp of becoming a household appliance whose applications are as much social as transactions-oriented.*[19]

By the time of Pew's follow-up study in 2005, 86 percent of American women between eighteen and twenty-nine were online, compared with 80 percent of men that age.[20] Men were still using the internet for a wider variety of activities, but women were far more prolific online communicators, sending and receiving emails for personal reasons that had nothing to do with work and approaching the new tools at their disposal as ones well suited for connection. Though men had been the early adopters of the internet, women were the early adopters of social media—in late 2010, just after the launch of Instagram, 68 percent of American women were using some combination of social networking sites, compared with 53 percent of men. By August 2012, the numbers had risen to 75 percent for women and 63 percent for men, and the gap didn't close until 2015.[21] Incidentally, One Direction had been the biggest band in the world for four years by then, and I was twenty-two years old, having the time of my life, friendless in my first apartment in New York City, scrolling through Tumblr.

THE REASON I WAS SO DISTURBED WHEN I WAS INCLINED TO look for the shrine to Harry Styles's vomit on Tumblr and couldn't find it is because I rely on Tumblr to provide me with my memory.

Tumblr had no system in place to archive or analyze activity on its platform before it hired its first "meme librarian," Amanda Brennan, in 2013, six years after the site launched.[22] But luckily Tumblr's basic premise—as a somewhat secretive space for identity exploration through multimedia—enabled a culture with a unique visual style and a predilection for "discourse" and historicizing. Stockpiling images and compiling them into "master posts," the basic work of archiving a cultural phenomenon, became one of the common recreational uses of the site—today, even for those wading past broken links and stabbing blindly for useful search terms, there are remarkable libraries of One Direction ephemera to be found. They're made up of GIF sets, an invention of Tumblr users, and organized with elaborate tagging systems that are possible only on Tumblr, where users can put spaces between words and write entire paragraphs legibly in a post's tags. Though they can be difficult to find, posts that are deleted are not necessarily gone, because reblogging a post and adding to it makes a persistent copy of it—totally unlike a Twitter retweet, which disappears if the source material is erased. At various points, users couldn't reply to posts at all without reblogging them onto their own page, turning every conversation into a public exquisite corpse.

The way Tumblr is built also explains why so many describe the site as formative in their political, aesthetic, and cultural taste, as well as their personal identity. Alexander Cho, an assistant professor of Asian American studies at UC Santa Barbara who researches how young people use social media, has credited the physical structure of Tumblr with the creation of its culture. In his 2015 doctoral thesis, he explored the reasons that queer young people of color gravitated toward Tumblr in its first several years of popularity, and how the site was used "to cultivate an explicitly anti-heteronormative, anti-white supremacist politics."[23] Tumblr was a creative new space that had little in common with other social media sites on which users were expected to maintain public profiles, and on which the ties between people or "accounts" were also public and could be explored in order to understand a web of connections. While Tumblr content *can* be seen and distributed widely, and there are certain Tumblr posts from many years ago that persist, reblogged by hundreds of thousands of people, it's rare for a Tumblr post to become well known outside of the insular world of the platform. When a blog disappears or its URL changes, there is no easy way to find it again. Tumblr's search feature is so bad it might as well not even exist. These design choices meant that Tumblr was impossible to simply drop in on and understand: "Tumblr, especially in the early days, seemed impenetrable, ruled by a code and norms that were never outlined anywhere officially, only intuited," Cho writes. "[It] feels almost as if it purposely gave the middle finger to established conventions of indexing, search, and persistence on the internet."[24]

The same design elements and features that foster

Tumblr's singular culture make it difficult to find cultural artifacts on the site. But this, too, is part of Tumblr's culture: for me, the shrine to Harry Styles's vomit is preserved by my resolve to wade through shards of information and broken links to find it. I should have prepared better—I should have reblogged the shrine years ago so that it would forever be part of my own page and I would never have to worry. Because Tumblr's primary interactive feature is the reblog, its primary mode of engagement is frantic stockpiling. Scrolling through the feed, users gather things to their pages—things that may be deleted later by their original creator but which anyone, after reposting, can single-handedly preserve.

The small thrill of understanding a meme comes from a feeling of belonging, but when years have gone by and the meme resurfaces, the feeling is also one of relief. For Christmas one year, my sister made me a sweatshirt with a Tumblr in-joke on it: a photo of Niall Horan trying out for *The X Factor* with a paper sign taped to his shirt, on which some production assistant had typed out his name, erroneously, as "Naill." Dredging up his tiny humiliation is funny because it's a callback to a time before the world knew his name, when only day-one fans could be expected to notice the error. Bringing it up again years later is a way of teasing him, even though he's not there to participate, and it's a way of teasing each other for caring so much about his life. It's also an offer of reassurance—we all feel this way, still, a decade later.

These are the best and most satisfying memes: the ones that require years of recall. I can scroll through my Tumblr feed today and sometimes be startled anew by the absurdity of "Wax Liam," the nickname the One Direction fandom gave to Liam Payne's horrifying wax figure at Madame Tussauds, which looks, frankly, like some kind of sex doll. The mouth is open, corners turned up, with a tongue visibly close to emerging—kind of like he's panting? But the eyes are dull and dead, with no smile creases. The effect is that the face looks pained and horny. It's been Photoshopped into any number of unnatural scenarios, including a tattoo on Zayn Malik's arm; an *Insidious* movie poster, overtop the faces; the "hide your kids" meme; a still from the music video for Christina Perri's "Jar of Hearts" (?); and a whole bunch of smutty tousled-sheet fanfiction scenarios. (In the fall of 2020, going about my workday scrolling, I felt a tinge of sadness upon seeing the news: One Direction's wax figures were being removed from the museum after seven years.) Yet Wax Liam is not easy to find if you are not already embedded in Wax Liam culture. It was never added to a formal archive or written about in a publication that would maintain such a thing. Know Your Meme, the de facto encyclopedia of internet culture for more than a decade now, does not reference it. There are only eight entries on the site that refer to One Direction at all. The meme repository of record is run by well-intentioned and detail-obsessed people, but everyone has blind spots. "Having a female voice on staff is very rare," Brennan told me when I was reporting on the site's ten-year anniversary.[25] (Before she was Tumblr's meme librarian, she interned at Know Your Meme for a summer.) Your best bet for links to Wax Liam, and details about his storied time on earth, come from messaging the operator of that invaluable blog bad1dimagines. "I like this blog a lot because sometimes when people ask about a specific thing (a picture or wax liam), you link it," an anonymous follower wrote to her once. "Every time I click a link I get this mini rush, because I never know where it will send me or what I'll be looking at. It's always more disturbing than what I could have imagined." (bad1dimagines replied with a smiley face shedding a tear.)[26]

When I wrote to the proprietor of bad1dimagines, she told me that she hadn't imagined her blog as an archive when she started, but considers that word "an accurate description of what it's become."[27] The blog started as a joke—of course!—but then people started to rely on it, so she started to take it seriously. And by creating archives outside of the purview of institutions or corporations, and in massive collaborative efforts with no barrier to entry or rules for participation, an amateur archive like bad1dimagines is, as Abigail De Kosnik argues in her 2016 book *Rogue Archives*, doing the work of democratizing cultural memory. "Traditional memory institutions were not designed to safeguard cultural texts that proliferate indefinitely" she writes.[28] Something like bad1dimagines is still reliant on Tumblr in a lot of ways, but it is not reliant on any formal archival system, and it *is* designed to "safeguard" a still-evolving cultural text, for as long as anyone is still on the site and reblogging its posts to make more and more copies. It can respond immediately to inquiry, replace links when they break, and fill in missing pieces of information before it becomes too eroded to be read by future audiences. It connects those who remember and those who are learning, allowing them to bond over the mutual project of digging up the good stuff.

Fans are engaged in archival work all the time because they're always engaged in a conversation of "remember when," presenting and building on their own oral history. (Where collective memory "used to mean the record of cultural production, memory is now the *basis* of a great deal of cultural production," De Kosnik writes.)[29] In the early days of One Direction, when several members of the band had girlfriends and Niall didn't, a random photo of him holding a leaf became another in-joke: it was passed around with a caption about "shipping" the pair known as "Neaf." In 2019, Horan posted a photo of himself standing next to a plant in his house, and "Neaf lives, never give up the ship" popped up on my dashboard. The first "Neaf" is the sort of event that would be compiled in a master post of stupid things Niall has done, or "best memories from early One Direction." (Today, you can easily find it, of course, on bad1dimagines.)[30] These archivists acknowledge their own limitations and unreliable memory, often admitting, "I can't find this," and then asking others, "But didn't this happen?" Sometimes, the best anyone can do outside of locating the original post is connecting with someone else who remembers the original post, and who may be willing to describe it for the record.

In my deluded attempt to locate the precise former roadside site of a large piece of paper, I failed. But in talking about it online, I succeeded in archiving the story once more. When you search for the shrine to Harry Styles's vomit, you will see a handful of stupid tweets by me. These tweets may fall, like so much else, into what the WELL cofounder Stewart Brand was the first to refer to as a looming "digital dark age," when cultural history that is maintained only at will by for-profit corporations erodes and falls away, leaving huge gaps in future generations' understandings of who we were.[31] But I like to think that someone else will make a copy of the shrine to Harry Styles's vomit. We'll never know an internet without it—thank god! On my phone, sometimes, I replay the clip of Harry Styles laughing at the puke poster. I ripped it from YouTube and saved it to my camera roll so I wouldn't ever lose it. "A little niche, maybe," he says over and over, while the studio audience laughs.

GABRIELLE KOPERA'S ORIGINAL PHOTO OF THE SHRINE IS easy enough to find, indexed dozens of times on Google Images. It's referenced in articles about "the moment Harry Styles knew he'd made it," which was supposedly the moment someone told him his vomit had been scooped off the ground and was up for sale on eBay.[32] In grainy, bootleg YouTube clips, it's pulled up on the big screen in the background of *The Graham Norton Show*, while Styles says, "Is this the puke thing?" The puke thing! In Tumblr's degrading and incoherent archives, it can be much harder to walk back in time to find the original conversations about this vomit, but they are there so long as you *know* that they are there. "My stupidity was immortalized," Kopera said when I asked her how she felt about her shrine's brush with online fame.[33] She'd known where to place the sign because she'd grown up five minutes away from the spot and recognized it instantly in the background of the photos—she'd been driving past it her whole life. The sign was only up for half an hour before other fans started tweeting at her, saying they were going to drive out to Los Angeles to burn or destroy it. (They felt she was encouraging the ruthless stalking of Styles by tabloid photographers.)

So she went back for it, grabbed it, and stowed it in the garage. (It's still there.) She was eighteen then, and the type of One Direction fan who would sometimes wait at the arrivals gate at LAX to catch a glimpse of the band. At the time, Kopera was bored: she didn't have the money for a four-year school and so she'd stayed home to work and to study at a local community college while most of her friends moved away. Being a fan of One Direction made her feel like she had something to do that wasn't a chore. At the very least, she would have something to say and people to say it to—something to care about and a way to spend her time. When she saw the photos of Styles throwing up, she saw them as a prank the universe had played on her alone. Here she was, one of his biggest fans in the world, a girl who had traveled for him and tweeted for him and thought about him for years, and he had barfed right in the middle of the drudgery of her life.

She was surprised that people misinterpreted the shrine so dramatically by assuming that she was crazy or malicious. She was also confused by the way it was covered in the media, as if it was something more bizarre than a comedy routine she was performing, primarily with herself as the audience. "The worst part for me about the sign was that news outlets kept saying his throw-up was being sold on eBay," Kopera said. Some of them strongly implied that she was the one who had scooped it up. "I never saw puke, nor did

I want to. I definitely never, ever tried to sell his throw-up. I never actually saw a listing on eBay, so I feel like that was made up." Oh well. You can't control the rumors and myths that swirl around the legitimate events of history. All you can do is preserve what you have. She keeps the photo on her Instagram account, and promised she would forever.

"It was more a joke about my life than his," she told me. Now it's a joke about mine, too.

Trending

IT WAS THE BEST OF WILD BLANDNESS: A MUSIC VIDEO THAT opens with a boy in nautical horizontal stripes—tapping on the steering wheel of a vintage VW Bug—and proceeds primarily with five boys jumping around and falling on each other, protected from serious injury by clouds of swooping hair. A song with the same chord progression as recent mall food-court hits like Owl City's "Fireflies" and Katy Perry's "E.T.," as well as several Beatles songs. All Abercrombie & Fitch and high-top Nikes. At the end of 2011, One Direction's dreamily offensive debut single, "What Makes You Beautiful"—"You don't know you're beautiful / That's what makes you beautiful"—was coursing through YouTube and American radio stations, charting higher than any song by a British act in fourteen years.

Within a few months, the phenomenon was compared explicitly to Beatlemania, and the boys were charged with causing waves of teenage hysteria—predominantly online—before a single show had been played on American soil. In March 2012, they performed on American television for the first time, appearing on *The Today Show*, swarmed by fifteen thousand fans at Rockefeller Center.[1] That same month, *Up All Night* became the first debut album from a British group to reach number one in the United States. In November, *Take Me Home* made One Direction the first boy band in U.S. history to release two number one albums in the same year. "It's a real moment," Sonny Takhar, then president of Sony subsidiary Syco Music, told *The Guardian*. "Social media has become the new radio. It's never broken an act globally like this before."[2] Harry Styles's suggestion that "famewise," One Direction was "probably even bigger" than the Beatles was not quite as scandalous as John Lennon's infamous insistence that the Beatles were "more popular than Jesus," but the claim was still interrogated by music critics and journalists. London's 5 News assembled an expert panel of radio DJs and "showbiz" reporters to assess it: "Well, they're the biggest pop band in the world right now, that's fair enough," BBC Radio 6 DJ Matt Everitt conceded. But the Beatles changed American cultural history, he argued. "I don't think One Direction are going to change American cultural history."[3]

By this time, One Direction fans were already boasting that they had stolen security camera footage from at least one hotel (to see Zayn Malik without a shirt on) and an Australian airport (so they could watch Harry Styles just sitting around).[4] They referred to themselves as hackers, and they acted as if they were above the laws not just of their respective countries but of reality itself. They bragged not only about leaking albums and breaking Twitter, but about things they could not possibly have actually done, like acquiring the ultrasounds of each band member in utero, as well as scans of their passports. They made One Direction into the biggest band in the world not simply by loving them, but by sowing chaos on every online platform they touched. Almost everything they did was worthy of media attention because almost everything they did had never been seen before and literally could not be explained. In 2013, one fan account "leaked" the penis sizes of every member of the band, insisting that Liam Payne's was more than ten inches long. For a year, another fan tweeted in character as "Liam's 10 inch," providing the Twitter bio "I AM THE OFFICIAL 10 INCH OF LIAM PAYNE."[5]

On Twitter, anyone who doesn't remember all of that is a "local." This is one of the more casually devastating labels one can acquire in the digital age. A local is a person who belongs to no subculture, understands no intricacies of online humor, follows only the accounts of people they know in real life—and maybe *The New York Times*?—and retweets only the most generic content. Most simply, and most often, a local is a non-stan. If you haven't been around since the early days of One Direction but buy a ticket to a Harry Styles concert just because you like his pants, you're a local, taking up space that doesn't belong to you. If you're confused by fan-made supercuts of Korean pop stars, proliferating in the replies to any viral tweet on any subject, you are a local. Locals have no identity, no allegiances, no personality, no charisma, no passions, no curiosity, and no reason to be on the internet at all. A local joins Twitter to share professional news, which they refer to as "personal news," and to retweet "inspiring" human interest stories. They love "relatable" content and memes that are long past relevant, and they're also, it's implied, kind of lazy. A local is a person who has not been bothered. They haven't felt moved to do the work of stanning. Maybe it's more useful to say what a local is not: A local is the opposite of the One Direction fan who started a new Twitter account in 2010—while the band was still just a contender on *The X Factor*—in order to share "facts" like "the boys blood types" (Liam: AB. Louis: O. Niall: A. Harry and Zayn: B.) and each of their heights, in inches and in centimeters (all are under six feet, and Niall is the shortest, at five foot seven, or 171 centimeters).[6] A local would never hang around, waiting for Niall to say that he can't calculate his rising sign because he doesn't remember what time he was born, ready to supply the answer (8:04 a.m.).

The corrective force acting in opposition to locals

is "Stan Twitter," a broad term encompassing all of the superfans of anything under the sun. (The word "stan" is taken from an Eminem song about an obsessive fan, but is sometimes also referred to as a portmanteau of "stalker" and "fan.") Looking at Twitter through the eyes of a local, you can certainly see that stans are there. You can sense their gravitational pull and the way they drag every conversation into their realm of relevance, making every day online about them and their wishes and their feelings on the many injustices of the *Billboard* charts. Locals roll their eyes at the antics of Stan Twitter, which seems always to be in hysterics and on the edge of a meltdown, as well as bent on dragging everyone else down with them. But they can't do anything about it.

WHEN TWITTER LAUNCHED IN 2006, IT WAS NOT OBVIOUS what it was for. Tweets were initially sort of like Facebook status updates, but what was the point of limiting your thoughts to—at the time—140 characters, and no pictures, when there was already a website that all your friends were on that did not impose those limitations? Why would anyone join a website that served them nothing but contextless, mundane messages from brands and a bunch of people—when they even *were* people, and not bots—they didn't even know? What was the point of moving into vacant space?

After the dot-com boom, technologists rallied

around the promise of "Web 2.0," a term coined by Darcy DiNucci in 1999. The new web, she wrote, in departing from the static web pages and passive browsing of Web 1.0, would be "understood not as screenfuls of text and graphics but as a transport mechanism, the ether through which interactivity happens."[7] In 2004, the tech commentator Tim O'Reilly organized a Web 2.0 conference to help developers and investors nail down the specifics and talk out the business model. To him, the new web would be about "harnessing collective intelligence" through activities like hyperlinking, tagging, and user-generated content. Where software companies used to talk about silent customers, they should now talk about users as "co-developers" of their projects. Logically, they should also engage in "real-time monitoring of user behavior," to see how their features were being used and when to add new ones.[8] Twitter was founded shortly before Facebook was made available to any person over the age of thirteen. Tumblr followed the year after. These applications debuted as blank slates, and the people who came to them filled them with culture. They innovated the language and rhythm and aesthetics and norms of websites that they didn't fully understand but saw instead as raw material.

As Nancy K. Baym and Jean Burgess document in *Twitter: A Biography*, the words we associate with Twitter today and use—for better or worse—in regular conversation, like "hashtag" and "don't @ me," were not the developers' own ideas but instead those of early enthusiasts.[9] In 2007, users started adding "@" as a shorthand when a post was intended to be read by someone specific, or to directly reference another account. This didn't really make sense until Twitter made @-replying a real feature a few months later. The hashtag made a similar journey to Twitter from Internet Relay Chat channels and early Web 2.0 sites like Flickr, Last.fm, and Delicious—where they were already in use to catalog conversation topics and make files more searchable. Twitter was initially reluctant to add hashtags to the site—cofounder Biz Stone said hashtags were "for nerds"—but they acquiesced when users pushed for it. The tags were made searchable in 2008, and the company started experimenting with using them to determine "trending topics" in 2009.

At that point, hashtags started drawing the attention of the types of people who later became known for caring deeply about directing attention on the internet. For those people, the crucial difference between Twitter and Facebook was that you could post to Twitter from a cell phone. A pre-smartphone cell phone. *Any* cell phone. You could text your tweets to Twitter. By 2009, Twitter's user base was young (mostly eighteen to twenty-nine) and female (21 percent of American women online had accounts, compared with 17 percent of men) and Black (26 percent of Black Americans online had accounts, compared with 19 percent of white Americans and 18 percent of Hispanic Americans).[10]

The young and the online moved to Twitter from other platforms and started to build it out. The staunchly anti-corporate and surrealist energy of "Weird Twitter" steered the site toward a default of absurdism, sustained by the constant retweeting of early accounts like @fart, known for hijacking brand campaigns with inexhaustible trolling; @leyawn, the sweet cartoon-bird man whose first tweet was "SOMEONE PUMP MY STOMACH ITS FULL OF EVIL"; and @dril, the source of such timeless-feeling phrases as "it is with a heavy heart that I must announce that the celebs are at it again."[11] As confused politicians, musicians, and movie stars joined the site to share total nonsense or graphic detail about the mundanities of living in even a very famous body, the idea of celebrity started to mutate. The unreachable were suddenly right here, at times even closer than we would like. "just got home, let out the dogs, within minutes they cornered,attacked and killed an opossum," Martha Stewart tweeted in 2009. "had to wash little bloody mouths .life on farm."[12] An untold number of brains were wrecked by one of Britney Spears's early tweets: "Does anyone think global warming is a good thing? I love Lady Gaga. I think she's a really interesting artist."[13] These disoriented extremely famous people were just like the rest of us: unnerved or moved by the events of our daily existence, deluded into thinking that projecting it outward would somehow be rewarding.

Black Twitter was recognized early as a major

cultural force on the platform. "What Were Black People Talking About on Twitter Last Night?" Choire Sicha asked on *The Awl* in 2009.[14] Black Twitter users were, for whatever reason, taking over the site during late-night East Coast hours, driving the course of conversation and the trajectory of memes for hours at a time, impossible to interrupt. The *Slate* columnist Farhad Manjoo asked several media and network researchers to explain the phenomenon to him and was told that young Black people were using Twitter "differently from everyone else" on the platform. They were creating dense clusters of interaction by following back most of the people who were following them, retweeting each other reciprocally, and replying to each other's posts quickly and often. "It's this behavior, intentional or not, that gives Black people—and in particular, Black teenagers—the means to dominate the conversation on Twitter," he concluded.[15]

Stan Twitter was molded by these three influences: the emotional valence of Weird Twitter, simultaneously detached and totally out of control; the public-private flattening of Celebrity Twitter, which promised that from now on we would always have access to a behind-the-scenes candor from anyone and everyone; and the tight networking and enthusiastic riffing of Black Twitter, which took the shapelessness of the site and gave it a conversational form. The type of densely connected networks that Manjoo noted—in which people with shared cultural reference points follow each other's accounts, becoming what's known now as "mutuals"—is crucial to fandom, which sustains itself by rapidly escalating the visibility of its passions and funneling attention to the celebrities and causes it cares about. The idea that hashtags could be used to elaborate on jokes or to sustain conversation on niche or insider-y topics preceded the rise of fan practices such as streaming parties and stan wars. The first major "update"—or news—accounts dedicated to individual celebrities appeared in 2009 as well. They were there mainly to share chart positions and curate paparazzi photos, but Stan Twitter also began taking shape around the idea that young users did not have to use their real name or real images of themselves in order to participate. In fact, it would make *more* sense and confer greater authority if they found a sufficiently rare or interesting photo of their "fave" to use instead. Stan Twitter was where Tumblr culture came to make itself known to a broader and busier internet. The most visible demographics were the young women who appeared to make up the majority of the fan bases for artists like Taylor Swift and One Direction, the young women of color who controlled the fan operations for Rihanna and Beyoncé, and the gay men who tweeted on behalf of Nicki Minaj, Lady Gaga, Ariana Grande, and others. Crossover and cultural exchange between "stan armies" happened predominantly through their warring—the Swifties taught everyone how to craft a narrative around their fave's persecution, while Nicki Minaj's Barbz demonstrated how to make memes that were funny enough to get their hero's personal attention, and Rihanna's Navy came to exemplify what a prestige operation could look like for Stan Twitter, having figured out its tactics and protocols long before anyone else.

For some fans, all of this was serious work from the beginning, even though their labor often put them at odds with the platform that was hosting them. The people who are the best at driving engagement and attracting attention are also the people who can lose their accounts in an instant for uploading a few too many seconds of a video they don't own; to stay in business, they have to act like they're in business. (They also tend to lose their accounts over repeated infractions of other rules—such as those against tweeting death threats at people.) The French Rihanna fan who started @TeamofRihanna in July 2011 referred to the account as "professional" when asked about it by *Paper* magazine.[16] The first major Beyoncé fan account, @BeyonceWeb, was created in August 2010 and developed a reputation for reliable, accurate news—a decade later, it has more than three hundred forty thousand followers, as well as the honor of being one of only ten accounts that Beyoncé herself follows on Twitter. The second, @BeyLegion, had been sitting on a Twitter handle since 2009 but grew its audience first on Tumblr. The mysterious Bey Legion leader moved to Twitter full time in May 2012 and was later interviewed about this successful cross-platform migration by the marketing blog *Brandwatch*. "What started out as a Tumblr page is now a global team operating multi-channel marketing across Twitter, Youtube, Facebook, and Instagram channels," the interviewer wrote.[17]

Twitter itself was abundantly aware of the business opportunity of stans. In 2010, tech journalists circulated a claim sourced to one unknown Twitter employee that 3 percent of the company's servers were employed solely to host activity related to Justin Bieber. "Imagine racks of servers dedicated to delivering [Bieber's] every word to 5.1 million users," the *Daily Beast* reporter Brian Ries wrote. "They exist."[18] As a claim, this does not even make sense, but Twitter wisely declined to publicly refute it. In 2011, the year Twitter introduced the ability to attach photos to tweets, Beyoncé announced her first pregnancy at the MTV Video Music Awards. Twitter's public relations team was quick to highlight how the reaction played out on the site—she'd generated 8,868 tweets per second in the moments after she threw open her blazer, rubbed her belly, and winked at the camera.[19] In 2012, Lady Gaga became the first person to hit 20 million followers—a milestone her online marketing company, ThinkTank Digital, had been anticipating for two years.[20] Her fans, who identify as "Little Monsters" under her care, often referred to her in those days as the "queen of Twitter," a title that she was also awarded by *Forbes* after she surpassed Britney Spears to become the most popular woman on the platform.[21] (In celebration, she recorded an inaugural address, in which she thanked her followers for making her Twitter royalty, waved a glowing blue wand, and vowed to "tweet and tweet again.")[22]

By the time I joined Twitter, as a college sophomore in 2012, the battle lines had been drawn: A person could be a Justin Bieber fan or a person could be a One Direction fan, or a person could be both—but if that were the case, they'd better cleave their personality in two and pick one half to keep off the internet. Hardly a day went by without the two fandoms jostling to get a spot among the trending hashtags, a goal even more tangibly possible and immediately achievable than the also important goals of winning chart domination and the highest ticket sales and the most appropriate recognition from award shows and the coolest photo shoots from the best magazines. The number one spot on *Billboard*'s Social 50 chart, which incorporated "buzz" from every major social media platform, toggled between Bieber and One Direction nearly every week. The rivalry was vicious and exhilarating, like college football except interesting. During a particularly noteworthy 2014 showdown between the two fandoms over a social media–based "Biggest Fans" honor at the MTV Europe Music

Awards, each side went so far as to create fake versions of the hashtags used to vote—tweaking a letter in their opponent's tag or adding an emoji, in hopes of pushing this version into the Trending Topics bar and confusing fans on the other side, hopefully sabotaging millions of votes.[23] "Gonna tell my kids this was world war 3," one Bieber fan tweeted five years later, with a screenshot of the leaderboard.[24]

This was also the year that *Billboard* introduced an annual competition called Fan Army Face-Off—a summertime online-only event in which stan factions were celebrated primarily for their ability to execute the pulling of levers, over and over and over. There were enough armies to fill up an entire March Madness–style bracket: Lovatics (Demi Lovato) and Selenators (Selena Gomez) and the Little Monsters and the Rihanna Navy and the Directioners in an arbitrarily drawn Eastern Conference, versus Arianators (Ariana Grande) and the Gould Diggers (Ellie Goulding) and the Beyhive and the Beliebers and the Barbz in the Western. The results were ridiculous and transparently warped by powerful fan armies voting for whomever their most obvious rival was paired up with in each round—unless there's another explanation for the Directioners losing to the Panheads (Skillet stans) in round one, or the Beliebers losing to the Victims (the Killers fans). The final champions were the VIPs, fans of the K-pop group BIGBANG, followed in second place by the Echelon, apparently the name for the fandom of Jared Leto's rock band Thirty Seconds to Mars.[25]

Whatever else you might say about it, 20 million votes were cast in the objectively meaningless contest that year. This, it was clear, was what Twitter was for.

ONE DIRECTION'S TAKE ME HOME TOUR STARTED IN FEBRU-ary 2013 and grossed $114 million, with six sold-out shows at London's O2 Arena as its centerpiece. Though it came out just before the end of the year, the band's third album, *Midnight Memories*, sold 4 million copies and became the bestselling album of 2013 worldwide. In a year-end post on the company blog, Twitter announced that three out of five of the most retweeted posts of the year were from members of One Direction. The posts they referred to were uniformly boring: Niall Horan celebrating his own birthday, with his signature punctuation artistry, writing "Yesss ! I'm 20 ! Wohooo ! No more teens!" Zayn Malik sharing a photo of Harry Styles sleeping, captioned "Harry wake up !! :D." The third was Malik's announcement that he was engaged to Perrie Edwards, a member of the British girl group Little Mix.[26] But the point of Twitter was for fans and faves to be in near constant contact—these little intimacies were what made it all feel real.

For One Direction fans, Twitter was easy to turn into a constantly refreshing scrapbook, and it was easy to start viewing the band's commercial success as a result of this labor. In 2014, Twitter allowed users to add GIFs to their tweets for the first time—One Direction's Where We Are tour was documented that way, almost second by second, by fans who uploaded from cities all over the world. Bringing in more than $290 million, it was the highest-grossing tour of the year, as well as the highest-grossing tour by a vocal group ever. When the band's next album, *Four*, came out that November, they broke their own record to become the first band in American chart history to have its first four albums debut at number one.

Social media researchers were obviously interested in the network of co-conspirators that made One Direction the most visible ongoing conversation on Twitter. These people lived everywhere, but they congregated in group chats to coordinate and strategize, and they never failed in their efforts. In 2016, Nicole Kelsey Santero, a graduate student at the University of Nevada, conducted a forensic analysis of a collection of One Direction–related hashtags that had been number one worldwide trends on Twitter the year before, including #HarryBeCareful, which referred to a rumor about an assassination plot against Harry Styles. ("Guys please rt this and make the boys security aware because we need to keep our sunshine safe," one tweet read.) The paper identified Twitter accounts that served as "hubs," defining them as "a small number of influential users" who were highly connected and motivated to spread these hashtags. The hubs were mostly personal fan accounts and moderately sized "update" accounts—based not just in the United Kingdom and the United States but in Portugal, Brazil, Greece, the Netherlands, Indonesia, Armenia, Lebanon, Mexico, Italy, the Philippines, and elsewhere. One particularly influential Zayn Malik fan account with over one hundred forty thousand followers and one Harry Styles fan account with about forty-five thousand were even traced to China, where Twitter is blocked.[27]

Critics of social media often point out that Twitter's functionality and engagement-juicing business model rewards dramatics and over-the-top rhetoric—suggesting that the platform is its cause. But it's also the emotional stakes of Stan Twitter that set the tone. Scrolling through my timeline at any given moment, theatrics are being pushed to ever more elaborate heights. "If taylor swift murders me DO NOT PROSECUTE HER !!!" one fan writes.[28] Another shares a photo of Harry Styles, captioning it "he's so sexy break my back like a glow stick daddy."[29]

The structure of stan networks is what makes them feel so unavoidable on Twitter—their slang is everywhere, their trends are filling up the sidebar, their wrath is coming down on anyone who makes so much as an offhanded comment about a pop singer whose latest single was not their best. This is how the mannerisms of Stan Twitter became the mannerisms of the whole site—through mutuals creating, as they did, thousands of denser, smaller networks knit together. Stan Twitter, of course, pushed the internet at large to use the word "stan," and sometimes to swap it with the self-deprecating equivalent "trash," and to parrot phrases like "we stan a legend" and "HER MIND," and to refer to people as "oomf," meaning "one of my followers," or an "IRL," meaning someone who also exists in one's offline life. A song has become a "bop" or a "banger." A good guy is now a "king," and a bad guy is now "over."

Gay stans popularized the light diss "your fave could never," as well as the unfortunate compliment "skinny legend" and the tongue-in-cheek practice of making ultra-violent demands of the things we love—"step on my neck," "run me over with your car," "break my back," "punch me in the face." Black Twitter introduced shorthand like "she snapped," to signify praise, then "she doesn't have the range," a casual put-down that blew up in 2016 and warranted explainers in *GQ* and *New York* magazine, to indicate cool dismissal. Black fans with a drag culture background introduced "wig" as an expression of enthusiastic surprise, and Black women popularized "tea" as a synonym for gossip. This language was appropriated by young stans, then more crudely by brands and white professional adults, before its adoption as the speech of Twitter at large. By 2020, the official Target account was retweeting BTS album sales numbers and adding, "We have no choice but to stan."[30]

IN 2018, A LADY GAGA STAN CONVINCED A BUNCH OF OTHER fans to make sock-puppet Twitter accounts and pretend to be middle-age women. "Radio hosts hate homosexuals and stan twitters, it's a fact," they wrote. "Make an account with a soccer mom selfie avatar."[31] This is charming because the only intention was to complete successful radio requests for Gaga's new single, but it's also a little bit chilling, because it demonstrates online fandom's allegiance to manipulation.

Stans have little regard for rules or terms of service. They manipulate the timeline in good fun, generally, and they sometimes do it with dubious methods that are traditions of darker online spaces. Their prodigious talent for amplification is not always paired with an interest in the truth, which can often backfire, and they've learned this the hard way. The notorious cesspool 4chan used fans' talents for escalation against them quite often in the early years of Stan Twitter, seemingly just to make a point about who *really* held the power to bend reality online. In January 2013, for example, posters on 4chan's "random" board conspired to prank Justin Bieber fans by circulating images on Twitter that would appear to show other fans slitting their wrists, paired with the hashtag #CuttingForBieber.[32] "You stop using drugs and we'll stop cutting," one fake fan account tweeted alongside a graphic image. "You make this world meaningless and we've lost hope." The hoax was debunked by media outlets, but not before it succeeded in setting off thousands of confused responses and trending on Twitter. The following year, 4chan came for the One Direction fandom by promoting the hashtag #SkinFor1D.[33] The idea was that One Direction fans could be duped into tweeting pictures of themselves naked if it were even suggested that this would in some way benefit the band. Trolls made more fake fan accounts, stole photos of naked teenage girls, and tweeted them until they started a trend. The hashtag was used one hundred ten thousand times in forty-eight hours, and though it didn't result in a whole lot of nude sharing, it did derail the fandom for two full days.

Years later, Stan Twitter has a seedy reputation due to its own history of aggressive trolling, inspired in part by tactics that were once used against it. If there's one thing that Stan Twitter is known for above all else, it's that when it turns against you, it turns bitterly. Once, alone in New Mexico after a breakup, drunk in an Airbnb on a Wednesday night, I tweeted a bland joke about an old Taylor Swift music video. "There's a reason you're drunk and alone," a stan spat back within seconds, though they didn't follow me and I hadn't tagged Swift in the tweet. *I love Taylor Swift!* I wanted to plead, but I knew it would do no good, so I simply went to bed. That kind of exchange is the most delicate of brushes with the bad side of Stan Twitter—like being blown a kiss, even. It was nothing.

I don't want to run through a full litany of the coordinated harassment campaigns that One Direction fans have executed throughout the years. But one memorable and well-documented incident happened in 2013, when they tweeted a baffling number of death threats at *GQ* magazine—the magazine itself!—after it published a condescending profile of the band and its fandom.[34] (The profile really was egregious, and described a typical fan as "a rabid, knicker-wetting banshee.") One fan's response read, "I want to fucking mutilate your insides, feed them to my dog and burn your body in my own personal raging hell."[35] (Everyone at the magazine's insides! And to one dog!) When Beyoncé fans decided that the designer Rachel Roy was Jay-Z's mistress based on a handful of vague clues, some of them wrote to her sixteen-year-old daughter, informing her that her mother should drink bleach.[36] Nicki Minaj fans pointed Minaj in the direction of the Canadian music blogger Wanna Thompson after she tweeted some light criticism of the rapper's recent work—Minaj wrote to her personally, calling her "ugly." After she shared screenshots of Minaj's message, Thompson lost her job and received death threats from fans, some accompanied by images of her young daughter.[37]

Over the years, stan harassment tactics have only

evolved to be weirder and deliberately more unsettling for those on the receiving end. In 2020, when Taylor Swift's surprise quarantine album *Folklore* was given an overwhelmingly positive review by *Pitchfork*'s Jillian Mapes, which contained perhaps two full sentences and one parenthetical of constructive criticism, fans immediately started suggesting that Mapes "sleep with one eye open."[38] They also doxed her by publishing her home address. Then they started tweeting images of Swift—edited to look like a demon, with an upside-down cross on her forehead or black maggots falling out of her mouth—accompanied by what they seemed to think was a hex, translated for indecipherable reasons into Amharic, the official language of Ethiopia. (The text, fed back through Google Translate, read something like, "Anyone who comes after the Queen of Darkness Taylor Swift will die alone and burn forever . . . You will never be happy and you will never sleep again.") They also spent days tormenting the Australian experimental musician Katie Dey, who had joked about the misfortune of sharing an album release date with Swift, tweeting "my ass is fatter than taylor's at least."[39] On Twitter and Instagram, they told her she was a "dumb bitch" and a body shamer and reminded her that she wouldn't sell as many records as Swift if she lived for two hundred years. They also reminded her of the Queen of Darkness stuff, obviously. "i knew my fat ass would ruin my life someday didnt think itd go down like this tho," Dey wrote in the midst of the storm.[40]

WHEN I TWEETED THAT I WAS WORKING ON THIS BOOK, THE response came in two phases. At first it was "congratulations!" from my friends and coworkers and former coworkers. Then, a few weeks later, it was something else: "Maybe One Direction fans should write a book about you instead, titled 'Why are you this obsessed with us?'" A segment of the fandom that was still irritated by an essay I'd written on the well-known conspiracy theory about Harry Styles and Louis Tomlinson years prior had heard about the project and signal-boosted it to each other. The replies came in one after another, until I turned off my notifications and started ordering glasses of wine. "Leave us alone," and "get a job," and "you're creepy," and "we're not here to feed this bitch," and "do better things with your time." "This needs to be stopped," and "she's not up to anything good," and "you're pathetic," and "girl go away," and so on. One person commented that I was probably just going to screenshot these replies and use them to make the fandom look bad, about which I had to admit they were right, even if they were misunderstanding how much I would rather not be in that position at all.

Fans are unavoidably part of Twitter's knotty history with abuse and coordinated harm. Stan Twitter has never been motivated to push entire groups of people off the internet, nor has it engaged in the same level of graphic violent threats or dangerous real-world attacks as those driven by explicitly hateful ideologies—which, during the "Gamergate" online harassment epidemic in the mid-2010s, usually took the form of calling SWAT teams to a victim's home address. But it would be irresponsible to ignore some similarities. In 2018, a team of MIT media researchers performing a postmortem on Gamergate explained how the site had once been turned into an "inescapable GamerGate experience" and described some of the "dark patterns" of Twitter, writing, "When one member sent a message, that message became a signal to [a] highly connected community that had been instructed to echo one another."[41] Stan Twitter harassment campaigns do not approach the level of Gamergate. Yet any kind of harassment at scale relies on some of the same mechanisms—a tightly connected group identifying an enemy and agreeing on an amplification strategy, providing social rewards to members of the group who display the most dedication or creativity, backchanneling to maintain the cohesion of the in-group, which is always outsmarting and out-cooling its hapless victims, all while maintaining a conviction of moral superiority. Twitter provides a platform for some of the worst habits of fandom.

Still, no matter how afraid I sometimes am of the whims of stans, I would never want to be a local.

Many or most stans don't participate in harassment campaigns, and being part of Stan Twitter is much more fun than logging on just to frown at politicians or congratulate acquaintances on their new jobs. When I'm doom-scrolling through a timeline full of terrible news and inane bickering, it's a treat to come across all-caps excitement or an ultra-niche joke. Or to wake up and find that there is a conversation going on and that I understand it, and that people are excited about something and I am too. This is the type of thing that can buoy a person for an hour or so at a time. In the same way that holidays give shape to formless years, album promotion and single releases give color to the days that line up one after another. There is a reason to stay up late. There is a reason to wake up early. There is something to do at lunch when you feel like you'd like to cry and take a nap. There are people who swear they *hacked into an airport security camera*, and aren't you interested to see what they saw, even if you find that totally weird and ultimately quite scary? I like Stan Twitter because it is so peculiar, even as millions of people participate in it and it *should* have become generic. "This is the 6th Christmas without One Direction," the anonymous account @1DPsychic tweeted on December 23, 2020.[42] Fair enough. "Niall Horan will be the first to go bald," it shared in January, no explanation.[43] "Louis Tomlinson will show us his wisdom teeth removal video," it promised in March.[44] I guess we'll find out!

In the summer of 2020, when coronavirus infections in the United States had not yet peaked, One Direction fans celebrated the band's tenth anniversary. I was in Brooklyn, living alone. Like many people, I hadn't seen my family in months. I had watched eleven seasons of *The Real Housewives of New York* in just under six weeks. I was in a new relationship, which had been robbed of the fun of meeting in bars or casually suggesting attendance at a friend of a friend's birthday party. We'd watched *Contagion* on our fourth date, sitting on my bed, speculating about what a respiratory virus could do to each of us. Like everyone I knew, I felt like I was living in the worst sensory deprivation tank of all time—completely deprived of human interaction, yet still constantly bombarded by news alerts. But the day of the One Direction anniversary, I started scrolling through Twitter and the world came back to me. There were memes I'd forgotten about and concert clips I'd never seen. It was all fresh—the first new thing in months, or the only special occasion of the year. I riled myself up easily, went out to the store—double-masked—in the pouring rain and bought ingredients for a birthday cake, as well as big cheap candles. I slid around my apartment making Martha Stewart's chocolate buttercream, and watched music videos on a laptop balanced on the edge of the sink. I felt like life indoors was enough again. I poured cake mix into a pie dish. I yelped when I scrolled past a screenshot of an old tweet: "help so my cousin got upset after reading a fan fiction where harry styles dies and now she's been peeling potatoes for 3 hours."[45] The text was accompanied by two photos of a teenage girl sitting on a couch, glaring at a potato, which she is peeling into a metal bowl. I clicked into another tab, clicked back, looked at it again, and laughed again. It was so perfect. The best short story I had ever read. Other people on the timeline were celebrating it too; they were in awe of its concision and hilarity, the way it felt like something that had happened to them personally. It *had* all happened to us, personally, and it was still happening.

This is the best of what Stan Twitter can do. It provides interludes in which it's possible to feel that there is such a thing as "community" on a website used by nearly 200 million people, or online anywhere. I love when girls tweet to see if anyone else is in the Los Angeles airport, flying home from the Harry Styles concert, feeling depressed that it's all over. (I am!) I love when it's Thanksgiving weekend and someone logs on to say that they put the new One Direction CD on in Mom's car, and as they did so they realized that there must be thousands of new One Direction CDs playing in thousands of moms' cars all over the world. (*My* mom's car!) I feel grateful every time.

The morning after the tenth anniversary, I pulled

up Twitter to start work, as usual, and felt the site diminished. Here we were, still grown-ups, still under orders to stay home and scroll. Here we were, nothing to do but our jobs. Nothing to look forward to except the 6:30 glass of wine that marks the end of the workday; nothing to search for except more advice on how to avoid contracting a disease. I read a tweet from a Harry Styles fan: "Yesterday was like a breath of fresh air after literally one of the worst years of everyone's life."[46] She didn't really need to explain what *this* day was like. It was terrible. With a stale cake in my refrigerator, I was bored again, and so tired—exhausted by 10:00 a.m. But for a moment, I was glad to know that even in my hyperspecific misery, I would never be alone.

Trash

WHEN I WAS NINETEEN, I HEARD A ONE DIRECTION SONG FOR the first time, and it ruined my life. This is how girls on the internet usually put it, and I like the way it sounds. *If the world ends tomorrow,* we say over and over, *just let One Direction know that they ruined our lives and we'll see them in hell.* On the band's tenth anniversary, one woman chastised her followers amid a day of festivity, writing, "stop celebrating . . . grow up if they didn't ruin you, you did it wrong."[1]

Some people will explain exactly what they mean: they've achieved utter and irrevocable financial precarity by designating an outsized share of their income to concert tickets, overpriced T-shirts, and collectible photo books, or they've become incomprehensible to their friends and family because of the degree to which they speak and think in fandom references and memes.

They didn't use spoons for three years because Liam Payne said he was afraid of them. They put a space before every piece of punctuation because of Niall Horan's baffling insistence on doing that. The only time they feel their brains flooded with serotonin is when they watch videos, as one fan put it, "about a stupid boyband that isn't even together anymore."[2]

Fans also know that this makes them a joke to some and an enrichment opportunity to others. The fully commercialized internet is built on an understanding of identity in which each of our characteristics is one that advertisers would be incentivized to track. Google and Facebook and their thousands of customers are probably equally or more interested in my affection for a pop star as they are in my coastal loyalties or the finances of my parents—though only insofar as it pertains to how I might spend my money and what I'll pause to look at for a while. This organizing principle of the internet cheapens all types of identity, reducing our lives in all their strangeness to a series of boxes to check and levers to pull before serving a targeted advertisement. But individually, we know that it's not so simple. When I say One Direction ruined my life, what I'm saying first and foremost is that they made my life much more difficult to explain. *One Direction ruined my life.* The word "ruined" expresses the indignity of love, and how it can careen us offtrack even under the best of circumstances. It's a satisfying and dramatic replacement for more feeble words like "changed" or "improved." To say that One Direction has ruined your life implies that they've had a greater impact than you would have chosen, even if you don't sincerely regret how things ended up.

Other times, I'll say it was Tumblr that ruined my life. The site was the home and incubator for fandom in the early 2010s, complementing its role as an identity accelerant—it provided images that gave form to the ideas that young people were having about themselves, as well as words that helped them describe burning feelings that might otherwise only smolder, or take much longer to catch light. Teenagers like me, who had come to the site to look at pretty things and collect interesting phrases, could often find themselves caught up in what the researcher Alexander Cho has referred to as the "cascading dynamic" of the timeline, then wind up somewhere completely unexpected.[3] In my mother's time, a would-be pop fan might hear a song serendipitously on the radio or on a friend's record player but would still have to actively seek out and pay for the physical media or concert tickets necessary to grow and sustain their affection. One Direction fans, telling their origin stories, typically start somewhere else: a YouTube video, which led to a rabbit hole full of more clips or a Tumblr dashboard mysteriously filling up with GIFs of boys they didn't recognize, which were so fun to watch that they could only dream of understanding their context. They recall becoming a fan in the course of a single breathless evening, entirely by accident, in one tab. "I was probably twelve or thirteen," Megan McNeeley, a One Direction fan from Cleveland told me. "We were just on YouTube watching random videos and in the suggested videos we saw one of their *X Factor* clips, so we clicked on it, and then we clicked on another one, and then we clicked on another one. We saw the 'What Makes You Beautiful' video together, and right away we were like, 'This one's my favorite, I want this one.' That was the start of it. It was just a night watching YouTube, and gradually I was like, *Oh no, they're the best thing that has ever happened.*"[4]

The "video diaries," a collection of blurry phone-camera videos taken on a set of dimly lit stairs while One Direction was on *The X Factor,* will come up eighty times if you ask one hundred random people how they fell in love with the band. These videos are just typical behind-the-scenes content, clearly an obligation that the band giggled and roughhoused through, and the source of some of the fandom's earliest memes, most of which are as unfunny as a nuclear family's inside jokes. (Louis says, "I like girls who eat carrots" in one, which somehow became a whole thing. He loves carrots!) "You've probably heard this a million times," Chiara Mueller, a fan from Germany stated. "I went on YouTube, and I went down a deep spiral of One Direction videos."[5] "They did those videos on the staircase, and then there was *so much* about them on the internet," Ashlynne Arnett, a fan from Kentucky, told me. "I just took an interest in them because that information was available, and of course Harry Styles is Harry Styles, and why not? I was curious. I wanted to know so much about them."[6] Jacob Gaspar, the fan from Ohio who told me that some people think his fandom is an ironic joke, said that he was "instantly hooked" after his sister showed him the *X Factor* diaries. "I thought they were the funniest people I'd ever seen in my entire life," he told me. "Then she played me 'What Makes You Beautiful,' and I was like, *That's fire, that's a fantastic song*."[7] These basically content-less stories are timeless, even though the mechanisms are modern—the experience of *becoming* a fan has never been easy to describe. Though social media popularized the idea of stan as an identity category, as well as the word "stan" itself, it hasn't clarified how a person transforms from "regular" to "stan." The commercial apparatus of the internet is interested only in *whether* I love One Direction, and not how or why I came to, a question around which there still is—and now I'm not only speaking for myself—plenty of mystery.

In the mid-1990s, the cultural historian Daniel Cavicchi spent three years interviewing Bruce Springsteen fans about where their love of Bruce had come from and how it had colored their lives. The resulting book, *Tramps Like Us*, published in 1998, is maybe the most thorough ethnography ever published about a single fandom. Cavicchi was particularly interested in "becoming a fan" stories and published many of them in full—some are hundreds of words long. He outlines two broad categories: the "gradual" transformation, in which devotional feelings work their way slowly into people's lives, and the "sudden" transformation, which involves a mystical change that seems to come out of nowhere. "One morning I woke up and I was a fan," said a woman named Laurie, who was thirteen years old in 1985 and had previously been bored by Springsteen. She'd made fun of his "I'm on Fire" music video whenever she saw it on TV. "I can't even begin to explain what happened because I don't know," she told Cavicchi. She borrowed her brother's copy of *Born in the USA* and listened to it over and over, then she borrowed all the other albums and memorized them. She said it must have been "predestined" that she would become a fan. "One minute I didn't care who he was and the next he was the most important thing in my life."[8]

The stories he collected were familiar to me, as a daughter of a Springsteen household. My mother was born in 1965 in Western New York, grew up on a dairy farm, and met my dad in a high school math class. (She'd first sat at the kitchen table with my grandmother and picked him out of the yearbook, noting his biceps.) For as long as *I* had known her, she'd been obsessed with Bruce Springsteen, and considered her fandom a cornerstone of her personality and life story. "I can tell you exactly when I became a fan of Bruce Springsteen," she told me over the phone one night. "I was sadly a late bloomer." She was nineteen, and she, like much of the country, fell for Bruce with the release of *Born in the USA* in 1984. The first concert of his that she attended was with my dad at the Carrier Dome in Syracuse, New York, about eighty-five miles from our hometown. "He was adorable, I'm not gonna lie," she said. "He was super exciting to watch onstage because he was having a blast. I fell in love and I just never left him." She started to say that it was a religious experience but then decided that was corny and ordered me not to include any quotes about it. "But that was it," she said. "I was done. There wasn't anybody else who has ever made me feel that way about their music." Cavicchi would label this a "self-surrender story," a category he created for the stories he'd been told that involved an easily recallable moment in which "indifference or negativity is radically altered."[9] These stories often read like accounts of religious epiphanies, and some of the fans who were telling them were, like my mother, almost embarrassed by their inability to describe the feeling without sounding extreme—it just seemed to swoop down out of nowhere in the same manner as romantic love or religious conversion. There was a before and an after, turning on a moment of transition from an old point of view, "dominated by ignorance and disenchantment," to a dramatically different one, "filled with energy and insight."[10]

WHAT DOES IT EVEN MEAN TO BE A FAN? CAVICCHI WAS frustrated in his attempts to find evidence of the word's evolution, though he noted that many scholars agree on a similar starting point. "The generally accepted origin is 'fanatic,' from the Latin *fanaticus*, meaning a religious and later a political zealot," he wrote in a 2014 essay. The word "fanatic" was used by American sports journalists in the late 1800s to mock baseball spectators, but the English were also using the term "the fancy" to refer to people who enjoyed spectator sports like boxing and pigeon racing, and it's unclear which one "fan" may have been abbreviated from, if either. He also pointed out that the practices we associate with fandom—collecting, cheering, following, fixating, celebrating, memorizing—were the habits of many people before anyone would have been called a "fan." There were "buffs" and "connoisseurs" and "devotees" and "maniacs," all of whom did certain things that some would count as fan activities. The whole chronology was a mess, he acknowledged: "Do the religious-minded 'music lovers' of 1850s urban concert culture or the unruly 'kranks' of post–Civil War baseball count as fans? Probably. But what about the weeping readers of Charlotte Temple in the 1830s?"[11] Today, it is even less clear what "fan" really means. The people in charge of entertainment properties or consumer brands consider anybody who pays money for the thing they produce a fan. In everyday speech, we say someone is a "fan" of anything they like, no matter to what degree. Coca-Cola refers to people who buy Coca-Cola as fans of Coca-Cola. During an average bit of small talk, I might refer to myself as a fan of shallots or not a fan of bell peppers.

The word "fan" is now synonymous with consumer loyalty; you could be forgiven for considering it a marketing word. Words like "stan" and, especially, words like "trash"—which started in early web fandom, faded out, and were revived on Tumblr in the mid-2010s, just as the commercialization of fans was reaching a new peak—are aggressively useless for marketing purposes, giving them their charm.[12] They signal derangement and depravity and they welcome confusion and disgust. To be One Direction trash is to be the type of fan who is devoted *beyond* the stereotype of asking Mom to buy a lunch box with Zayn Malik's face on it, or to put up the extra cash for VIP tickets at some arena sponsored by a car company. Trash is gross. One Direction trash make weird jokes tinged with sex and violence, and though they recognize the fact that they've been seduced by a commercial product, they don't care, nor do they respect its sanctity. They belong to a collective—a landfill of trash, a world of trash, heaping with loyalists to the biggest boy band in history. One Direction ruined their lives.

The One Direction trash openly complain about the demands that the band places on their time or on their wallets. Years into the band's "hiatus," every time a solo member of the band announces a tour or a new line of merch, Twitter becomes a chorus of jokes about blowing through rent money, or signing up for a new credit card, or skipping class and work to wait in a digital Ticketmaster queue undisturbed, or writing an elaborate PowerPoint presentation for parents who will need to be persuaded to fund a bus trip to the nearest major city. That being a fan interferes with a person's ability to be financially responsible or perform some of the more mundane tasks of adult life is part of what makes it fun, but it's also a source of conflict. Women who indulge in frivolities like One Direction concert tickets are often seen as spoiled teenagers (wasting their parents' money), or irresponsible adults (refusing to put that cash in a savings account), or inappropriately self-interested parents (who should be spending everything on their children). And the financial imperative of fandom is not just a personal strain; it also leaves the impassioned open to exploitation. It turns a core piece of a person's identity into something that can be bought and sold. Calling yourself "trash" is a way of accepting all of these external characterizations, as well as pointing out that they don't matter.

"There's an inherent contradiction in fandom, and it's one that everyone lives with," says Henry Jenkins, a media scholar at the University of Southern California who is known as the father of fandom studies because of his 1992 book *Textual Poachers: Television Fans & Participatory Culture.* "At one level, fans are ideal consumers," he told me. "They're deeply invested in the performer and they'll buy all kinds of merchandise related to that performer. But fans reject the basic relationship that is set up by the industry. They're always trying to push beyond the basic exchange of money. The entertainment industry is a tool or mechanism for fandom, but it's not what fandom is."[13] Fans intuitively understand the difference between the official product and their highly personal use of it. They might call themselves One Direction trash to accentuate this distinction outwardly, but individually it's very obvious. Personally, the moments when I've spent money on One Direction do not stand out as important ones the first One Direction T-shirt I bought at Heinz Field was very ugly, I felt. I've since lost it. Who cares? Much more important was a moment at a rooftop party in Brooklyn in 2019, when I was suffering from the typical emotional trauma of being perpetually on Tinder, and was surprised to find out that the host had slipped "Best Song Ever" into the Spotify queue just for me, as well as to discover that I still remembered a bit of the music video choreography I'd memorized in a college dorm room six years before. Would I have started dancing to anything that day otherwise? Probably not!

In his 1987 book *Glory Days: Bruce Springsteen in the 1980s*, the journalist Dave Marsh described the commercial hysteria around Springsteen's 1984 to 1985 U.S. stadium tour. Tickets had to be purchased over the phone at the time, so the late summer and early fall of 1984 was a season of phone systems crashing all the way down the East Coast. When tickets went on sale for a stadium show in Chicago, Marsh wrote, the phone companies had to power on the computer systems they usually used "to handle calls to towns hit by tornadoes."[14] Naturally, ticket scalpers were having the time of their lives. The tickets were so valuable, the possible profits so tempting, that local cops were even accused of participating. New Jersey Bell suspended five employees for "wire-jumping," bypassing busy phone lines to buy their own tickets, and the state assigned undercover police to stop scalpers around the Meadowlands Sports Complex outside New York City. But none of this has anything to do with fandom, really. Marsh also recalls a conversation he had with Springsteen about the marketing for one of his tours, which had enraged him to the point of ripping down his own posters. "Springsteen believed deeply in the inherent worth and dignity of popular music and in his own responsibility to its traditions, which he was convinced had saved him from a life of frustration and fury," Marsh wrote.

"A businesslike attitude toward that sort of thing is not appropriate," he remembered Springsteen telling him. "I want our band to deliver something you can't buy."[15]

IN THE SPRING OF 2019, A TAYLOR SWIFT PARODY NEWS account called @LegitTayUpdates tweeted an explanation to its followers for a recent absence.[16] "As most of you know, I haven't been very active in the past couple of months because I was in prison," she wrote. But everything was resolved and new Taylor Swift updates would be coming soon. When one of @LegitTayUpdates' followers asked her how she had *wound up* in prison, she responded glibly, "I refused to join the IDF lmao." (Service in the Israel Defense Forces is compulsory for citizens over the age of eighteen.)

The three-tweet story went viral, and @LegitTayUpdates was interviewed anonymously by a slew of publications, including both *Vogue* and the democratic socialist quarterly *Jacobin.* To the latter, she joked about how Swift had "scammed" white Republican fans by collecting their money for years and then declaring herself a Democrat. She also corrected the record, saying that many Swift fans are LGBTQ or people of color, despite the media's fixation on white teenage girls, and that a politically minded Swiftie is not the anomaly that her press cycle was making it out to be. "I think the smartest people I know are Taylor Swift fans, to be honest," she said. @LegitTayUpdates became one of the most beloved figures of 2019 internet culture, and admirers called her "timeless" and "iconic" and "influential," as well as "the only person" who did anything good all year. In January 2020, when it seemed as though the United States might start a war against Iran, there were more tweets: Americans might protest by dodging any potential draft, like that one Taylor Swift fan, a *hero.* @LegitTayUpdates received some backlash from pro-Israel factions of the internet, but took them in stride, announcing, "I never thought I'd see the day [my] main enemy would be Zionists but Tayliberal Swift really did bless me I guess!"[17]

She seemed to enjoy the attention and to revel in the opportunity to surprise people with what registered as an unlikely combination of identities: superfan of Taylor Swift and objector to occupation. Sometime later, her account disappeared—for unknown reasons—but admirers kept wondering after her. They hoped that Twitter hadn't "censored" such an indelible figure. (In 2021, another Taylor Swift stan claimed that @LegitTayUpdates had left Israel and gotten tired of Stan Twitter; according to the Internet Archive's Wayback Machine, the account was suspended from Twitter sometime between May and July 2019.)

I like this story because it reminds me that all combinations of identity are equally unlikely, and we can only be experts in our own. Some of the stigma of fandom comes not from cruelty or genuine disdain but from that simple fact—almost everyone is too complicated to be quickly understood. Abby Armada, the woman who accidentally bit into a glow stick at a One Direction concert, told me she came to the fandom through fanfiction. Then she started watching a bunch of YouTube videos. Then she went to a few shows. Then an old friend who was living in Puerto Rico went through a bad breakup and they both flew to Miami on a whim, for thirty-six hours, for the last stop of One Direction's 2014 tour. All of this happened shortly after Abby got married, and so it confused her new husband. "My husband got jealous. Isn't that crazy? I think because he didn't get it," she told me. "We had straight-up fights about it."[18] Looking back at the other fandoms she'd been part of, she could see that it was a pattern. When she was a kid and her mom was really sick, she'd become devoted to Hanson. When she first moved to New York in her midtwenties and didn't know anyone, she'd gotten really into the *Sherlock* fandom. "I think I was just coping with being an adult and having this weird change happen," she said.

After she figured this out, she explained it to her husband. "I told him, 'I feel like I lost a part of myself, not because I'm married to *you*, but because I'm going through a life transition. I'm not trying to replace you with Liam Payne or Harry Styles, I'm just trying to cope.'" She's aware that people find it goofy or even abnormal for a woman her age to be invested in a boy band—a boy band that, I'll say it again, does not even exist anymore. She's also aware that some people are jealous of her ability to talk so openly about something she really cares about. "I'm a thirty-three-year-old woman, I just don't give a fuck anymore," she told me. "I know there are things I like. I want to talk about them and go have a good time. I'm a millennial and I'm going to die."

When Cavicchi wrote his book, it was still up for serious debate whether the adoration of a pop star turned a person into an idiot. The cultural anxiety around popular culture at the time—which has relaxed now, even if it hasn't totally disappeared—was that it was a homogenizing force that turned every participant into a mindless consumer. But in speaking to hundreds of fans, Cavicchi found something different. These people were exploiting the ultra-popular things they loved in order to become more completely themselves. "Springsteen fans' conscious discussions of self making do not indicate that popular culture is shaping their identity but rather that they are shaping their identity with popular culture," he wrote. "The importance of fandom for personal identity is not so much about the disorder caused by the mass media as it is about the order found in devotion."[19]

Previous generations of women would not be so

public about their fandom as Abby or @LegitTay-Updates, or even the pseudonymous powerhouses of One Direction Tumblr. Until recently, a lot of fandom—especially for women who were no longer in their teens—was a stay-at-home secret. For example, on the cover of Janice Radway's 1984 book about women fans of romance novels, *Reading the Romance: Women, Patriarchy, and Popular Literature*, a woman with big hair and a red sweater sits curled up alone on a floral couch in front of matching floral drapes, with a pile of children's toys visible behind her shoulder. She's reading a novel, which has an illustration on the cover of a man kissing a woman's neck, but she's doing so covertly, alone in the middle of the day. Radway's book was about secrecy, but she was also one of the first scholars to suggest that fandom could be studied without pulling it out of the context of daily domestic life. Daily domestic life was, in fact, what motivated some kinds of fandom, she discovered. The women Radway interviewed articulated their disappointments with the artistic limits of the novels they loved, but they made the case for enjoying them as an indulgence and as a distraction from the sharper disappointments of the real world. They used the books "to diversify the pace and character of their habitual existence," she wrote.[20] In previous studies of the plight of the house-wife, women reported feeling lonely and isolated, and described their social roles as ones that precluded the pursuit of self-interest or personal pleasure. Some of the women in Radway's study were remarkably frank: "I especially like to read when I'm depressed," one told her.[21]

These women read romance novels, typically, in near total secrecy—most of them didn't make public declarations of their fandom, and many of them talked about being careful not to read when their husbands were around. (One woman told Radway that her husband wouldn't let her read anything after he was ready to go to bed, but she would sometimes take a full day off from housework to read, as a "very special treat.") Radway was careful to define what her subjects meant when they said reading was an "escape." They were using the term two different ways, she wrote. "Literally, to describe the act of denying the present, which they believe they accomplish each time they begin to read a book and are drawn into its story," but then also in a broader, more figurative sense, "to give substance to the somewhat vague but nonetheless intense sense of relief they experience by identifying with a heroine whose life does not resemble their own in certain crucial aspects."[22]

Two decades later, the researcher Laura Vroomen profiled Kate Bush fans—a very different cohort of women who often identified as feminists. She interviewed women in their late twenties and early thirties, noting that while there had already been many studies about teenage girl fandom, there was a dearth of research into the role that fandom might play later in a person's life. What she found was that women who admired Kate Bush for her feminism and her independence "were not always able to translate this into powerful positions in their own lives." They talked about listening to Bush's music when boyfriends or husbands weren't home or were occupied by something else in another room. "Kate Bush is what I'll put on when I'm alone in the house. And I've got some time," one told her. They talked about resenting the men in their lives for not understanding, but they only rarely mentioned rebelling against the arrangement. "An ex-boyfriend was jealous of how, when I got sad, I wouldn't indulge in it with him, I would go and drink or listen to Kate and dance around my room until it's completely gone," one woman said. "I'd be sort of singing out of tune at the top of my voice, like [the song 'Cloudbusting'] or whatever, and then walk back in the room and I'd feel great and I could see that he was like numb."

For decades, scholars had been debating whether popular culture made a person into a rebel or an acquiescent. Vroomen was interested in the way lifelong Kate Bush fandom showed a middle way: neither "spectacular resistance" nor resignation to "being dull and trapped." While they were self-proclaimed feminists, many of the fans she spoke to took care to differentiate themselves from *other women*, who were usually young and silly and devoted in the wrong way to the wrong things. They didn't always call themselves "fans," even, because of the frivolous connotations they thought the word carried. Still, they copped to allowing the music of one woman to inform their identity over the course of their lives. Adult fandom, Vroomen argued, could not be chalked up to nostalgia or lingering loyalty—it was significant and specific to a new phase of life.[23]

Today, women still have complicated feelings about making their fandom public. Angela Gibbs, a mother from Alberta, Canada, told me that she avoids talking about her love of One Direction with anybody except her teenage daughter, Olivia. She fell for them while watching TV late one night, maybe three in the morning. The next day, she woke up her daughter—nine years old at the time—and they drove thirty-five minutes to Calgary, the nearest city, to buy a copy of One Direction's first CD. After listening to it on the drive back, they went on YouTube to watch the videos and figure out which voice was which. The band immediately became a shared passion. At the first concert they flew to Vancouver to see, Olivia was so exhausted from all the excitement that she fell asleep in the middle of the show, her mother remembered. Years later, during the band's last tour, Angela pretended that there wasn't spare money to go this time, and they'd have to miss it. "I was so good," she said and laughed, recalling her acting performance.[24] But of course, she'd really managed second-row floor seats and a hotel room in Toronto, and it ended up being one of the best nights of their lives. She doesn't have any good photos of it because she was shaking too much to focus the camera. "We sat there after the concert, and we actually had to sit there and just *be* for a moment because it was so overwhelming," she said. *"I can't believe that's over. I can't believe that happened.* We hugged and we cried, and we laughed, and we just talked and talked and talked."

The morning we spoke, years later, Harry Styles had just released the first single from his second solo album. Olivia was still sleeping. "My god, child, wake up!" Angela said in a showily strained voice, then laughed. "I want to play it for her. I can't wait. I just get so excited about it." As her daughter gets older, she's developing new interests and becoming her own person, but One Direction is something Angela and Olivia can still talk about. It ties them back to that time when they were so close. Angela's friends and coworkers don't understand any of it. They tease her about being a grown woman who loves a boy band, or they simply roll their eyes when she talks about it. "I am not the kind of person to be consistently hitting myself in the head with a hammer. You learn not to bring it up," she told me. "It hurts my feelings when my coworkers or friends make fun of me . . . whatever. So I just don't talk about it, which is hurtful in and of itself."

The adult fans of One Direction I met during the research for this book all told me the same thing: they don't talk about fandom with people who are going to make fun of it, so for the most part, it's easier to talk about it with other women on the internet. Liz Harvatine, a fan from Los Angeles who's in her early forties, does this mostly in a Slack server called "1D for Olds." One day, I called her and she told me how she became a fan of Harry Styles. Someone on the internet had pointed out that a character in the Rainbow Rowell novel *Carry On* was dressed like Styles, so Harvatine looked him up out of curiosity. "I was feeling quite depressed and for whatever reason I gave myself permission to lay in bed all day," she said. She started watching videos. "I exhausted all of the solo stuff, so I was like, okay, now I'm going to watch video interviews of One Direction and I have to listen to the songs and I just added more and more until I found myself in the condition I am now, which is just, you know, ridiculous."[25]

She was added to the Slack group after another member stumbled across the Harry Styles–themed quilt she'd made for a local quilting contest and posted on Instagram. That moment was a big deal for her because she'd previously heard rumors of the group's existence but had no idea how to go about joining. It was a little bit magical, she told me, "to be invited to a group that was previously known to me but completely invisible," and especially "to be in a space where you know everyone is an adult and you can act like an idiot about cute boys and their music." I knew exactly what she meant because I, too, had read about and heard about the Slack server but couldn't figure out how to get in until I learned, by chance, that another woman at the company I worked for was already part of it. When I talked to Harvatine, I was sneaking time away from my desk and sitting on a bench outside my Manhattan office. We talked over each other, and spoke in shorthand, though we'd never met. We were grown women, laughing about how a boy band had ruined our lives. "If people are instantly turning up their noses . . . I know who those people are," she said. "They don't get any of this side of me because they don't deserve it."

MY MOM HAS SEEN BRUCE SPRINGSTEEN IN CONCERT "around ten times," in Syracuse, Buffalo, Rochester, and New York City. She saw him on Broadway after entering the ticket lottery every day for weeks; she dropped what she was doing and took the eight-hour Amtrak ride down to New York without blinking. She took me and my sisters to see him in Rochester in 2012—the Wrecking Ball tour—right after she finished chemotherapy for breast cancer. "Taking you girls was really exciting for me. That concert had a lot of meaning," she said. "That was the end of my chemo, that was wanting you to love him like I did." When all four of us were kids and she was a stay-at-home mom, she still went to see Springsteen every chance she got. "Those years were kind of a blur," she told me. "But those nights I was able to see him were always special. Rejuvenating, I guess."

As a kid, I memorized the lyrics to "Thunder Road" to make my mother happy. I knew she loved Bruce Springsteen, but I didn't really understand why. I even resented it a little bit. I remember one summer afternoon when I was very young, we spent a few hours working in the community garden behind the church, then drove the vegetables to a food pantry in the nearby city. As usual, I'd probably spent the whole time heavy-sighing and stealing sugar snap peas (eating them in one bite, unwashed). In the minivan, a sticky heat and the smell of rotting fruit put a whine behind my eyes that made it hard to see straight. I remember feeling nauseous, bitter, wanting to cry, when she rolled the windows down and turned up "Jersey Girl," draping her wrist on the crusty rubber coming out of the car door. The song has a line about dropping your "little brat" off at her grandmother's for the night, and even though I wouldn't have been able to put it into words, I'm sure I could sense that she was somewhere else when she was listening to it.

When I try to demonstrate how fandom has worked in my life, I always use the same example: Harry Styles has a song that's kind of about abortion.[26] The song is called "Kiwi"—I do not know why—and it's a song about a woman who chain-smokes "cheap" cigarettes. She is also described, somewhat unfortunately, as "hard liquor mixed with a bit of intellect," and "such a pretty face on a pretty neck." The chorus is "I'm having your baby / It's none of your business." It's not clear if Harry Styles is saying this in character as a woman he is dating, which would kind of make sense, or if he's saying this in character as himself—maybe a joke about how much fanfiction has been written about him in which he is pregnant. The song is archetypal rock 'n' roll, lots of obtuse references that seem to be to cocaine and weed, and lots of guitar played in a screechy, dramatic fashion. "I'm gonna pay for this!" Styles—now in character as a sort of confusing type of guy—says a few times. Maybe he means he'll regret some of his actions vis-à-vis drug use; maybe he means he will be subsidizing a routine medical procedure. Who knows?

The song came out in 2017, and in 2018 I accidentally got pregnant. This was sort of an interesting scenario because my boyfriend at the time wasn't really in love with me the way I was in love with him, and being pregnant by accident even for a few days made me very sad. It's not that I thought I would like to give birth to his baby at twenty-four years old, or that I wanted to have any babies ever, but what I distinctly didn't enjoy was the way it made our undeniable lack of a long-term future feel immediately real. Of course I would get an abortion; of course we would be together for a little while longer; and then, of course, the rest of our lives would unfold separately. I found out that I was pregnant on a Thursday and then I had two margaritas; I made an appointment for an abortion the following Tuesday and spent a few days in a funny little haze. I journaled. I drank at a German bar and watched soccer. I attended a dinner party in honor of the anniversary of a Lorde album. I sliced, fried, and ate an entire eggplant. I went to a scary movie by myself and sobbed through the whole thing—I had to hold my hand over my mouth so that the rest of the audience wouldn't think I was making noises just to be freaky.

And I listened to "Kiwi." I listened to it while I walked to meet an editor for coffee, minutes after taking a second pregnancy test in the bathroom of a famous diner. I listened to it after I called my boss and told her I was taking the rest of the day off. I listened to it while I sat on the couch and touched my boobs and ate a hamburger. I listened to it in my bedroom while I drank red wine and imagined texting my sisters. I listened to it while I wandered, sweating, up and down Eastern Parkway in cutoff shorts, waiting for my boyfriend to get back from the beach so I could tell him what all had gone on. And I kept listening to "Kiwi." I listened to it on the train on Tuesday morning, tapping a foot, swaying in oversized jean shorts. "I'm having your baby! It's none of your business!" On the walk through Soho, with the early-morning sun making my armpits dampen under my sweatshirt. During the wait outside the Planned Parenthood building, across the street from a modest knot of protestors. On repeat. My boyfriend showed up twenty minutes after the time I'd asked him to be there, and he did not ask me how I was paying for anything, but he did bring me an apple and an off-brand Fig Newton. I cried because he was late, and I listened to the song again in each of the four waiting rooms I spent time in that day. I don't remember if he said he was sorry, but seeing as he sat there for six hours and didn't eat the apple or the off-brand Fig Newton, I just assumed he cared about me a lot.

Three days later, I went to see Harry Styles at Madison Square Garden with my sister, who was nineteen at the time and in her second year of college. Before the concert, I took her to dinner in Koreatown and told her I'd had an abortion earlier in the week. I tried to say this in a way that conveyed exactly how I felt about it—it's not a big deal, but I have some complicated feelings, and I'll talk about them, but not in a weird way, and only if you have a true curiosity. *I'm having your baby! It's none of your business!* Then she taught me how to use chopsticks. We had our palms read by a psychic who could not tell that we were sisters. The psychic said I would be going to California. We walked to Madison Square Garden and bought T-shirts with Harry Styles's face on them. We waited for Harry Styles to sing, and when he did, we jumped up and down like two girls. A woman in the audience had a sign that said I'M WITH CHILD, and Harry Styles read it aloud from the stage. He asked her how pregnant she was, and she screamed back that she wasn't pregnant. He said, "You're holding a huge sign that says, 'I'm with child.'" She screamed something else, and he said, "You're trying? Well, we're all trying." It was hysterical to me. Very funny! I wasn't with child either! I was a virgin at my first One Direction concert, I reminded my sister—I was a little drunk!—and now I was at a Harry Styles concert as an adult woman who'd just had an abortion, and that was funny, but also, I guessed, statistically likely to be a common experience.

I stomped my foot, and it was like sucking my thumb. I was marking time, I thought. Today, I'm twenty-four and in love and it doesn't always feel good. Last year, I was lonely. Next year, I'll be lonely again. These songs will sound right, even if they hit me differently. I felt almost entirely normal and almost exactly like myself. When I spoke to Daniel Cavicchi, it had been more than twenty years since he'd interviewed the Springsteen fans. I asked him what he remembered as the most common thread throughout their accounts of loving Bruce, and he told me: "It wasn't strange and bizarre, it wasn't twisting people up. I found that it was actually doing the opposite. It was helping people become less twisted, and to cope."[27] Whenever I hear "Kiwi," I am back wandering around Brooklyn in an early summer heat, rehearsing my sentences with a straight face, getting ready to say "It's okay" out loud. I'm back in the arena, taking videos of my sister. These kinds of memories are such small things, important only to me, the same way the specifics of my mother's Bruce Springsteen fandom—sustained since the early 1980s as a grand gesture of solidarity not with New Jersey's working-class men but with her teenage self—are important mostly to her.

When my mother talks about listening to "I'm on Fire" as a nineteen-year-old, I think I know what it was like, but it's hard to imagine your mother as a person. My mother is my mother. My parents met in high school, and they were married well before the age I am now. That night on the phone, I asked her if she thinks about when Bruce Springsteen will die, and she started crying, so I did too. "I honestly can't imagine a world without him in it," she said. "It would make me feel even older than I already feel. It would be the end of my youth. Because even if he's not running around onstage anymore, it's in my head. When I see him, I'm nineteen." How else do you get to be nineteen forever? Is there an easier way to do a quick check and remember who you are?

The boyfriend who was late to my abortion eventually broke up with me, obviously. It happened in a dramatic fashion on New Year's Eve. I'd celebrated the beginning of the year in the freezing rain on a rooftop with a bunch of people he knew and I didn't—he'd invited me to the party and then not shown up. As the hours had worn on, I'd had plenty of time to see what was coming, and when he finally arrived, fifteen minutes after midnight, he said something absurd to me in the street. Then we took a car back to my apartment and went to sleep, and on New Year's Day we broke up some more. I cried straight through the following workday, and on into the weekend, and I went through a monthslong period of screaming at my mother every time we spoke on the phone. *I'm unwell*, I told her. I couldn't handle it. I couldn't live inside my own head. I felt, because it had been so long since she'd dated anyone other than my dad, and because anyone she thought she loved in early high school probably didn't even count, that she'd really robbed me of something. She had deliberately refused to have an experience that would make her useful to me now. I'd been a well-behaved teenager, and I'd never rebelled in the home. Never had so much as a sip of alcohol until college, never called my mom a bitch. Now, as an adult, I was drinking five nights a week, and I really felt a white-hot fury. I knew that this was embarrassing, but I couldn't stop myself. If it weren't for her, I would know what to do.

But then, drunk one night, in a cab going over the Manhattan Bridge, I asked a friend to play "I'm on Fire" for me on his phone. With one arm out the window of the car, I pictured my mother sitting alone, a teenager on a farm, woozy and terrified by whatever it was that kept her up at night, which I'll never know about. *What kind of pain did she dull with this song?*

I wondered. *Can I do that now?* I didn't think so. But I had to admit that listening to those words—*sheets soaking wet, freight train through the head, hey little girl*—felt like sucking on a piece of ginger after the longest bus ride of all time. There *was* "a six-inch valley through the middle of my skull." That was a classic enough feeling to be captured by a pop song, and classic enough for me and my mother both to feel it, decades apart. For a few moments, I let my head droop onto my own shoulder. Then I sat up and sang quietly along, and of course I knew every word, because that's what my mother would expect of me.

Promo

IF YOU WANT TO SEE A SONG HIT THE TOP OF THE *BILLBOARD* charts, it's not enough to just listen to it. You should also bookmark a master post of every radio station in the United States (and the United Kingdom, and Ireland and Mexico and Italy and Ecuador) that takes requests via Twitter or online contact forms and petition them to play it—politely, followed by a thank-you, but over and over. You should pull open half a dozen YouTube tabs each morning and leave them churning in the background of whatever it is you're compelled to superficially spend your time doing. You should print out flyers with QR codes and plaster them all over your town. You should buy the song on iTunes as many times as you can afford it, juicing the numbers by sending gift downloads to everyone you know. You should tweet and tweet and tweet. You should feed the song through the Shazam app over and over, asking

"What is this?" despite the fact that the song is by this point more familiar to you than your own pulse and, however much you love it, more grating than your own voice.

If you don't live in the United States—the only country whose streaming numbers count toward *Billboard* chart positions—you could figure out how to convince the streaming services that you do. On Tumblr, instructions for how to game the system are easy enough to come across. All you would have to do is delete Spotify from your computer, download a proxy server or a VPN, turn it on, change your country to the United States, sign up for a free Spotify account, and fabricate an American zip code—or so the instructions say. From there, everything is taken care of for you. Someone else has already created a playlist with the song on it at least five thousand times. You can just hit play. Is this illegal? Perhaps. But it's common practice among fans, many of whom see it as a way of inverting expectations of what a pop music fandom can be. Though the critique of the music they love is that it demands nothing but passive listening and tacit acceptance of played-out storylines and chemically engineered hooks, their diligence is a counterpoint: they are still breaking something. When Harry Styles fans employed these tactics to juice the numbers for his first solo single, "Sign of the Times," in 2017, I asked a fan named Tessa why she was doing it. "I got involved because I love the DIY attitude," she told me.

"It's taking things in your own hands as a fandom." It was even, she ventured, a bit "punk."[1]

There's no reason to interrogate whether One Direction is actually punk, but it is fun to point out a couple of similarities, including the fact that neither were merely widely observed phenomena—they were *scenes.* The scene in One Direction's case was online rather than downtown or in basements, but it had its own language and culture and signifiers of belonging. There were other tactical and creative similarities between this pop music fandom and the musical undergrounds that came before. The wealth of music zines in the 1990s, for example, came from geographically dispersed, passionate, lonely outsiders who both gushed over and critiqued their idols on handwritten pages. They were not for profit (in fact they lost money), they were collaborative (participatory, transformative), and they were decidedly amateur. They weren't always political, but they were serious about wasting time. They labored unproductively or counterproductively on something that most people considered emphatically dumb. "Creating a zine can define work—and the sense of time that accompanies it—in a way that is markedly different from that which is common in daily labor," the historian and activist Stephen Duncombe observed in his 1997 book *Notes from Underground.* He also remarked that stealing images and words from various sources, cutting them up, and putting them somewhere else was an act of rebellion in itself, and a way for the rebels of the day to make "the mass media speak their own underground language."[2]

One Direction fans' relationship with the entertainment industry is adversarial, but mostly because they think they could run it better. Literally: in 2015, there were two separate fan efforts to buy One Direction out of their record label contract. Both were widely covered by a bemused press, who wondered how fans could claim to have stumbled upon a copy of the band's management contract, and who would know how to look for a buyout clause, and was this effort as implausible as it sounded?[3] The fans who did it were responding to the obvious misery of Zayn Malik—who had recently left the band—and to the grueling tour and recording schedule they feared would eventually break the remaining members of the group. They reasoned that they would need $87.7 million to make it happen, and they further reasoned that with the number of One Direction fans in the world, if everyone contributed two or three bucks, this could be accomplished quickly. If they were in charge, One Direction would be permitted to slow down, and therefore One Direction would remain healthy enough to never stop.

The general attitude of One Direction fans—both during the band's existence and during the solo careers of individual members—is that entities like "management" and "the industry" suffer from a lack of imagination. What fans have in mind is not just commercial success for the stars they love, but the more complicated aim of bringing One Direction to the world, in service of the world, and to prove, in turn, something about their own taste and intelligence. The internet lets them make One Direction into a shared project in which we are all involved—in which *every living person* is considered a candidate for becoming involved. Whether someone makes money off of this at some point is incidental to that aim, and whether the media chooses to take it seriously or not, it will be compelled to observe it, and when your friends say this boy band isn't very good, you'll invite them to argue with millions of people who have nothing else in common and can't all be wrong.

AFTER ZAYN MALIK'S UNEXPECTED DEPARTURE FROM THE band—he dipped out with a terse Facebook post in March 2015, a day on which the internet screamed and screamed in unison and I drove around my college town in the rain playing "You and I" on a loop—One Direction's record label opted not to release any more singles or music videos from the last album he appeared on, the band's fourth album, *Four.*

This irritated a certain faction of fans who had hoped to see a big promotional push around "No Control," a sexy eighties-rock banger cowritten by Louis Tomlinson and Liam Payne and various other people. It featured Tomlinson on lead vocals in a chorus for the first time ever—a big deal for those who had selected him as their favorite from the beginning and had so far received very little validation of this choice. It also featured a bunch of graphic lyrics about morning sex. ("I don't want to wash away the night before / And the heat where you lay / I could stay right here and burn in it all day," for example.) While everyone on Tumblr was moping about Malik's departure and what already looked to be the band's looming demise, a then twenty-three-year-old London-based fan named Anna Franceschi shared a proposal: "I would like this fandom to gather together for a project I thought about while I was coming back home on the overground on a working day," she wrote. "The project is releasing No control as the first One Direction DIY single." Sony wasn't going to do it, so logically, the fans should do it themselves. "We should decide a date as the release, promoting it through twitter and tumblr and facebook," Anna suggested. "This fandom is born and raised throughout these platforms, promoting the band just like when they were kids at The XFactor shouldn't be hard at all."[4] She tagged the post "#sorry it's just a silly idea" and "#it would be nice [though]."

A team assembled on Tumblr overnight. The professionals—referred to in shorthand as the collective "1DHQ"—were dropping the ball. They were failing at their most important task, which was bringing One Direction's most openly vulgar song to every corner of the earth. The fan-organized "social media exposure campaign" would kick off "immediately" and end with a massive effort hours before the Billboard Music Awards. The ultimate goal was not entirely clear, but the energy was electric. "1DHQ is like that lazy partner you were paired up with for a school project, so you have to do the whole thing yourself," one fan joked.[5] And with that, Project No Control was off the ground.

Instructions for supporting the project circulated on Tumblr and Twitter throughout the week: fans planned to buy the song on iTunes as many times as possible on their invented release date, May 17, and then came up with the idea of gifting the song to fans who didn't have credit cards. Everyone who participated was expected to keep "No Control" on repeat on streaming services, request it on the radio, keep it trending on Twitter, Shazam it repeatedly, submit it as a write-in candidate for *Billboard*'s "Song of the Summer," create fan art for it, and boost each other's efforts constantly—obviously. "This momentum cannot stop after tomorrow," one fan wrote the day before the unofficial release. "Otherwise it will completely flop, and we'll be completely run over by the release of 'Bad Blood.' We need to keep this up for at least a week."[6] They made Google Forms to pair up people who were willing to buy an extra copy of the song with people to give it to and encountered a major problem almost immediately: there were too many people willing to buy the song multiple times and not enough who were signing up just to receive it. "I had the idea of buying 30-40 gift copies for fandom members who couldn't do so for whatever reason, and then suddenly loads more people started stepping up and volunteering to sponsor copies too!" one fan wrote. "WE HAVE A PROBLEM THOUGH. Loads of sponsors, not enough recipients!"[7] That issue didn't last long. The next day, requests for gifted copies were pouring in from Albania, Iraq, Indonesia, Lebanon, Lithuania, Poland, Thailand, and anywhere else you can think of. The organizers needed sixty-seven copies of "No Control" for Indonesian fans alone.[8]

"No Control" reached the top of *Billboard*'s Trending 140 chart—a ranking of songs that were most talked about on Twitter—and fans successfully lobbied more than sixty radio stations to start playing it, including BBC Radio 1 and Z100 New York. The eerily sentient Tumblr account for Denny's even got in on the promotion: in response to a fan question about how the restaurant chain felt about "No Control," it replied, "it should be the next single."[9] When the band appeared on *The Late Late Show with James Corden*, Corden brought the campaign up, saying, "I have received so many tweets from your fans about this that I fear if I don't ask you about it, they might kill me."[10] In June, One Direction added the song to their tour set list and performed it live for the first time in Brussels, Belgium. At a tour stop in San Diego in July, Louis introduced the song, saying, "We want to thank every single person in the 'No Control' campaign, that was sick. Incredible, incredible, again, thank you so much." They played the song as part of their set for *Good Morning America*'s summer concert series that August, and two weeks later it became the first non-single to win a Teen Choice Award.[11] Discussing Project No Control, the BBC Radio 1 host Nick Grimshaw used phrases similar to the fandom's own. "They're taking it all into their own hands," he said. "This is like punk all over again." *LA Weekly* ran a headline heralding One Direction's transformation into "a DIY band."[12]

I CAME ACROSS "GIFTING BLOGS" WHEN I WAS WORKING AS A social media manager, scrolling through Tumblr looking for interesting viral content that could be repackaged into more viral content—it was the golden age of viral content. When I first talked to the fans who, at that time, were collecting money to gift copies of Harry Styles songs, they explained to me that it had once been a painstaking process. Gift organizers used to spend weeks making spreadsheets and setting up matches.

But a fan known only as Becca came up with an automated solution to erase this problem. She started working on it in August 2015, when fans were gifting copies of "Drag Me Down," the lead single from

One Direction's final album, and the system officially debuted with the release of "Perfect" that October. There was one form for signing up to give a gift and another form for signing up to receive one, each feeding into separate pages of a spreadsheet. The simple code that she wrote would group the data by country and then, as she explained it to me, "walk down each side looking for an open spot. The first open gifter spot gets paired with the first open receiver spot and the match is noted on each side. Once it gets to the end of the file and has gathered all the new matches, it gets the gifters and sends an email with the emails of the people they should gift to." There was no money being exchanged, so she was never nervous about the system being scammed. But it could send out seventy-five emails per minute, so she did sometimes get nervous about blasting out typos or other errors. The system has been used a few dozen times; new projects can be "generated with the push of a button, and then running matches is a push of a button, so over the years it's been low maintenance."[13]

Becca's system was also used for the April 2016 fan campaign Project Home, which was a continuation of Project No Control, this time promoting a bonus track from One Direction's final studio album, *Made in the A.M.* These gifts always came with specific conditions. Matches between "Home" gifters and recipients were facilitated on a rolling basis, but gifters were asked not to send the song out until April 29, "for maximum chart impact." Those who received gifts were asked to redeem them by May 5 or they would be surrendered and re-gifted to someone else, again to "maximize the impact of our project on the song's chart performance."[14]

This project failed to sway any of the people who were legally or financially in charge of One Direction's career. To this day, it's a source of pain for many fans that "Home" was never released as a single, and never received a music video beyond the amateur one they provided for it. This is just one of many sustained beefs fans have with the choices made around the promotion of One Direction's work—the beefing has become, in itself, part of the performance of One Direction fandom, and clinging to old wrongs is a way of hanging on to the experience of being a fan of One Direction long after they stopped making music. Five years after the band's last album came out, one fan announced on Twitter that she would "never" stop pressuring Ben Winston—the director of many of One Direction's music videos—to release the "finished(?) and buried" music video for the song "Infinity." "It had been started but not finished," he wrote in reply, to the surprise of fans. "Label changed course."[15] That response was retweeted more than thirteen thousand times, and the replies are full of all-caps outrage. They are very direct: "JUST HAND IT OVER. WHATEVER IT IS."[16] Release what you have! This is not hard! How about you just share access to your Google Drive! "ben have u seen the [videos] this fandom makes?" one of the top replies asks. "we don't care if its not edited chile we're shitty editing connoisseurs."[17]

When fans undertake high-lift projects, they don't tend to assume that they'll be 100 percent successful. They get something out of the exertion in any case. In 2017, when I talked to fans who were trying to boost Harry Styles's debut single, "Sign of the Times," to number one on the charts, most of them knew that it was not going to work.[18] The maximum that any of them could listen to the 5-minute, 20-second track was 270 times in one day. It would take thousands of fans really committing and following through on a promise to stream without respite for the effort to have any real effect, but only a few hundred people even liked the Tumblr post with the instructions about streaming. The Harry Styles Promo Team account created for the purpose of promoting "Sign of the Times" was eventually suspended from Twitter. The song debuted on the *Billboard* chart at number four.

But by this time, doing "promo" was a ritual, and failure was not exactly failure—superstition demanded that the process continue despite the results. If they *didn't* do it, Styles might feel it somehow. "The primary goal is just to support the individual members of the band as they release solo material, and to let them know that we're still here as a fandom and looking forward to hearing their new material," a fan named Chris told me at the time.[19] "We're just being supportive of him and of each other."

The identity of the fandom was reliant on continuing to do this. In the same way that fans transform One Direction's image with fanfiction and fan art, they transform their own image by playing with expectations and flouting the rules. Media presentations of punk music scenes or underground art movements or, in this case, a legion of so-called screaming fangirls give these groups a sense of collective identity, even and especially if the groups disagree with the way they're depicted. This is true for all kinds of subcultures. "Derogatory media coverage is not the verdict but the essence of their resistance," the sociologist Sarah Thornton wrote in her 1995 book *Club Cultures*, a history of dance clubs and raves.[20] As much as Project No Control was about promoting a One Direction song out of love for One Direction, it was also about refuting the media's portrayal of what One Direction was, and who the people who loved them were. The song was *adult*, lovingly and sarcastically referred to by its promoters as a "boner song." (Part of the chorus is "Waking up / Beside you I'm a loaded gun!") The call to action wasn't just to bring attention to one song; it was to bring attention to the fact that the band members were adults and serious musicians, and that the fans were adults now, too.

THERE'S A STORY I'VE BEEN TELLING ANYBODY WHO WILL listen—and because it makes no sense, that's no one.

It's about the mystery woman who passed out thousands of pictures of a pregnant Harry Styles on several college campuses in Utah in 2019.

The mystery woman who passed out thousands of pictures of a pregnant Harry Styles on several college campuses in Utah in 2019 is known around Utah Valley University as "the Harry Fairy." My tour guide through this saga was Olivia Diaz, a student journalist at UVU who spent months on the story. She was twenty-six when we spoke, and she'd grown up on Tumblr. She had a familiarity with the Larry Stylinson agenda—the imaginary romantic relationship between Harry Styles and Louis Tomlinson—from whatever had been reblogged onto her dashboard over the years, and she was a casual fan of One Direction when the band was at its peak. "It was a big deal for me when they came out with the song 'Olivia,'" she said. "I was very excited about that."[21]

Diaz was an education major and the editor of the arts and culture section of the university paper. One day, waiting outside a lecture hall for her next class to start, surrounded by students doing what students do—stare at phones, stare at laptops, stare at each other—she saw a woman with a high, messy bun dash through the space dispersing small pieces of paper all around her as she went. "I can't stress enough how tiny they were—they were like two inches by an inch and a half, they were so little," she remembered. "I figured, *This club is giving out free food or there's an event on campus*, but someone picked one up and I looked over and there was this picture of pregnant Harry Styles." She thought about it all through class—pregnant Harry Styles!—and decided it was a story, even though, strictly speaking, at the time it wasn't. Then one day, Diaz was walking to her car and a mysterious woman dashed past her through the campus parking lot. "I didn't think anything of it, and then I got in the car and there was a picture stuck in my car," she said. "I was like, *Oh my gosh, that was totally her*."

So she pitched the story. "As Halloween approaches, there's something spooky happening at UVU," she wrote in the campus paper a few days later. "No one knows how or why, only that everywhere you go, there he is. That dazzling smile, that artful tattoo sleeve . . . the one hand perched on top of a full, pregnant belly. It's Pregnant Harry Styles."[22] In writing it, she became invested in it. As Halloween approached, it *did* start to feel that there was something spooky happening at UVU. Diaz had easily figured out that the image came from a 2015 tweet captioned "First exclusive baby bump photo of the mother of Louis Tomlinson's child." But there was no other information. It seemed like the flyers could be a joke—or propaganda—about Larry Stylinson, and it also seemed like the flyers could have no explanation at all.

Not long after, a couple of other editors for the paper were hosting an informational booth at a club fair. A mysterious woman approached them—bun high as ever, sunglasses covering her face indoors, as usual—and blew a handful of pregnant Harry Styles right in their faces. Diaz spun the saga into a YouTube docuseries that involved questioning a volleyball coach, a janitor, and the student body president. There were disappointments, dead ends, red herrings. The newspaper filed a request to get the security camera footage from the club fair and tried to use the blurry images to deduce who the Harry Fairy might be. "We got a couple of imposters DM-ing the newspaper's Instagram saying they were the Harry Fairy," she told me. From Twitter, she learned that the photos had been distributed on other college campuses in the state, including Brigham Young University. "There was this girl from BYU who actually came in and did a video interview and said she was part of a street team for Harry Styles, that the photos were part of a PR campaign for his upcoming album. She was like, *Oh, everything will make sense when the album comes out.* And it came out in December and of course had nothing to do with anything." (That girl was also *not* the Harry Fairy.) Then the campus shut down because of COVID-19. There were no more interviews. No more leads. No more tiny pictures of Harry Styles everywhere. They were pretty sure they had finally figured out who the Harry Fairy was—by zooming in on a T-shirt she was wearing in the security camera footage, which happened to have the logo of a student organization on it—and Diaz wanted to confront her in a final installment of their documentary video series about the chase. But too much time had passed and nobody else was invested anymore. "It couldn't happen," she said. "It's a cold case."

Actually, no matter how much time had passed, at least one other person was still invested. I was living alone. It was a pandemic. I was drinking martinis out of jam jars on my fire escape and hoarding cans of fruit cocktail in case things got so bad it would become impossible to buy dessert. I wanted in on a mystery. I thought about the Harry Fairy if I saw a piece of paper on the ground. *Homemade flan for sale? Oh, I wonder how the Harry Fairy is doing. Canned food drive next Sunday? Oh, that would be a great way to distribute tiny photos of a pregnant Harry Styles.* I started messaging UVU students on Instagram, pretty much at random—anybody with long hair who belonged to the student organization that Diaz had connected HF to. For the most part, these teenagers did not even open my messages, which I guess I understand. But one day in August, I watched the docuseries again and realized that I had missed something completely obvious—the Harry Fairy had given the student journalists a burner email address with which to contact her. I had no idea if it was still active, but I wrote to her in a bit of a frenzy. She responded with an email that began with a laugh in all-caps, nine "HAs" long.[23]

I asked if I could call her immediately, worried that if I didn't talk to her within an hour she would disappear forever. She agreed. She picked up the phone. The Harry Fairy, who wanted to remain anonymous, insisted that there was no profound explanation for the photos. I was nervous while I was speaking to her because she seemed totally unperturbed, almost pitying of my interest. Her voice came through as friendly and a little froggy, girlish but low and surprising, like Gigi Hadid's. When she was in high school, she'd been a One Direction fan herself. She'd seen the photo by chance, part of an inside joke among friends. She'd loved it. "I saw it and I wanted everyone to see it," she said. "I wanted everyone in the world to see it, you know?"[24] As a teenager, she'd used her parents' printer to run off thousands of copies of the image, distributing them around her school and around neighboring high schools she traveled to for track meets. When she got to college, she kept going. She used almost all of the free printing credit given to her by the school and printed thirty-five photos per page. Over the years, she estimates, she's printed tens of thousands. She planted the photos at her own college, and at nearby BYU, where she convinced some students to let her use their IDs to access the library printers. She drove up to Salt Lake and spread more. With a friend, she traveled to Las Vegas and hit the University of Nevada. There are pregnant Harry Styles photos everywhere she's gone, she told me. "I always have a pouch with me and wherever I go I just leave a few. It's my little bread-crumb trail."

Talking to her, I felt like I'd been sent to the seaside to put the color back in my cheeks. When it was my full-time job to write about fandom, I'd leaned on the tech angle. I'd said, *These are the first people to think of faking an IP address for such a goofy reason.* But the Harry Fairy was handing me something else. Even alone, even in secret, there must be a reason to do what we do. When the student paper started investigating her, she thought it was funny at first. Then she got confused. What were they investigating? The images speak for themselves.

Whenever someone approached her on campus, having figured the mystery out, she denied it. "I wanted the focus to be more on the Harry Styles picture than it was on me," she told me. Her favorite place to plant Pregnant Harry Styles is in places where he won't be found for weeks or months or even years—hidden corners, or in between the pages of dusty library books. "Someone will find it in however long and be like, *What the heck, who put this here?*" She laughed. "It's kind of everywhere. That's what I want it to be, I want it to be everywhere." And that's how it was for me when I saw the flyers. I thought, *What the heck?* I wondered, *Who put this here?* I laughed about it for months, thinking, *Why would anyone do this? Could they even tell me if I asked?*

Secrets

"PEOPLE WHO DON'T KNOW FANDOM, DON'T KNOW ONE Direction, what they do know is Larry Stylinson," says Ashley Hull, a fan from Brooklyn who's in her early thirties.[1] When she became a One Direction fan in her twenties, her friends didn't have any real interest in what she was doing. But they would ask: Have you heard about this? Do you think they're sleeping together? That they're married? "I stay perfectly on the margins of the conflict," she said. "Maybe in 2013, 2014, it would have seemed worth it to argue with them online but at this point they believe what they believe, and nothing anyone says is going to convince them otherwise."

"Larry Stylinson" is the name given to the imagined and hoped-for romantic relationship between Harry Styles and Louis Tomlinson, as well as the name of a conspiracy theory. If Styles and Tomlinson are secretly married, and have been for years, it stands to reason that powerful forces are preventing them from being publicly in love—the media is certainly implicated, as is anyone who has worked closely with One Direction, particularly in the early years of their career. On Tumblr, image collages have "proved" that Tomlinson's longtime girlfriend Eleanor Calder was actually three *different* people—triplets named Eleanor, Tina, and Gretchen—all cast in the role of *fake girlfriend* by the band's label. When Harry Styles dated Taylor Swift for a few months at the end of 2012, "Haylor" became a flash point pitting those who considered themselves fans of both artists and enjoyed the relationship against those who believed Styles was delivering coded messages promising that Swift was nothing more than a tabloid diversion tactic. (A particularly well-known GIF, which shows a slowed-down second of concert footage, purports to show Styles looking at a picture of Swift held up by someone in the crowd, then miming a slow and deliberate pinch of his chin—*beard*.)

Larry Stylinson is also the subject of thousands of pieces of fanfiction, but there's a difference between imaginative stories and a literal-minded conspiracy theory. Larry truthers, who call themselves "Larries," believe that Harry Styles and Louis Tomlinson fell in love when they met on *The X Factor* and that various powerful figures within the entertainment industry have been forcing them to conceal that love for the last ten years of their lives. This theory became popular enough to reach the ears of its stars, which is when it started to drive a wedge between fans who believed and fans who didn't. Before we spoke, Hull sent me photos of half a dozen portraits she'd painted of Styles and Tomlinson individually. Back in 2012, she'd blogged about One Direction on LiveJournal and read fanfiction about them to kill the time during her first postgrad summer. But the evolution to serious speculation about real-world events was disturbing to her. "I find it really toxic," she said. "Fanfic is always part of fandom. I'm fine with people reading about the five of them or different variations, but *Oh, we need to tweet at them, they need to see this* . . . No, they don't."

Though fandom shaped Tumblr, the affordances of Tumblr shaped fandom in return. The medium caused something big to happen: the blossoming of a conspiracy theory that might otherwise have stayed the private secret of a small group of fans. It was allowed to grow in a semi-controlled environment that gave it just the right amount of oxygen. Tumblr was accustomed to academic and theoretical discussions of media, and was ready to play with the premise that famous people might also be read as texts. It was a place for piling up images until they revealed some kind of significance, and it distinguished itself from both the fully mainstream Facebook (which required that users present their full legal names) and the fully chaotic

4chan (which allows users to generate a new anonymous ID with every post) by encouraging users to build up followings under pseudonyms that could eventually become something like personal brands without the consequences. It had a culture of submitting and responding to anonymous questions, which allowed the curious to experiment with the theory before they were ready to announce their interest to the rest of their online circle. It had a spirit of debate and a tolerance for disagreement, but it was also cliquey and it had a norm of wielding shame as a weapon; in retrospect it's obvious how it could split a once somewhat cohesive group cleanly in two. When I spoke to Hull two years after our first conversation, during the coronavirus pandemic, she wondered if I'd noticed that Larry Stylinson was trending again. "The conspiracy theory will continue to prosper no matter the evidence that is given," she said. "It's a line of thinking I compare to QAnon believers. They see what they want to see."[2]

The Larry Stylinson theory has mutated many times—bit players come and go, media attention waxes and wanes—but at its center is a simple love story. Two boys from regular upbringings were thrust into the public spotlight together, and fell for each other as they came of age, happy at times, trapped at others. ("I'd marry you, Harry," Louis Tomlinson jokes in an *X Factor* behind-the-scenes video diary filmed in the fall of 2010.) Every flirty joke and gesture of intimacy between the two has been collected and collated into hundreds of YouTube compilation videos and Tumblr master posts. After *The X Factor*, Styles and Tomlinson lived together briefly in an apartment in London. That was the closest they ever were in public, but the many meticulous timelines of their relationship published to Tumblr by amateur researchers have several other major events in common. There was the "White Paint" weekend, the name given to the frenzied conversation that took place on Tumblr in the fall of 2012 after Louis Tomlinson wore white face paint for Halloween and Harry Styles was photographed with what appeared to be white paint in his hair the following day. Then there was an incredibly grainy video of two people who appear to be Tomlinson and Styles, swaying toward each other, possibly kissing, filmed in a bar in New Zealand in April 2012, which is still cited as the ultimate "proof," even as believers admit that it looks as though it was filmed on "a graphing calculator," "a first-generation Nokia phone," "a potato," or "a sock." There's the "Blue Bandana Incident," a reference to a Twitter project in 2014 that asked fans to wear a bandana corresponding in color to their favorite member of the band. When Harry was photographed wearing a blue one—Louis's designated color—at least ten times in the following year, it was widely interpreted as a wink to the fans: you're onto us.

During the biggest years of Larry, following a bunch of One Direction–related blogs on Tumblr and then scrolling down the dashboard was like watching an information war play out in real time. There were GIFs of Harry Styles falling over onstage next to GIFs of Harry Styles supposedly staring longingly into Louis Tomlinson's eyes before falling over onstage. Then there were paparazzi photos of One Direction doing whatever, right next to paparazzi photos of One Direction in which any dark-haired woman with glasses standing a moderate distance away from them was deemed a member of their "management," tasked with stalking them. At the time, the heteronormativity of mainstream media was a major topic of discussion on Tumblr across most fandoms. This complicated conversations about Larry Stylinson because it could be used as a cudgel, and Larries often ended disputes by asking pointed questions about why nonbelievers felt the need to "protect" the boys from gay rumors. The mysterious author of a monumental Tumblr text titled "The Harry+Louis Treatise"—which has been deleted but is well known enough to be archived piecemeal across the site in reblogs and on the Internet Archive's Wayback Machine—collates all of this alongside dozens of other pieces of evidence. In a disclaimer, it also states: "I do not think it is inherently homophobic not to [believe] in Larry. If you don't see it, you don't see it. But I would honestly question how hard you are looking." Refusing to look hard enough was "at best, aggressively heteronormative."[3]

The progressive politics that were popular on the platform at the time were appropriated as weapons by both sides. Those who disputed the Larry narrative would often spit back that Larries were misogynists who methodically tore down Styles's and Tomlinson's public love interests as frauds and fame-chasers, revealing an anti-woman bent. This was fair, but the Larries' advantage was the work they were willing to put in. The Harry+Louis Treatise contains literally hundreds of links to GIFs. The sentence "There is an outrageous amount of evidence of their jealousy; here is a bit of it," as it originally appeared, had a hyperlink to one super-slowed-down GIF or video on every word. "This moment of Louis smacking Zayn's hand away from Harry and this one of Harry reacting to Zayn feeding Louis are particularly hilarious," it continued, linking twice more.[4] Master posts include photos of Harry with what seemed to be the letter *L* written on his hands and arms in pen in the early years of the band. The sheer amount of *stuff* could be overwhelming. On one Larrie Tumblr, a timeline of "Larry" events from only the month of February 2012 has 207 items. "The way they look at each other, man," the treatise reads, again putting a hyperlink on every word, each to a different looping image of the two making eye contact. Some GIFs are so important, they receive their own write-ups: one of the most famous Larry GIFs shows Styles seated behind Tomlinson during an interview, reaching over the back of a couch his arm rests on to graze Tomlinson's upper arm with two knuckles. "This is small. This is subtle. This is not for the camera or the fans. This is for them."

Two sides of an unresolvable dispute took shape through endless sniping in anonymous "Ask" boxes, accusations of bad behavior that would circulate with screenshots of proof piled up in the replies, and a new custom of putting "DNI"—or "do not interact"—requests in one's Tumblr bio, specifying which group a person wouldn't even be able to stand seeing in the likes on her posts. There was endless debate, often unfurling in academic language, over what did or did not constitute internalized misogyny and what could or could not be considered homophobic. Larries referred to Calder as "Elebeard" or "Elewhore," or at their most polite, a "glorified dog sitter."[5] They tweeted at members of Tomlinson's family and covered his sisters' Instagram pages with questions about when he was going to come out, when he was going to be "free." Non-Larries had solid arguments against these kinds of behaviors but would often also pathologize the believers as "disgusting" or "mentally ill." The non-Larries came to be labeled as "Antis" and some of them grew into that label, defining their fandom disproportionately as a counterpoint to someone else's, which they had deemed inappropriate.

The fandom splintered into named and easily recognizable camps, and a standard set of terminology was solidified around the second half of 2014. The Larries were the truthers; a "dark Larrie" was a secret Larrie.[6] (Antis would often accuse Larries of deliberately blurring the line between themselves and regular Larry shippers, who were interested only in fiction. They would sometimes even comb Archive of Our Own for Larry Stylinson stories that were written by Larries and then publish lists in case their followers wanted to avoid them.) Antis, the stans who openly disapproved of Larries, were the primary opposing force. (Today, there is a small but noticeable number of publicly contrite ex-Larries, who sometimes express lingering affection for the "idea" of Larry, but more often become full-fledged Antis, writing long "leaving a cult"–style posts about how they extricated themselves.) There were a few subgroups: Larries believed that Styles and Tomlinson were officially together and always had been, while "Houies" thought they had been together at some point and had broken up; some Larries also used the term "Weak Larrie," for wishy-washy believers, sometimes as a joke. Today, on the outskirts of the feud there are "Harries," who are fans only of Harry Styles (not of Louis Tomlinson) and do not believe in Larry, but are often referred to as "Het Harries" by those who do. (This title is crueler than it immediately appears, because it's meant as a crude suggestion that anybody who doubts Larry is just obsessed with the idea of having sex with one of the men themselves.) An even smaller faction is known as "Rads"—fans of Louis who are now convinced that Harry and his team are out to ruin Louis's career.

There is some room, mostly in offline conversations, to equivocate about Larry. Mina Hughes, a student from Texas, told me she didn't *identify* as a Larrie, but she was invested in the story. "I am a grown-up, and I am self-aware enough to know that it's really childish to want total strangers to be dating," she told me. "I don't care if it's true or not." But she has fond memories of the love story because she first came across it when she was seventeen, right after she'd moved to Oregon by herself—Larry was a comfort then. "Now it just calms me down to think about them, because I'm so used to doing that."[7] Abby Armada considers herself an Anti, but still has a soft spot for Larry fiction, which she has written plenty of herself—her most popular story is about Harry and Louis falling in love while working at a restaurant, where Harry is a baker. "I think when you go down that rabbit hole, there's five minutes of your life where you're like, *This could be true.* I was never one of those people who took those five minutes and made it my whole life," she told me. The point where it becomes ridiculous, to her, is when Larries start talking about the clues hidden in Styles's and Tomlinson's outfits. "Not everything is a secret code," she said. "They are giving these two really famous idiot boys too much credit."[8]

For the power players on both sides of the dispute, however, there is little room for uncertainty. The most well-known—you could say infamous—Anti goes by Skye.[9] She's a One Direction fan in her midthirties who lives in Houston and runs a small network of media properties called Shit Larries Say—a Tumblr, a YouTube channel with about eighty videos, and a podcast, which started in 2020 and set out to pick apart a new master post by a well-known Big Larrie. ("Big Larrie" is an iteration of BNF, or "Big Name Fan," a term as old as organized fandom. It's used to identify fans who are famous within fan spaces and have some level of authority and influence.) She often singles out individual posts from Big Larries and dissects them line by line, which is why they talk about how she's pedantic and pretentious and "obsessed" with them. (To be fair, she does spend an awful lot of time correcting their grammar.) When I suggested to her that she might be fixating on the Larries, she said she was fine with that characterization, but clarified that she has higher aspirations.[10] She told me that she's been interested in misinformation and conspiratorial thinking since the beginning of the 2016 election cycle, and that she considers Larries a valuable case study.

Years ago, Skye identified Larries as an existential threat to online fandom in general, and her opinion of them is that they're even more malicious than most have previously imagined. They confuse people, she argues. A new fan can go on Archive of Our Own to read shipping fic about Larry and have no idea that she's reading a story by someone who also spends serious time blogging on Tumblr about "stunt" girlfriends and secret contracts. Skye spent years participating in various media fandoms on LiveJournal before she became a One Direction fan, and she sometimes speaks like a traditionalist. "The fandom with One Direction, they don't know what's acceptable, what's not, what lines should exist," she told me. "That's not shipping, what they're doing." Em, another well-known Anti and One Direction fan in her forties, cohosts the *Shit Larries Say* podcast and has a similarly lengthy background in fandom. "Fans just have no boundaries now," she told me. Confronting the subjects of fic was not something that happened in fandoms she participated in before the age of social media. "That would be the equivalent of going to a fan convention and sticking porn in someone's face. But it happened day in, day out on Twitter."[11]

Meanwhile, the Big Larries hold court—dismissing hypotheses they don't like, elevating the ideas they do, condescending to anyone who misses a piece of information, making the decisions when it's clear that the grand theory has to make a major pivot. The undisputed Larry expert is a One Direction fan in her late forties who has gone by several Tumblr usernames and is also in charge of a charitable organization that raises and donates money to various progressive causes on behalf of the fandom. (When I asked her to speak with me for this book, she declined to be interviewed and said, "Everyone hates us until they need us for something."[12] Because she expressed concern about being doxed or harassed, I am referring to her as Lisa, a pseudonym.)[13] She fields questions nearly every day from new Larries who don't have the same knowledge of a decade's worth of lore—if she's in the mood, that is. Otherwise she might simply command them to "scroll down." Her bio explains that she has been part of the fandom since 2012 and a Larrie "since day 1."[14] She offers commentary on every event in the wide world of Harry Styles and Louis Tomlinson—noting the movements of their friends, acquaintances, romantic partners ("stunts," as in PR stunts), and anyone else who could be believed to know anything about them. She does not engage with people like Skye. "We don't talk to them. For ANY reason," she wrote in an exasperated response to a question about the Anti crowd, and Skye specifically. "I've been here a billion years . . . anything they want to 'learn' about is probably within the bowels of my blog, which they are on 24/7 anyway LOL."[15]

BEFORE THERE WERE LARRIES, THERE WERE "TINHATS." Since the beginning of online fandom, there have been people who are alienated from their communities because of their insistence that two celebrities are in love, without proof and sometimes despite public denials. Tin-hatting is not the same as real-person fanfiction, but that's part of the reason there's a stigma against it—it undercuts the typical defenses of real person fiction, which is a sensitive topic and usually requires writers to point out that they would never show their work to the stars involved, that they know what they're creating is just imaginary, and that it's meant solely for fun and as a creative enterprise.

There was a strong taboo against using real people as characters for fan stories until the internet loosened the rules. (The fan studies scholar Henry Jenkins learned about RPF while researching his 1992 book *Textual Poachers* but didn't include it for this reason; fans specifically asked him not to blow their cover.)[16] By the time of email listservs, things had started to open up a bit. Real person fiction about *The X-Files* actors Gillian Anderson and David Duchovny was particularly well documented in the 1990s, and its popularity surged alongside that of slashfics about '90s boy bands and the classic '90s duo Ben Affleck and Matt Damon. But even then, most fans agreed that real person fiction was acceptable only if writers never "broke the fourth wall" by alerting the subjects of the stories to their existence. And of course, it was all supposed to be fiction.

Partly, this was because fans had to be careful: the ability to disseminate these stories widely, for free, carried with it the risk of backlash. In the early aughts, fandom's reliance on a small number of for-profit platforms also made hosting and sharing real person fiction much harder than it is now. In 2002, the popular site FanFiction.net banned adult content and real person fic, and the founder, Xing Li, gave hardly any explanation for the decision, offering only a perfunctory apology.[17] In 2007, LiveJournal's purge of various types of explicit content—an event known colloquially as "Strikethrough"—while not specific to RPF stories, eliminated another popular choice of platform for what fic writers lovingly refer to as "smut."[18] The subsequent exodus of fans from LiveJournal is often cited as a primary driver of Tumblr's growth—there were no rules about content there. Around the same time, the nonprofit Organization for Transformative Works built and launched the fanfiction repository Archive of Our Own, which was similarly welcoming. With more places for RPF to thrive, the taboo started to erode.

The change was also sped along by the rise of the *Lord of the Rings* film fandom in the early aughts. Many of those fans were interested not in Tolkien characters but in the actors who played them, and they wrote book-length stories on the internet about the love between Orlando Bloom and Viggo Mortensen, or Dominic Monaghan and Elijah Wood. "It was *Lord of the Rings* RPF that brought RPF to mainstream fandom recognition," the researcher Anna Martin wrote in a 2014 thesis paper on real person fiction.[19] In 2002, when a fan asked the series' star Ian McKellen if he found fanfiction "slanderous," he replied that he found "nothing harmful in sharing fantasies about favorite characters or their interpreters," and that "even real person stories seem unobjectionable as they are clearly fictional."[20] This was a huge moment for RPF writers, representing hard-won acceptance and a validation of their art, but the peace didn't last long. A year later, some "Domlijah" shippers became convinced that the dream relationship between Dominic Monaghan and Elijah Wood wasn't fiction after all, but an elaborately covered-up tragedy. They became the very first "tinhats."

Domlijah truthers would make photo essays called "picspams"—someone with an artful eye could easily arrange photos to evoke a certain emotion, perhaps thrill, at witnessing an affection that was being hidden, but not well. They'd create litanies of images of the actors jumping into each other's arms, kissing each other's cheeks, looking at each other from any distance. This practice became a precedent. After *The Lord of the Rings* came *Supernatural*, an unexpected hit about two brothers who hunt monsters—the brothers, Sam and Dean Winchester, became a popular subject of slash fiction. (There are hundreds of thousands of stories on Archive of Our Own tagged #Wincest.) Nearly simultaneously, a real person shipping community paired the starring actors, Jared Padalecki and Jensen Ackles. Then, truthers started talking about the very "real" relationship on the "spn_gossip" board on LiveJournal. By then, the word "tinhat" was in wide use, as was the word "het," as slang for a nonbeliever.

There are people in the One Direction fandom who were old enough to remember that all of this had happened before. Em told me she started writing fanfiction and making GeoCities fan sites in the late 1990s, back when she loved NSYNC. Much of that band's fan activity took place in mailing lists run through Yahoo Groups, where fans often discussed which members they would like to see together and exchanged real person slash fiction. The fiction didn't bother her at all. What did was the moment when people first started saying, *Wait, actually this is real.* "It split the community," she said. "There would be people who would read your fanfiction and be like, *This is great and really describes who they are,* and people would feel uncomfortable, like, *I'm just writing fanfiction, what are you talking about?*"[21]

To Em, speculation about a person's sexuality was a corruption of fandom's purpose. In the late 1990s, conjecture about the sexuality of celebrities was a preoccupation of gossip bloggers and conservative commentators, and it was a sordid fascination—a public piling-on of pressure and judgment, an unfeeling attempt to force reluctant people to come out. In the mailing lists, there were a lot of people who claimed to be insiders "saying, *No, no, no, he's out to the band, everyone knows about it,*" implying that it was a condition of Lance Bass's recording contract that he stay closeted to the outside world, she remembered. "After the band broke up, he basically confirmed that he hadn't been out [before] and that all of the speculation made him really uncomfortable," she said. "And I felt like nobody learned from that." Her interest in Larry Stylinson came from a concern that history was repeating itself. To her, it was a stretch to say that Larry truthers were "fans" at all—they were selfish, single-minded, and dangerous.

"ALWAYS IN MY HEART @HARRY_STYLES," LOUIS TOMLINSON wrote on October 2, 2011. "Yours sincerely, Louis."[22]

A decade later, this tweet and historical moment are referred to as simply "AIMH." October 2 is celebrated as #AIMH day every year. The hashtag has been used an unknowable number of times, but hardly a day passes without it, and as I write this, I can flip to Twitter and see its latest use—eight hours ago. The tweet is a miracle and a mystery. Year after year, Tomlinson elects not to delete it, which—if his public denials of Larry Stylinson are to be believed—has brought him nothing but grief. Why does he keep it? It stays up, it stays iconic, and it stays proof. This is the appeal of Larry: it's all right there. It's a love story you can click through over and over.

Larry is a conspiracy theory about forces as well known as the U.S. government or the scientific community: the entertainment industry and "the media." But more than that, it is a conspiracy theory about grown-ups—adults with money, adults with power, adults who could convince two teenagers that they could never be publicly in love, but who could never quite dissuade them to stop signaling to the thousands of quiet, diligent spectators spending their days online, swapping evidence, listening closely. ("Look, they're paying attention," the Harry+Louis Treatise promised in 2014, referring to the couple that its author was fighting to save. "They know what we're talking about.")[23] If they were proved right, nothing would change except two lives. Two people that no one in the fandom personally knew would finally get to be happy. ("Larries reveal complex forms of desire that appear to belong more to the collective—the desiring community—than to the individual," the cultural studies scholars Hannah McCann and Clare Southerton observed in 2019. "Far from lusting after their boyband idols, Larries desire *desire* itself.")[24]

Angela Gibbs—the mother I spoke to who bonded with her daughter over One Direction—had a different kind of investment in Larry than the Larries who ruled Tumblr. Going back to the moment she became a fan of the band, watching TV in the middle of the night, she told me she was struck by the intimacy between two of the boys—one with curly hair, one wearing suspenders. She didn't know their names yet, but they were the reason she wanted to go out and buy a One Direction CD the very next day. There was something about them. "Louis and Harry have a special place in my heart for sure just because I was like who *are* these boys? I wanted to find out more because of those two," she explained. But when I asked if she thought they were in love, she equivocated. "It felt like there was something more between them, more than a friendship, but not necessarily a romantic love, just affection for each other," she said first. Then, "I don't know. I think maybe yes. But it'd be okay if it wasn't true, you know what I mean? As long as they're happy—if they're together, if they were or aren't, or whatever."[25]

This was a common feeling among One Direction fans early in the band's existence, and one they were largely robbed of once the conspiracy theory was codified as serious business. The problems started when "Larry Stylinson" made its way to Harry Styles and Louis Tomlinson directly, in questions from curious journalists, and in tweets from Larries who wanted to let them know they were standing by. They laughed it off for some time, but eventually stopped appearing alone together on camera or in the corner of a stage. ("There's no secret relationships going on with any of the band members," Zayn Malik said in a 2015 interview. "It's not funny, and it still continues to be quite hard for them. They won't naturally go put their arm around each other because they're conscious of this thing that's going on.")[26] After the band went on "hiatus," they were seen in the same place in public only once, shortly after Tomlinson's mother died.

As the two became more guarded about their interactions, the fandom's divisions became more bitter, and Larry Stylinson took on another common element of internet conspiracy theories: symbolism became key, and any direct, contradictory evidence could be subordinated to it. The denials were not denials, but messages to watchful fans that they should start paying closer attention to the things that could not be read by anyone other than them—most notably a series of apparently matching tattoos. The Harry+Louis Treatise section on tattoos begins: "I've found that the tattoos are often enough for people to believe in Harry+Louis."[27] Styles got a tattoo of a ship shortly before Tomlinson got a tattoo of a compass. Tomlinson got one of a piece of rope; Styles got one of an anchor. When Harry got a tattoo of a rose, the fandom speculated as to whether Louis would get one of a dagger to complete a common tattoo design with supposed connotations of tragic love. When he *did* get a dagger tattoo, in November 2014, it proved them right. It got easier to see why it might be better to ignore Tomlinson's public denials—which were so flat and boring and crude—in favor of a subtext that was rich and interesting and romantic.

In September 2012, Tomlinson's frustration with the harassment of his then girlfriend Eleanor Calder culminated in an event referred to as "the Bullshit Tweet." The full tweet, posted by Tomlinson, reads: "Hows this , Larry is the biggest load of bullshit I've ever heard. I'm happy why can't you accept that."[28] To Antis, it was enraging—proof of what they'd feared, that the shippers had gone *far* too far. To Larries, it meant that the real Louis Tomlinson was not in charge of his Twitter account, and that someone else was tweeting for him. They started referring to Tomlinson by different names depending on which medium he was—or wasn't, really—speaking in. Tweets that denied Larry were sent by @Louis_Tomlinson. Words in magazines were spoken by Print!Louis. Neither of these people were Louis Tomlinson himself. (Although they could be if that happened to be reassuring—as when Tomlinson followed a Larry shipper on Twitter, supposedly to reassure the entire community.)

Written two years after the tweet, the Harry+Louis Treatise contains a long parenthetical explaining the Bullshit Tweet away yet again:

> *For what it's worth, on the second anniversary of Bullshit Day, as it were, Harry posted a photo of two guys—one in blue, one in green, which are the colors associated with Louis and Harry—and captioned it "Strong." Which happens to be the title of a song everyone knows the Larries think Louis co-wrote for Harry. So was it Harry's own little commemoration of Bullshit Day? Maybe. Either way, would he absolutely know that the Larries would read any use of "strong" like that as a reference to the song, and thus to Louis? Yes.*[29]

The division between Antis and Larries was aggravated by this kind of reasoning, but outside scrutiny was arguably even more destructive. In August 2013, Larries were embroiled in an internet-age disaster. One night, Twitter lit up with the hashtag #RIPLarryShippers—seemingly out of nowhere, One Direction fans had somehow become convinced that Larries were committing suicide. But there was an explanation: the hashtag trended for two days following the debut of a documentary called *Crazy About One Direction*, on British public television Channel 4.[30] The documentary had featured several interviews with Larries and prompted more than three hundred thousand tweets within the hour of its first airing. The Larry community was furious that their "private" world had been made public; the rest of the fandom was furious that it was associated with Larries. Amid the chaos, a rumor emerged that Larries were committing suicide in response—with the number of such deaths starting at fourteen, then rising to twenty-eight, and then to forty-two. Hardly any of the tweets contained any information about where the rumor had come from, but it was so widely circulated that even Liam Payne addressed it, writing, "Not really sure what's going on right now I just hope everyone's ok xxx."[31]

The event was covered by publications as mainstream as *The Atlantic*. "The Internet is mourning," the reporter Alexander Abad-Santos wrote. "No, not because of the horrific situation in Egypt, but rather because One Direction fans believe 42 fans killed themselves in response to a British documentary."[32]

The internet culture site *The Daily Dot* debunked the rumor and traced it to a nonsensical tweet from a week before the documentary aired.[33] Still, this was before widespread literacy about viral misinformation. (A year after #RIPLarryShippers, some fans still used the hashtag #ProjectNeverForget to commemorate the fictional deaths.) Daisy Asquith, the film's director, watched #RIPLarryShippers trend for two days and panicked over the possibility that some fans might really have harmed themselves. She was relieved when the claim turned out to be baseless, but she was still shocked by all that had happened. Unrelated to the #RIPLarryShippers drama, fans also uploaded reaction videos to YouTube with the tag #ThisIsNotUS—more than half of the videos were in protest of the fans chosen to be featured in the documentary. The girls in these videos were not Larries and argued that the film should have focused on "normal fans who have never met the boys and have boring lives," Asquith summarized in an essay published in 2016; more than a quarter of them talked about how Larry Stylinson is a topic that does not belong on television.

Larries apparently hadn't understood how all this attention from the outside world would feel until they felt it. People were making fun of them, and the rest of the fandom was furious because they felt Larries gave them a bad image—being a fangirl was a bad enough image already. "The hierarchies, taste policing, and internalized shame within the fandom collide awkwardly with the projected shame and derision that is applied from the outside," Asquith wrote. She had "outed" the Larry ship, she realized. "Moving Larry from Tumblr to television decontextualized it and had a destabilizing effect on the fandom, who were already arguing about its significance." Even though Larry shipping happens on public Tumblr accounts, and many of them are indexed by Google Search, fans were shocked to see that anybody was looking. All of the fan art that Asquith used in the documentary went through the proper clearance process with individual artists, but fans who watched it assumed that she must have stolen it. Their criticisms were often about "trespassing," and taking something out of an insulated context to turn it into a spectacle for outsiders. "Larry in private fan spaces is fun, clever, and naughty, but seen through the public eye it suddenly feels embarrassing and stupid to fans," she concluded.[34]

#RIPLarryShippers was a brief panic but it was also, in hindsight, a point of no return. Larries were dragged into the spotlight on television, a medium that was all wrong for them. A conversation that was native to the internet and seemed to have some kind of internal logic when discussed on Tumblr was then presented in a format in which it made no sense. It was obviously something that a general viewing audience was going to reject, and that rejection was going to have to inform this group's self-image. So, shaken up by the events surrounding the documentary and the public's new awareness of them, Larries were forced to choose: shame or doubling down.

They chose the latter and cobbled together evidence that September 28, 2013, was Harry and Louis's wedding day. This was confirmed to them when Styles tweeted a lyric from a Joni Mitchell song: "We don't need no piece of paper from the city hall."[35] To ritualize reminders of this wedding, the number twenty-eight became yet another symbol for Larries. It was already the number on Tomlinson's soccer jersey, which explains why he had a two and an eight tattooed on a pair of his fingers, but now it was also the date that bound Larry together for life. They looked for the number everywhere. Years later, Styles posted a photo on his Instagram of a billboard with the LA zip code 90028. That was a reference to his wedding anniversary, they claimed. Years after that, Tomlinson tweeted the word "Always" and captioned a selfie "You"—February is the second month, and these posts were on the twenty-sixth day of the month, which adds up to twenty-eight. In 2017, Tomlinson released his debut solo single on the same day that Styles's film *Dunkirk* premiered in the United States—July 21. July is the seventh month, etc. These were meager things, but these clues were all that was left after One Direction announced an indefinite hiatus and Tomlinson and Styles stopped appearing together or speaking to each other in public, and after the whole world turned against Larries, who were only telling a love story.

• • •

LONG BEFORE THE NEWS MEDIA BECAME SERIOUSLY CONcerned about deceit and manipulation on YouTube or the algorithmic wormholes on the platform that lead people to take up strange beliefs, Larries were circulating as fact doctored videos that "proved" Larry Stylinson was real. Even those that were presented as unedited raw footage, like the notorious video of Styles and Tomlinson sharing a drunken kiss in a New Zealand bar, were carefully and misleadingly framed.

The audio in the New Zealand video is essentially unintelligible, the only clear phrases coming from the woman holding whatever recording device took it. The captions were added by someone listening to what they wanted to hear—you can't *actually* hear Tomlinson yell the word "Boyfriend!" Yet it appears on the screen as an uncontested caption. You can't hear a "Woman #4" saying, "Oh my gosh, they're kissing," either, but that appears on the screen, too. To watch the video and read it the way Larry shippers would like it to be read, you have only to approach it the way you would any chaotic clip from reality television, with captions provided by off-screen producers. If you trust the person who's presenting it, you would have no reason to question it.

Em, the cohost of the *Shit Larries Say* podcast, noticed early how Larries worked to create a completely original reality through the media that they put on their timelines. After Tomlinson called bullshit on Larry—literally—she was shocked and disturbed that nothing changed in the Larry world. "Instead of diminishing, they became more defiant," she said. "That was a thing I had never seen happen before."[36] From that point on, she was uneasy about participating in the fandom on Tumblr at all, having noticed that Larries were behind many of the biggest blogs and the most popular fandom projects (including, to some extent, Project No Control). "I didn't want to interact with those people, but they were overwhelmingly the creators of content," Em told me. "At that point, they were propagandists. You almost couldn't get media, or fanfiction, or the GIFs, or the captioned work, or the paparazzi photos or things like that unless it was filtered through those eyes. I just felt like, *Am I crazy? Am I the only person seeing this?*"

To her, it was obvious the Larries' constant close-reading and refusal to accept anything at face value had curdled into obsessive self-interest and a hard lack of empathy. She remembers the spring of 2014, when a clip called "the weed video" was leaked. Blown up by the tabloid media, the video shows Louis Tomlinson and Zayn Malik in an SUV in Peru smoking what appears to be a joint—in it, a voice that seems to be Tomlinson's also says a common British abbreviation of the n-word. The use of the slur dominated conversation among the fandom on Twitter and Tumblr for days. "I'm a Black woman and the slur in the weed video hurt me profoundly," Em said. But for some Larries this was not a betrayal of One Direction's Black fan base—it was simply another chess move on the part of "management." They were forcing him to do things that would make him look bad, and he was probably tortured by what they were having him do. Because of their worldview, it was impossible for Larries to even engage with the possibility that Black fans were pained by the revelation, having conditioned themselves for years to think only about one perspective.

"I felt like it was a culmination of this kind of mindset of not being able to engage with reality," Em said. "I felt like the fandom didn't have my back." So she took a year off, and when she came back, things were even worse. In the summer of 2015, she watched the One Direction fandom destroy itself forever over a new theory, called Babygate.

Proof

LOUIS TOMLINSON COULD NOT HAVE GOTTEN BRIANA JUNGwirth pregnant in 2015 because he was and is in love with Harry Styles. The pregnancy was fake and the resultant "baby" was at first a doll, then replaced with either an actor or a child secretly supplied by a member of Jungwirth's immediate family. Whatever Jungwirth and Tomlinson did was because of a contract drawn up in secret by the people in control of Tomlinson's life. The charade will someday "end," and then Styles and Tomlinson will finally live free. These are the core tenets of belief in the Babygate conspiracy theory.

"When Babygate happened, I was really embarrassed. It really made us look bad," Mina Hughes told me. But she could still see where the theorists were coming from. "I would never say they're faking a kid, but her pregnancy was a weird one." There were rumors that Jungwirth doctored pregnancy photos that belonged to other people for her own use, which Larries attempted to verify and eventually just presented as unquestionable. "People say the first photo Louis posted was very clearly edited," she told me. "A whole lot of suspicious stuff."[1]

On August 4, 2015, One Direction performed on *Good Morning America* and then sat down for an interview. Tabloids had reported two weeks prior that Jungwirth was pregnant, and Simon Cowell and Liam Payne had both confirmed the news personally, for whatever reason, but Tomlinson had yet to speak about it. Cheerfully, as if this were not the case at all, the co-host Michael Strahan said to him, "From one father to another, I want to congratulate you on your upcoming fatherhood."[2] Tomlinson gave the sort of pained smile of a person who is having the "Happy Birthday" song sung to them in an office context, but he didn't hesitate to respond. "Thank you, obviously it's a very exciting time," he said. "I'm buzzing, thank you."

The "Babygate" tag first appeared on Tumblr that day. Prior to Tomlinson's "I'm buzzing," Larries could convince themselves that the tabloids were making stuff up, which tabloids are known to do, and that Cowell was egging it on for whatever nefarious reasons, and that Liam was simply confused. But now that Tomlinson had spoken, it had to be code. And speaking code means: conspiracy. The fact that Jungwirth and her family were unused to an intense level of media attention and were inexperienced with crafting a public image only added fuel to the fire. Every awkward move or odd choice of words was scrutinized by thousands of fans looking to see something sinister. (Jungwirth's former stepfather, Danny Fitzgerald, for some reason confirmed the pregnancy by sending screenshots of text messages from Jungwirth's mother to *Buzzfeed News.*[3] The undeniably tacky maneuver was made stranger by his choice to refer to Jungwirth by her first and last name in text messages to her own mother.) They also started digging, in hopes of finding a counter-narrative. They looked back at the hundreds of hours of concert footage from earlier in the summer and found something interesting: On June 27, at a show in Helsinki, someone in the audience had thrown a baby doll onto the stage and Tomlinson had picked it up. In GIFs pulled from a video, Liam Payne can be seen mocking the way that Tomlinson is holding the doll—by the ankle. Then Tomlinson laughs and yells, "It's not real!" before throwing it back into the crowd. There were plenty of these incidents. On July 12, two days before Jungwirth's pregnancy would become public, Tomlinson had tweeted, "And I owe it all to you." Maybe you know that this is a lyric from Bill Medley and Jennifer Warnes's "(I've Had) The Time of My Life," a song made famous by the 1987 film *Dirty Dancing*, and that it was also a clue. "You know, there was a pregnancy in that movie, too," one fan wrote. "People assumed Johnny was the father because he was 'close friends' with the mother. He wasn't."[4]

Hardly anything Tomlinson or Styles said or wore or carried or touched—past or present—escaped notice. There was so much to sift through, hundreds of amateur sleuths could each make a splash by digging up something fresh or making a novel connection. But because Tumblr follower counts are private, a handful of pseudonymous bloggers were able to speak as authorities to audiences that it was impossible to ever quite judge the size of, making that authority difficult to question. There was Lisa, as she said, from the very beginning. There was also a Big Larrie who had been a well-known British sex blogger in the early 2010s and wrote under the pseudonym Sex at Oxbridge (or SAO for short). She started writing about Larry theories on *BuzzFeed*'s unpaid community section in early 2016 with the intention to use the clips in an application for the site's editorial fellowship, she told me. But *BuzzFeed* deleted all of her posts a few weeks later (writing in an email that it was because she'd used the site to promote her personal brand), and she shifted to Tumblr and a private newsletter full-time.[5] Her style was unique, sometimes crass, and people seemed to like her because she was a little bit glamorous and because she framed Babygate as an academic pursuit, often emphasizing that key Larries were older fans who were professional adults or university students.

"I've done my research," she wrote in 2016. "Please educate yourself. Larries may be fuckin' wild, but we're statistically the more intelligent critical thinkers of the fandom."[6]

SAO made waves by connecting Babygate more intimately to Simon Cowell. She suggested that Tomlinson was going along with a plot orchestrated by Cowell, but signaling clues to the fans all the while, and taunting Cowell at the same time. The first photo of Tomlinson holding his child was in black-and-white, which fans believed was a choice made to cover up sloppy Photoshop. His shoulders were an "odd shape," and his eyelashes looked too thick. A tattoo looked smudged. And then SAO found a black-and-white photo of Simon Cowell holding his baby on his chest in nearly the exact same pose.[7] (The rest of the Cowell theory is way too confusing to explain, but it hinges on Tomlinson carrying around a 2011 pop psychology book called *The Psychopath Test.*) "I am a very thorough researcher and just took all the information that I had at my disposal and presented my conclusions," she told me years later. "I wish I was completely wrong about everything because the reality of a situation in which these guys have been controlled and manipulated since they were teenagers is a horrific thought."[8]

Though SAO also emphasizes that she uses only publicly available information to inform her conclusions, different writers have different approaches. Some claim to have privileged information, or walk through every hypothetical about every detail in their story until it's easy to forget that they're speaking hypothetically at all. These theories are often broken out into their own master posts, which tend to be thousands of words long and contain hundreds of links, as well as dozens of tangents into "if this, then that," splintering in all directions. For example, though Lisa does not believe that Briana Jungwirth was ever pregnant, she has entertained thought experiments about the possibility. She meticulously re-created the pregnancy timeline, starting with Tomlinson's arrival in Los Angeles on May 4, 2015, then rattling off each night that he was photographed out with Jungwirth (May 5, 7, 9, 11, 15, 22). From there, she offered piecemeal calculations of a stranger's menstrual cycle: Jungwirth's mother said she was exactly thirty-four weeks pregnant on December 24, 2015. The last day of Jungwirth's last normal period would have been April 30. "Assuming a normal cycle, Briana would likely have been ovulating May 12th to May 16th." The estimates are printed alongside a chart of three months' worth of Jungwirth's speculated periods, and the most likely date of "conception"—in other words, staged conception—would have been May 11, the night that Jungwirth and Tomlinson attended a party hosted by Snoop Dogg. The reason for all this math is to prove its impossibility. Jungwirth's mother started following *People* magazine's *People* Babies page on Twitter on May 18, the day she made an account—suspicious to Lisa, as, if the pregnancy were real, Jungwirth would "have only started missing her period around May 18th."[9] A photo from the Snoop Dogg party was used on the cover of the U.K. tabloid *The Sun* when the pregnancy was announced—again suspicious because *The Sun*'s U.S. editor at the time, Peter Samson, was married to Ann-Marie Thomson, head of public relations at One Direction's record label. Also suspicious because blurry clips of paparazzi following the pair out of the party show Jungwirth slowing down at the car door—maybe she was waiting to be photographed, knowing that the photo was key to the stunt.

Ultimately, suspicion and paranoia won out, but they weren't uncontested. In the hours after the pregnancy was announced on *Good Morning America*, there was caution in the Larry fandom—even sympathy for Jungwirth. Some wrote about an obligation to "protect" her, and to keep an eye out for anyone criticizing her unfairly.[10] "i am expecting every single person to shut that shit down," one wrote. This didn't last very long. By the end of the day, the idea of Babygate as a "stunt" had taken shape, and Jungwirth became an undeniable villain. "She's revolting in every way," one fan wrote.[11] Another bought the domain name BriaJungwirth.com, and dedicated it to "expressing disdain for Briana Jungwirth and her band of losers." The same fans who had sworn not to attack Jungwirth for her role in a public relations nightmare were soon passing around what they thought might be her sex tape, and publishing photo collages intended to prove that she'd gotten lip fillers and a nose job while pregnant. They refer often to her "new face," and imply that she is using Tomlinson's money to keep it up. "The question is how is she paying for [these] procedures?" Lisa asked in 2020. "Babygate truly seems to have been an opportunity to get a 'makeover' for Briana at Louis' expense." In the same post, she annotated images of Jungwirth's body. "The bikini photo below does seem to show recent implants," she wrote. "They don't appear to have 'dropped' yet—when implants are first inserted they tend to sit higher and not 'hang' as naturally, looking more like round balls attached to the chest."[12]

In fact, *every* photo of Jungwirth came to be loaded with significance. There was the blurry screenshot of a video taken at a family Christmas dinner, where her pregnant belly is obscured by a table and difficult to make out. (It's usually placed side by side with a photo of another pregnant woman sitting down, belly popping forward like a watermelon.) There are the photos of Jungwirth on Halloween, six months into her pregnancy, belly visible but not obtrusively so, side by side with a photo from three days later, where it looks enormous. There she is at a passport office—what could be the significance of that? There she is backstage at a One Direction concert in all black—why was it posted by someone who is followed on Twitter by Simon Cowell? There she is—or is she?—in a gray-scaled photo of her pregnant body from the neck down, suspicious because it chops off her head. The analysis continued long after she gave birth. Briana Jungwirth goes outside in January 2016, staring at the ground, a blanket over her newborn baby's car seat carrier—"heeled boots and a mini skirt a week after birth," the Tumblr caption reads.[13] The next day, she goes outside in leggings: "Heels and tights a week after birth."[14] A few weeks later, a friend posts a video of her eating a taco in the back seat of a car, wearing a long-sleeve shirt with a keyhole back: "I can only imagine not wearing a bra when you're meant to be producing milk is a bit uncomfortable."[15] These were once the images that a young woman took or had taken as reflexively as any of us ask for photos of our lives, and now they were shreds of evidence.

The Babygate theory actually was convincing if you looked at it for a short time—when *BuzzFeed* published an explainer, it went viral because of how much fun readers had believing it.[16] "There's no way they would make up a baby," Megan Collins, a fan from California, told me. "But then I found myself starting to be like, *Oh, there are pixel differences between this photo and that photo.*" She had to snap herself out of it. "I was like, wait, that's insane, who would make up a fake baby? What value is there in that?"[17]

At first glance, Babygate was also just a gossipy

good time and an opportunity to toy with an elaborate puzzle. But the theory that Briana Jungwirth was some failed criminal mastermind faking a pregnancy for vague reasons wasn't an isolated story. It was similar to conspiracy theories about Meghan Markle or Benedict Cumberbatch's wife, Sophie Hunter—both of whom have been baselessly accused by Tumblr users of physically abusing their husbands, faking their pregnancies, and trafficking drugs.[18] These theories draw on blind items from well-known celebrity gossip sites and exploit the air of mystery surrounding anonymous contributions to online discussion. Over the last ten years, they've developed a common set of characteristics: The "victims" of the conspiracy tend to be famous men; the villains tend to be women. The women are sometimes acting on their own, but more often they're a pawn of industry—a distinction that never earns them any sympathy. The victim is almost always being blackmailed because of a secret sexual identity, and the victim's personality has almost always been changed somehow by the torture they've experienced. When they do things the fans don't like, it's because of that personality shift, but they would go back to the way they were before if only they were freed. (In Tomlinson's case, Larries were upset by his transition into wearing more athletic wear, going out to parties, and being photographed with women, all part of a fake bro-y persona demanded by the industry.) The conspiracy theorists also tend to claim that they have personal sources who provide them with privileged information, and that they have expertise in a vast array of subjects like photo editing, psychology, obstetrics, contract law, passport protocol, journalism, etc. They usually claim to be progressive feminists, and insist that even their most personal criticisms of the women at the center of their theories are not misogynistic—it would be misogynistic *not* to call these women out on their many misdeeds.

They espouse a deep distrust of the media—a distrust that preceded the peak years of "fake news" discourse—and rely frequently on the idea that technology can be used to fake basically anything. Apart from the small circle of famous people they have chosen to defend, they see most people in the public sphere as self-interested, driven only by a desire for profit—journalists and music industry executives are likely to tell whatever story benefits them financially or in their abstract quests for power. This attitude has rubbed off even on Larries who don't participate fervently in Babygate. "It's very difficult, you know, especially when the media is involved," Angela Gibbs told me. "It's difficult to know what's real and what isn't and what's Photoshopped."[19]

Though Larries mostly want to keep to themselves, they sometimes tangle with the outside world in startling ways. They're wary of betrayal, and they never let go of a grudge, as demonstrated by their public feud with Richard Lawson, a writer and critic who was once their hero. Writing cultural criticism and celebrity gossip blog posts for *The Atlantic* and then *Vanity Fair*, he'd become interested in celebrities who were popular with the young, extremely online generation. The stories were weirder and more interesting than your typical Brad-and-Angelina fare, and he thought Larry was "an interesting development," he told me.[20] Here were all these girls ignoring the point of the commercial boy band—that they were supposed to have crushes on the boys themselves—and insisting instead that two of the boys were together. He didn't dig too far into it, but he decided it was fun. He started making stray straight-faced jokes in his writing about Larry being real just to entertain himself. He thought of it as a wink to whoever might be reading, and he assumed everyone was just being playful.

On Tumblr, Larries noticed immediately and became Richard Lawson *fans.* He was "larry af," and "a fucking gem." Everyone loved him, which I know because one of the most reblogged posts from that time says, "everyone loves richard." He engaged with a few of them on Twitter because he thought it was fun, he told me. "It seemed like a transgressive kind of modern thing that this was a theory going around." But the Larries weren't playing—they thought he was a whistleblower or the lone journalist speaking truth to power, and they expected more from him. In the spring of 2016, Richard went on a vacation to London with his sister, which some Larries found out about because they were monitoring his Instagram. Deducing that Styles and Tomlinson were also in London at the time, they decided that he was there to interview them both and write a *Vanity Fair* cover story in which they would come out. "That went from idle speculation to asserted fact among the Larry community within a couple days," he remembered.

Richard tweeted apologetically that this was not what was happening. He kept joking about Larry throughout the summer, even tweeting at Mike Pence to ask if he thought Larry was real. But around that time, other One Direction fans started writing to him on Twitter to explain the full drama of the conspiracy theory. "I was like, *Oh, well, this has gotten darker*, or maybe it was always darker than I thought," he said. "Basically, I disavowed the whole thing and was like, *I really thought this was a joke. I didn't know how serious it was.*" The Larries turned on him immediately, calling him manipulative and a liar and a shill and homophobic, even though Lawson himself is gay. On Tumblr, he was accused of using Larry for "click bait," and labeled "arrogant," "uneducated," and "insensitive." He was shocked by his own failure to realize how deep Larry Stylinson went, years after he thought he understood most things about life online. He never mentioned Larry publicly again, but you can still find

Larries talking about him. "That silly Richard Lawson guy . . . he got badly burnt by the Larry fandom," one explained several years later for the benefit of those who might be new to things.[21]

THOUGH BABYGATE FOCUSES ON THE IMAGINED CRIMES OF one twentysomething woman, its investigation is often framed as an opportunity for the empowerment of women.

"The problem with babygate was that [the powers that be] assumed that the fan base consisted of teenage, impressionable girls who wouldn't be able to put 2 and 2 together," one Larrie wrote in 2020. "They learnt that we couldn't be fooled." Larries—because they are women—will be willing to wait as long as necessary for Babygate to end, she argues, the same way they—in a grand historical view—waited for everything else. "We waited for the right to education, we waited for the right to work, we waited for the right to vote, we waited to become *Dr. Who,* we waited for the nails to dry . . . we'll wait for the other shoe to drop."[22] This hardly makes any sense, but there is an appeal to the argument, as it reframes a pursuit that appears irreversibly misogynistic as, to the contrary, empowering for its participants and possibly for women everywhere. The truthers insist that they aren't puritanical; they are all for personal choice. But they can't seem to stop themselves from fixating on individual personal choices, and they evaluate the women involved in their conspiracy theory based on the way their choices reveal them to be indecent caregivers. (Imagine the conversation about the night that Briana Jungwirth accidentally set the sleeve of her sweatshirt on fire while livestreaming on Instagram. *With her child sleeping upstairs!* Horror, from the people who insisted the child was a plastic doll for almost a year.) They are worried about how the women they don't like are giving women in general a bad reputation, and they are most of all worried about how the women they don't like are hurting men—manipulating them with false images, hoarding their attention, exploiting them for financial gain.

Now, I know some of the Larries' impulses more intimately than I would like. Hunting for the artifacts they've left, some deliberately obliterated from the public record, available only in clunky cached versions or merely rendered unsearchable by the decay of Tumblr, I've sometimes felt the frenzy of a person digging up evidence and connecting the dots. After all, I was taking notes. I was talking about women I didn't know and whom I mostly couldn't even picture, who I saw only as spectral limbs, weaving plots behind the surface of my everyday experience of the internet. I found myself saying things like "This explains everything," using my hands to make shapes in the air so my friends and family might grasp what I was dealing with. I wanted to lay it all out so everyone could understand. But the reality of Babygate is that it can't really be explained and set aside. That's why there are new master posts every year. It's the articulation of a fantasy—our fascination with celebrities is not primarily about their wealth or their beauty, Anna Martin argued in 2014, but of living "a life in which love is the only concern"—and it's the expression of an insurmountable divide.[23] One Direction fans all came to Tumblr for the same reason, but Babygate allowed them to wield that desire as a weapon against one another, for no reason at all.

WHEN MARY WAS IN HIGH SCHOOL IN THE BALKANS, MILLING around with her classmates at recess, she overheard someone argue that Harry Styles was definitely bisexual and dating Louis Tomlinson. "The impatient way she said it made it clear to me that she questioned the intelligence of anyone who disagreed with her," Mary told me.[24] When she got home from school she looked Larry up on YouTube. "Cue romantic music, millisecond clips of them looking at each other, decent editing, I was hooked."

She made a Tumblr and a Twitter account, each devoted to Larry, and she selected only Larry accounts to follow. All of her One Direction news came from whatever Larries reblogged, and from the Larry Stylinson tag. She immersed herself and became part of the community. "There was an intense 'us vs. them' mentality," she said. "Poor Larries. All of us just blogging about two boys in love." It was around this time that she started identifying as queer, and though she didn't want to be out in her offline life, she was proud to be out online. She joined the online collective Rainbow Direction, which was dedicated to LGBTQ+ visibility within One Direction fandom, and was added to a Telegram thread for Rainbow Direction insiders that was *all* about Larry—they analyzed every GIF, every tweet, every quote, every way that Larry could possibly come out. "Looking back, it was all so far removed from everything they said or did," she told me. "But that's conspiracy theories for you."

For the years that she was involved in Larry, she hardly ever saw a photo of a woman Styles was dating in real life. The Big Larries ignored "stunts," and they wouldn't reblog updates or photos about "beard" relationships, she said. If Harry spent time with openly gay friends, that was ignored too, because it didn't fit a narrative of him as an oppressed gay man. Anytime Tomlinson talked about his girlfriend in an interview or told Larries off on Twitter, Mary didn't hear about it. Those tweets didn't get shared on her Tumblr feed—or if they were, they were attributed to "@Louis_Tomlinson," the fake Tomlinson. "Unless it was something cute," she said. "Then we ignored the fact that it's supposedly management tweeting for him and it was all *sweet, pumpkin, precious, oppressed Louis, he's shining through despite their best efforts to break him.*"

But when Tomlinson's son was born and it was obviously his child, Mary snapped out of it. "The homophobic and sexist stereotypes I was arguing against were the same ones I was perpetuating," she realized. She'd spent two years saying "It's happening" and waiting for them to come out, and for what? She resented that she had wasted her time, but also that she'd soured her entry into the queer community. "It taught me a lot about myself," she said. "Through all the ugly things I said as a Larrie, I learned a lot of things I need to work on." When we first spoke, she called it a growth experience, but later she revised. "It's mostly a lot of regret."

Now Mary still keeps an eye on the Larries, because Babygate is far from over. A new generation of Larries is posting on TikTok and starting celebrity gossip accounts on Instagram. A Reddit forum dedicated to Larry Stylinson had fewer than three hundred members from 2012 to 2018, but experienced a growth in membership starting at the beginning of the pandemic, making a steep climb to six thousand members a year later. (The tagline is "A community for those who know the truth.") In the spring of 2020, Lisa published an updated Babygate primer for the uninitiated, writing, "This document aims to explain why people think Louis is not the father of Freddie, even four years after the announcement."[25] Larry Stylinson started trending again on Twitter around that time, and new Tumblr gossip blogs sprung up like weeds to discuss Styles's fake relationship with Olivia Wilde, known in these spaces as "Ho-livia."

Larries suffered from outside scrutiny and from internal policing, but they've made conspiracy thinking easy for the next group of fans. There is no *one* fandom community to deal with now because of the way Babygate ripped it in half. And over the years, the Babygate taboo has eroded, particularly in spaces like TikTok where attention metrics reward absurdity. There has already been a Babygate 2.0, centered on Liam Payne and the singer Cheryl, and more recently a Babygate 3.0, centered on Zayn Malik and Gigi Hadid. (Some One Direction fans believe that Zayn Malik and Liam Payne are the band's second secret couple.) "I can't believe they're trying to pull off a Zigi baby," one person wrote after Gigi Hadid's pregnancy was announced. "Zigi is literally the most obvious PR stunt of all time."[26] Another, who appears to believe in all three Babygates, offered their predictions about how the ruses would end: Tomlinson would get a paternity test, Payne would simply admit that he "knew from the beginning" he wasn't the father of his child, and Hadid would have a miscarriage, they wrote, acknowledging in a parenthetical that "this sounds harsh."[27] (Hadid gave birth to a daughter in September 2020.) The format of the original Babygate let these new theorists move quickly. They use the same style of posts—annotated photo collages, screenshots of incriminating digital evidence, etc. But they spread these things to more platforms than the last Babygaters, and are comparatively shameless.

Within days of Hadid's pregnancy announcement, a popular Instagram account was circulating a speculative timeline of her menstruation cycle and possible conception dates. At the end of the post, there was a caution: "If zayn confirms [the pregnancy] in his social media dont worry, he doesnt really have access to his [Instagram] or twitter, it is all his teams."[28]

Belonging

ON MAY 25, 2018, NIALL HORAN—THE SOLE IRISH MEMBER OF One Direction, who is two months older than me, and who has spent roughly the same portion of his life dyeing his hair blond as I have—tweeted, "Cmon Ireland ! This is your day to make another great decision. Please do right by the great women of our nation."[1]

There was also an Irish flag emoji, and yes, Niall Horan sometimes puts an extra space between the last word of a sentence and its punctuation, and sometimes he doesn't. There was something moving about it to me, even though there was hardly anything to it. I know that this is not good: activists and citizens make historic social change over the course of generations and decades. That Niall Horan tweeted in support of reproductive rights is one result of that work, and not really a meaningful contribution to it. Still, from where I was sitting, in a country where nearly

80 percent of the population agrees that women have the right to abortion yet it is functionally illegal to get one in many states, it was a fun surprise to see Horan treat the statement as natural. If the right to abortion is popular, why *wouldn't* a pop star tweet about it? Why don't more?

At one level, this feeling is a result of our very modern obsession with reconciling our politics and our consumer choices, which we regularly remind ourselves is impossible, usually when tacitly giving ourselves permission to continue shopping on Amazon. At another level, it's parasocial relationships 101: I want a famous boy, who I grew up with, to understand and support me, because that is what I feel like I have done for him. It's about coherence. When Elon Musk started dating Grimes, the *New Yorker* writer Naomi Fry described an odd kind of disappointment, expressed mainly on Twitter by people who had loved the indie weirdo's garish and otherworldly experimental pop music, and who had set themselves in principle against technocrats and libertarians and ego men like Musk. The pair had met via Twitter exchange, the context of their personas and politics flattened into some viral quips about something nerdy. "What if ideological distinctions still mattered and were not so easily swept away by a levelling torrent of information and capital?" Fry asked. "What if anything still meant something?"[2]

The experience of being on Twitter, the site of all

these emotions and contradictions, is an experience of futility. My fellow scrollers and I spend our time in an endlessly refreshing feed alerting us to injustices big and small, most of which we can't do anything about. People with large follower counts are said to have a "platform," which feels like the thing most proximate to power. We know that our political system is horribly broken, and so maybe we develop a sense that our true representatives are not those elevated to power at the ballot box, but the ones we have elected far more democratically. With our millions of patient streams and endless tweets, we're laboring out of love, but we also expect something in return: we come to see it as crucial that our values be reflected, to the letter, by those we have chosen and feel we can influence.

There has never been a time when pop music was truly apolitical, but today we are literally asking Cardi B to talk about the dispersal of economic gains through a population. Harry Styles was pushed to give his personal feelings on Britain's exit from the European Union, and every few months there is another Twitter thread about his failing to be sufficiently critical of Israel. (When his Muslim former bandmate Zayn Malik tweeted #FreePalestine in 2014, he was met with death threats.) Rihanna's politics have been consistently unimpeachable, while Lana Del Rey squandered the goodwill around her 2019 opus *Norman Fucking Rockwell!* by subsequently dating a cop. Even as we say these things don't *really* matter, we stew over them constantly. When we talk about celebrities having politics, we're writing fanfiction all the time. For example, One Direction—the first internet boy band—was aligned fairly early on with Barack Obama—the first internet president. There is literal fanfiction about Harry Styles and Barack Obama falling in love, of course (search term "Hobama"), but there were also real-life scenes that were blown up beyond their significance. After Horan became famous, he was asked often about a statue of Obama he kept in his backyard. "I like him out there because you can see people doing a double take then looking confused," he said in a 2011 interview. "He's beginning to feel the effects of the weather though. I don't think he's supposed to be left in the open."[3] Styles quipped that he would buy some special "varnish" for Niall's next birthday, to refurbish the president. The following summer, Horan jumped on the statue, ripping its arm off.

None of these boys are American, yet their allegiance to liberal politics in the States became part of a pop culture narrative that continued after the end of Obama's presidency. Horan, in particular, made a habit of offering commentary on President Trump that delighted his fans. He told an anecdote about One Direction leaving one of Trump's New York hotels, years prior, after Trump got angry with the band for refusing to take promotional photos with a friend's daughter. This was picked up as a #Resistance narrative, even though the boys had refused simply because they'd been very tired.[4] "Wish you would use common sense before you open your mouth," he later replied to one of the president's incomprehensible and illogical tweets about the coronavirus pandemic.[5] It was a silly jab, making Horan just another of the thousands of Twitter users who hovered in Trump's mentions, waiting for an opportunity for a viral clapback. Yet it was a charming image—sweet Irish golf jock standing up for his tragic American fan base, doomed to live here all of the time. "Nothing but respect for MY president," many of his fans wrote in reply. I pressed the little heart underneath it as well, even though I knew we were all at the mercy of Trump's mouth, regardless, and that Niall Horan legally can't be president, never mind that he shouldn't be.

Then summer came, and Trump referred to Black Lives Matter activists who were protesting the murder of George Floyd as "thugs." "THUGS ??" Horan wrote, "these people are protesting against the fact that one of YOUR animalistic white policemen kneeled on George's windpipe and forced him to stop breathing and killed him?? THUGS???? Are you listening to yourself?"[6] This was different from the insignificant anecdotes so many fans, myself included, had sketched a narrative of Horan's political ideals around previously. Here he was putting real emotion into sloppily typed phrases, expressing what had to be sincere solidarity with a country of which he is not a citizen. On the mechanisms of what was happening, it was not going to have much of an impact. But for some of the young Americans who had been swarming the streets for days, had this cute Irish boy ever been someone they'd cared about, perhaps it felt like something, for one second, to know that he'd been affected.

Styles and Horan both enjoy participating in a kind of American political cosplay: in 2020, Horan also tweeted that he wished he could vote in the presidential election, and Styles wrote that if he could vote in America, he would "vote with kindness."[7] (Become citizens, cowards!) While this could reflect an independently arrived at sense of personal responsibility to speak on matters of import in a country where you own property and reside for much of the year, fostering friends and business relationships, it seems more likely that Horan and Styles were pulled this way by the internet's highly attuned networks of desire.

Fans are aware of this power. When Harry Styles's fans lobbied him to publicly align himself with the Black Lives Matter movement, the fandom researcher Allyson Gross wrote that they were "seeking explicit representation of their own political will, and mobilizing his image for their own political use." She identified this as a form of populist politics and observed that the fans wanted to play "a direct role in developing his political meaning."[8] After years of work elevating the members of One Direction to their positions of relative cultural influence, fans have started to realize the significance of what they've done. They selected these boys to represent them, and now they want to be represented.

GABRIELLE FOSTER HAD BEEN A FAN OF ONE DIRECTION since she was eleven years old.

"We all come from different backgrounds. We all bond over Harry, but we don't personally know what's going on in each other's lives," she told me. "I just want there to be more representation for everybody."[9] Now in her early twenties, Foster is one of the better-known "Black Harries" on Twitter, as she was one of the first Black Harry Styles fans to organize efforts to win his public alliance with the Black Lives Matter movement.

This took a longer time than many people seem to remember. In the fall of 2017, a fan threw a Black Lives Matter flag onto the stage at a Styles concert in London, and Styles ignored it. His fan base was used to him accepting pride flags and dancing with them onstage, as well as giving an opening monologue about how much he valued the support of women. It didn't seem like an accident that he'd left the flag on the floor, untouched, even as sections of the crowd were holding up Black Lives Matter signs. He was known for *noticing* things like that—he would often read off the signs in the audience and banter a bit with the people who had written odd ones. Many fans responded with anger. "Use your fucking platform," one tweeted afterward. "You're enabling hypocrisy."[10] Others were deeply hurt. "I love Harry, he's my safest place, but I feel so disconnected, so unsupported," another wrote.[11] Some taunted him with a play on his own song lyrics, from the (horrible) song "Woman": "You flower, you feast" became "You flower, you white feministe."[12]

Young people who were raised to understand network effects speak reflexively about the power that comes with having a lot of followers and a central cultural position, or a platform, which is not so much a stable object or trait but a privilege granted by interconnected groups of real people and should therefore be used judiciously. Black fans of Harry Styles were not arguing that he should support Black Lives Matter only because it would be personally affirming; they saw it as his moral responsibility as a person with a high public profile. But many white fans joined in the conversation only to suggest that Black fans were asking for too much, that Harry couldn't support every political cause, and that a concert was not a protest. After the initial uproar, Styles posted a black-and-white photograph of some of the signs on his Instagram, captioned "Love."[13] To white fans, that gesture was supposed to be enough. In June 2018, when Gabrielle organized a huge showing of mass-printed paper signs at a show in Hershey, Pennsylvania, white fans tweeted at her about it in rude confusion. This was resolved already, wasn't it?

"The projects we put on all through the tour, it started to feel hopeless at some point," she told me. "It was a constant attack toward Black fans, we're getting attacked and we can't get the recognition from Harry." Gabrielle went to a second concert, in Washington, D.C., and splurged for a ticket in the standing-room pit at the edge of the stage. She brought a Black Lives Matter flag with her, and planned to toss it up to Styles, to see if he would pick it up. "I was very hopeful," she told me. "He was directly in front of me and he was talking to someone near me. I threw it at his feet, and he looked down at it, accidentally stepped on it, and walked away. So that kind of crushed me." Her mood got worse when some of the girls in the crowd around her insisted that she had only herself to blame for the disappointment. She'd kept the flag crumpled up so he couldn't see it the whole show, they told her, and then she got mad at him for not noticing it that one instant? She shot back that she'd held the flag open over the edge of the barricade for hours. The night was ruined, and she went home in a rage. "I was really upset in the moment," she said. "I had a picture of him standing on the flag and I was so mad. I had even considered just unstanning completely because it was so awful. I went off the rails."

After a long drive back to Virginia, she cooled down a bit and checked her Twitter messages. Many of her friends in Styles fandom had sent her clips of another Black Lives Matter flag on the Jumbotron at a different show, or of Styles holding the flag up in Boston, and one of him yelling, "I love every single one of you. If you are Black, if you are white . . . Whoever you are . . . I support you."[14] Eventually, she decided that Styles did care. But she never quite forgot that moment of despair. "I wish he had done something sooner," she told me. "It still gets thrown in Black fans' faces to this day by other fandoms. *Well, your fave wouldn't even hold the flag*, or something like that."

FOR BLACK FANS, A PART OF WHAT MADE IT SO IMPORTANT for Styles to pick up the Black Lives Matter flag was the fact that Black women had never been part of the popular idea of who One Direction fans were.

Similarly, for years, queer fandom of One Direction was overlooked and poorly understood by other fans, the media, and sometimes, it seemed, the band members themselves. In 2015, Payne introduced the song "Girl Almighty" on a tour stop in Columbus, Ohio, saying, "It is about trying to find that number one woman of your life, which none of you can relate to, because most of you are girls." The backlash against the comment was quick, and Payne was apologetic but defensive, tweeting several times about the unfairness of calling him homophobic, and saying it was "annoying" to be criticized after trying his best to make people happy. "Lol this is so insane the more I read I'm like wtf have u ever said something in the wrong way I'm sure every person here has lol," he wrote in one of the messages.[15]

The stereotype of the screaming, hysterical teen fangirl is harmful to fans who may indeed be teens and screaming and girls. It's also harmful to the many fans who feel they don't fit into even the basic contours of that caricature and may not be welcome at all. "As a cisgender male and a queer person, it just felt like One Direction fandom was a club I wasn't in," Tyler Scruggs, a fan from Georgia, told me. "It was something that was more for girls, and at the time I was still in the closet, so being an unabashed One Direction fan came with a lot of social hurdles."[16]

The visibility of LGBTQ+ fans became a priority for Kat Lewis, a fan from Europe who is now in her midforties. "Boybands are marketed with a majority teenage female public in mind, and the assumption is that these female teens are all heterosexual and therefore the band should be sold to them as 'romantic interests,'" she told me. "That assumption can make LGBTQ+ fans feel like they are not seen, like they don't matter. It can make other fans and the press forget they are there."[17] In 2013, she set up the Tumblr account Take Me Home from Narnia as a "safe and enjoyable space" for LGBTQ+ fans who felt overlooked. Later that year, she started talking to two friends, who go by Ellis and Li, about how to take this idea and move it offline so that these fans would be visible in the real-life spaces of fandom as well. These conversations led to the launch of Rainbow Direction in 2014—an organization with the explicit goal of bringing rainbows "to every single show on the Where We Are Tour." They started by posting it to Tumblr as a fandom "challenge." "We figured we'd get the most people involved in the campaign if we'd make the options to join in as diverse as possible," Lewis said. "If you wanted to knit a rainbow hat you'd do that, if you wanted to draw a poster, you'd do that. Craft wristbands or dye your hair or do rainbow makeup." The first person to sign up was in Sweden, she remembered. The first person to bring a rainbow sign to a show was in Colombia. The group hosted meetups where they decorated banners, signs, and T-shirts, doled out rainbow flags, and worked on other handmade crafts to distribute at shows. "Physical shows are at the core of what it means to be a fan of music," she told me. "This is where you experience your fandom to the fullest, this is where fandom is celebrated, so that's where you want to fully be yourself and feel fully accepted."

The effort was praised by *Teen Vogue*, *The Advocate*, *Pitchfork*, and other outlets, and seemed to be warmly received by One Direction members themselves—during the 2015 On the Road Again tour, Harry Styles frequently accepted rainbow flags from audience members. "Rainbow Direction was not easy to ignore," the researcher Bri Mattia wrote in 2018. "Not only did its ideology become dominant, but the band itself, in response to Rainbow Direction's efforts, began attaching the same meaning to their concerts"—at six sold-out shows at the London O2 arena in 2015, the lighting design was modified so that the stage was bathed in rainbow colors during the performance of "Girl Almighty."[18] Soon, fandoms for other pop groups, like Little Mix and BTS, were making similar efforts. In 2016, groups of Rainbow Direction members attended vigils for the Orlando Pulse victims, as well as pride events in London, Paris, Berlin, Stockholm, and Helsinki, among others. Even years after One Direction stopped performing together, Rainbow Direction planned actions at shows on the solo tours. Before the pandemic hit, there were supposed to be four individual tours in 2020—Tomlinson, Payne, Horan, and Styles—and Rainbow Direction were going to bring rainbows to all of them.

But it wasn't always so simple. The dark element in the Rainbow Direction story is its unavoidable politicization in the ongoing Larry wars. Among many fans, there was a general perception that the Larry drama was too entwined with Rainbow Direction for the two to be considered separately. The founders always maintained that the effort was not associated with the Larry Stylinson theory—or later with Babygate—and Lewis said they were asked about it "frequently enough to be annoyed by having to explain ourselves again and again." She declined to tell me if she had any personal interest in Larry, though I'd noted that she had sometimes reblogged Larry content. Rainbow Direction's policy was that everyone be neutral while "on the job," she said, in order to keep the movement inclusive. Volunteers were supposed to be accepting of all ships; shippers were supposed to keep their ships off of their signs. "That was not always easy to enforce," she admitted. "When you participate at a concert, and you bring rainbows, [we said] *don't put your ships on your T-shirt or poster.* Of course, people would wear what they wanted, some did not stick to that rule, and we'd get criticized for that."

The way that some Antis reacted to Larry theories, and to even the smallest affiliation between Larry and Rainbow Direction, sounded homophobic to Lewis at times. "There was a small subsection who were adamant that they needed, in their own words, to 'defend' the boys against these accusations," she told me. "Some called the rumors 'vicious.' Those words, that attitude of gay rumors being seen as possibly the worst thing that could happen to someone, did have a very negative impact on the LGBTQ+ people in the fandom." The confusion and conflict around Larry undermined Rainbow Direction's effort by making the two appear inextricable to those who weren't paying careful attention, and the toll was significant.

Near the end of One Direction's final tour, Liam

Payne told *Attitude* magazine that there had been "loads of rainbow flags" at the band's shows that summer, in celebration of marriage equality in the United States. "But I think that was mainly because people think of the Louis and Harry thing," he added, "which is absolutely nuts and drives me insane."[19]

THERE IS A TERM FOR THE TYPE OF FAN WHO WILL NEVER criticize their fave, never hold them accountable for anything, and coddle them forever as if each day is freshly the day they were born. It's "cupcake," and the Harry Styles fandom has many of them. It also has what Black fans refer to as "KKK Harries"—white fans who refuse to cede any ground in the fandom and prefer to pretend they're the only people there.

When Harry Styles agreed to perform at a Super Bowl preshow in the midst of conversations about the NFL's legacy of racism, Black fans were startled and tried to put pressure on him to change his plans with the hashtag #HarryBackOut. Supporting Black Lives Matter with a sticker was not enough, they argued, if it didn't reflect a principled dedication to living those politics. Some white fans were annoyed too, but it seemed that most of their annoyance was directed at the fans who wanted to prevent them from enjoying a rare television performance by their favorite star. They offered "friendly" reminders that Styles is a singer, not a political activist. Black fans were asked to qualify and defend their desires over and over—they do love him, they don't think he's racist, they just want him to do better, maybe he's not a political activist but he is an adult man who is capable of processing information and altering his behavior, if he cares to. (The show was canceled due to inclement weather.) Many of them also wrote about how tiring it was to be a Black Harrie or a Black stan in general. "When you're a fan of somebody and the fan base is mostly white, you might feel a little ostracized," Ezz Mbamalu, a twenty-three-year-old fan from North Carolina told me. "People try to get on you about *Why do you listen to them? That's not what Black people listen to.* You get pushed down even more."[20]

Black Harries had a big moment when Styles released the single "Adore You" in 2019—it was an upbeat, charming love song with a lyric about "brown skin and lemon over ice." These few words turned Twitter into a party, as Black fans were elated by what they viewed as much-delayed representation in Styles's work. "THE BLACKS HAVE FINALLY WON!" Ezz tweeted, "ADORE YOU WAS WRITTEN ABOUT A BLACK WOMAN."[21] The celebration lasted all night, and for self-described "Harries of colour," this event was "going in the history books."[22] But almost as soon as Black women started tweeting about the lyric, white fans were replying and subtweeting, suggesting that Styles could have just been talking about a woman with a tan. Or, after the release of the "Adore You" music video, which followed Styles as he cared for a large pet fish, that it could have referred to scales. "It's like, let us enjoy one thing," a Black Harrie named Elul Agoda told me. "He writes two words about us and that gets taken away from us too."[23]

Black fans sometimes abandon the main Twitter timeline when these types of dismissals happen and move to group chats for Black Harries only. There, they can organize to make themselves visible in the broader fandom in careful and coordinated ways, such as with the hashtag #BlackHarriesMatter. For several years, on the first of every month—in honor of Styles's February 1 birthday—Black fans tweeted selfies in Harry Styles merch, or styled in a Harry Styles aesthetic, or just smiling, paired with the hashtag, so that their faces would take up space in the broader fandom's timelines. The idea, Ezz told me, was to say, *We're here, we're visible, we care about Harry, we're not going to be pushed aside.* "I think it's cool to go into the hashtag and see other people who look like me, that have the same interest as me, which is Harry Styles," she added. But even that effort has received pushback from white fans, some of whom will go so far as to comment things like "White Harries Matter Too," while others mask their questions in politeness, saying they love the hashtag, the photos are gorgeous, but why is it important to say this?

"It's tiring," Gabrielle Foster told me. "But it's

also like, we got to let it be known. Black Harries Matter."[24]

IN AUGUST 2019, IN HIS SECOND *ROLLING STONE* COVER story, Styles told the journalist Rob Sheffield that he had struggled with Black Lives Matter because he hadn't wanted people to feel like he was virtue signaling. He inched into participation by putting a BLM sticker on his guitar. "When I did it, I realized people got it," he said. "Everyone in that room is on the same page and everyone knows what I stand for. I'm not saying I understand how it feels. I'm just trying to say, 'I see you.'"[25]

Eventually he would be stirred to do more; he tweeted links to bail funds when demonstrators were arrested during the George Floyd protests, and participated in a Black Lives Matter march himself in Los Angeles. The Styles fandom organized itself to support the protests as well, in an assiduous way that reveals how fans have started to think about the relationship between their pop culture loyalties and their politics. Many removed his face from their avatars and replaced it with a Black Lives Matter fist. They canceled the #BlackHarriesMatter tag that June, and all other usual fandom activities, preferring to stay focused on helping protestors. When I spoke to Black fans during that time, they sounded energized—they were excited that K-pop fans were popping out in such numbers to support them, even though typically the two fandoms couldn't possibly have less to do with each other.[26] They were also relieved to see Styles participating, and glad that he had attended the protest without deliberately calling attention to himself over Black protestors themselves.

Activism in a fandom context has often been concerned with visibility. The causes tend to be identity based, and the aim is often to win from the stars in question some explicit recognition that these identities exist within their audience, that they are important, and that both star and fan are aligned with a broader political movement related to this identity. But the choices that Styles fans made during the protests of 2020 reveal a shift or logical progression in this thinking. Fandom activism has been mostly visibility based *so far*, but it could still be a precursor to something bigger: visibility is a starting point for activism, and not its end goal. "Pop culture doesn't really change the world," the labor organizer Teo Bugbee wrote for *SSENSE* that summer. "It's a product to be consumed, an indulgence. But the gift of pop is that it actualizes a fantasy: visions of a world that doesn't yet and maybe won't ever exist."[27] Harry Styles fans didn't imagine that they would erase the structural problems of the societies they lived in by calling attention to themselves, or that being seen by people who like the same music as they did was overtly political. They just wanted to be respected for their dedication and to be seen for all the things they are other than fans of Harry Styles.

Just as stereotypes can hurt all kinds of fans, elucidating the diversity of fandom can help all kinds of fans, too. Jessica Pruett, a gender and sexuality studies scholar who completed a Ph.D. in culture and theory at the University of California, Irvine, in 2021, wrote her master's thesis on lesbian fans of One Direction. "Thinking about lesbian fandom of One Direction helps reframe how people think about One Direction fandom in general," she told me. "It's a lot more complicated and weird than people think it is. It's not a straightforward thing of *Oh, of course girls have crushes on the boys and that's why they're fans.* It's not just lesbian fandom that's more complicated than that—it's all fandom."[28] (She recommended a Tumblr account called 1Dgaymagines, which is short-form self-insert fanfiction for queer women fans of One Direction.[29] Among the most recent stories on the blog: the boys of One Direction are your best friends and help you woo a sexy vampire who lives in a castle on a hill; Harry Styles asks you to decide who to let into the Met Gala; you start a community garden.)

When the goal is visibility within a fandom, the external result is clarification: if Black women love One Direction too, then this is not just a white cultural artifact; if queer fans love them, then this is not just a cheap ploy to exploit heterosexual teenage hormones; if adults love them, then this is not just a phase that a person eventually grows out of. When the goal is to use a fandom's numbers and organizational capabilities to lift a political cause, the external result is also a clarification, one more like an adjustment of a lens that brings something into clearer view: selecting a pop star to love was never a political tactic, but an expression of optimism that anyone can be changed. To hope that Niall Horan deeply cares about my rights is to hope that the other men I love do. To expect that Liam Payne understands why there are so many rainbow flags in the crowd is to believe that anyone should. To want Harry Styles to wave a Black Lives Matter flag onstage is to believe that the world is shifting, and to ask him to do it is to insist on it. We don't need to be told that these men are more a reflection of us than we are of them.

10

Power

ONE AFTERNOON, AT MY DESK IN THE FLATIRON NEIGHBOR-hood of Manhattan, bored out of my mind, I watched the Facebook CEO Mark Zuckerberg give a speech at Georgetown University—the subject of which was his choice not to fact-check political ads—and was startled by the comments streaming down the side of the livestream. "You're looking very handsome and dashing . . . Looking very sweet and cute . . . Lots of love for you." It ended with a fire emoji and a peace sign. "This man left an indelible footprint in the sands of time. Thanks a lot for this wonderful platform called FACEBOOK." When I messaged some of the commenters, they talked to me about loving him, calling him a "great hero" and complimenting him on being very young.[1]

There is no such thing as fan internet, because fan internet *is* the internet. We don't see these things happening until they've happened: Now every time a pop star or a real housewife or a woman politician makes a quip, it winds up the subject of homemade merch and reaction GIFs. When a man is seen doing something endearing—eating Flamin' Hot Cheetos with chopsticks, leading the country of Canada with some amount of competence—he becomes "the internet's boyfriend" for a season. When a girl does something interesting on TikTok—a dance, a funny face, a well-executed bit about how golf courses are causing the destruction of the planet—dozens of Instagram accounts dedicated to her pop up overnight. We love to *fan* so much, we'll take nobodies and make them into stars, just because they filmed themselves skateboarding, drinking cranberry juice, and listening to Fleetwood Mac, or simply because they yodeled for a few minutes in a Walmart. We trot out a new icon every week, adulating them until they do something worthy of a fall, or until we forget. We stan everything now, from Supreme Court justices to new flavors of sparkling water. I have recently stanned a local news blog, a stranger in the comments of a YouTube video, my own sister, a friend's puppy, and a bottle of skin-contact wine.

Fanning is the dominant mode of online speech, and the vitriol of defensive fans is the dominant mode of shouting people down on social platforms. When anybody, anywhere, says something critical about Taylor Swift, they know what kind of week they're in for. When a famous person's name is trending on Twitter, it hardly ever means they're dead—it usually means that some sizable group of online people has turned on them, called for their cancellation, and announced a so-and-so-is-over party. When President Trump announced that he and his wife had tested positive for the coronavirus, the replies to his tweet filled up with the same nonsensical fake hexes, translated from English into Punjabi or Amharic, that Swift fans had been using in the months prior to harass music journalists.[2]

Fandom is the dominant mode of commerce—the backbone of the influencer economy, the force behind the bizarre rise of self-aware Brand Twitter and the dizzying ascent of a handful of pop stars whose personal fortunes are larger than the yearly budgets for some small cities. Brand loyalty has been rebranded as fandom, as has passive consumption of all sorts of media, from HGTV to Spotify playlists. The word "audience" slips seamlessly between concert halls and follower counts. The word "love" drifts around like a leaf.

THE SUBCULTURAL THEORISTS OF THE 1970S AND '80S understood "youth culture" as a matter of class. They were interested in the skinheads, rockers, "mods," and "teddy boys" of postwar England, subcultures that mostly centered on new genres of music and a masculine working-class identity.[3]

These subcultures were newly visible because of the rise of mass communication (i.e., television) and mass culture. They were fashion based, and emerged at the beginning of the era of mass consumption. Scholars were concerned about superficial displays of commonality and solidarity replacing legitimate class-based political action, even as they were curious about the way that new subcultural identities could help a person shape a view of the trajectory of their life, "plans, projects, things to do to fill out time, exploits," and so on. These years were the first in which teenagers were considered a significant demographic independent of their parents, and the media began to fret over their behavior. Though theorists found the rockers and the skinheads fascinating, they, too, worried: "There is no 'subcultural' solution to working-class youth unemployment, educational disadvantage . . . dead-end jobs . . . low pay and the loss of skills." It was all, when it boiled down to it, a waste of time and energy.[4]

These were also viewed almost exclusively as subcultures for young men. Girl culture, or "bedroom culture," was not discussed until 1976, when Angela McRobbie and Jenny Garber wrote a now famous criticism of subcultural studies as a field: "The absence of girls from the whole of the literature in this area is quite striking, and demands explanation."[5] It was either that girls hovered on the edge of male subcultures, or that they weren't interviewed by male researchers, or that they weren't there at all. And if they weren't there, where *were* they? McRobbie and Garber looked at the home and found that girls were doing entirely their own thing within the constraints that had been placed on them. "They may be marginal to the subcultures, not simply because girls are pushed by the dominance of males to the margin of each social activity, but because they are centrally into a different, necessarily subordinate set or range of activities," the pair wrote.[6]

The idea of bedroom culture is that subcultural activities can happen anywhere, and that they often happen in private. "One of the most significant forms of an alternative 'sub-culture' among girls is the culture of the Teeny Bopper," McRobbie and Garber wrote, though it was difficult to study because the girls they tried to interview often made fun of them or refused to provide useful answers to their questions. Fandom could "easily be accommodated" in the home, and had a low barrier to entry—anybody with a bedroom, a record player, access to magazines and to a social circle of similarly interested girls could participate. It was low-risk, and though it was set up around highly manufactured pop acts and commercial products, it was low supervision and therefore freeing. The theorists called it "a meaningful reaction against the selective and authoritarian structures which control the girls' lives at school." Bedroom culture was subversive, and required avoiding surveillance by parents, boys, or unfriendly peers.[7]

This is not to say that they found it empowering, exactly. McRobbie and Garber referred to fandom as a "passive" subculture and believed the "personal and autonomous area" available to preteen and teenage girls was more like a consolation prize, "offered only on the understanding . . . [of] a future general subordination."[8] But they revised that stance in a 1991 update to the essay, recharacterizing girls' at-home fandom practices as more "resistant" and more interesting than they'd previously recognized.[9] Today there is a whole body of scholarship on bedroom culture. Thirty years after the original essay was published, Mary Celeste Kearney reviewed its legacy and then filled in its largest gap, declaring girls' bedrooms "sites of cultural production," not just consumption. Historically, she argued, researchers had been focused on consumerism, and had "[ignored] subjects' remarks about playing guitars or writing poetry."[10] By the time of her writing, girls were not only in their bedrooms looking at magazines and listening to records—they were also using the internet. At least 20 percent of American children had internet access in their bedrooms, she wrote in 2007, and girls were surpassing boys in online activity. They were using it to email and instant message, but they were also using it to blog and design websites, and eventually to broadcast themselves. Far from petering out, as the well-examined subcultures of the 1970s did, bedroom culture lasted and grew and changed with the times.

Girls were "problematizing the conventional construction of the bedroom as private," Kearney wrote, "by using this space not only as a production studio, but also a distribution center."[11] Today, the internet is home to fandom *of* bedroom culture itself. The girl stars of Instagram and YouTube and TikTok let others into their private spaces to watch them create that culture, and they're followed by mini stan armies of their own. The latest innovation of bedroom culture is to be fourteen, sitting in your room, making an Instagram account dedicated to cataloguing the clothes that another girl wore while she was dancing on TikTok, also in her room. The whole web is created in a girl's image now. What all of this means is still fuzzy—modern mannerisms and language and platforms of communication are styled to make more sense for fan culture and girl culture than for almost anything else, but does that effort translate into power for anyone in particular?

DURING THE BLACK LIVES MATTER PROTESTS IN THE SUMmer of 2020, following the murder of George Floyd in Minneapolis, fans of BTS and other K-pop groups achieved national attention for their efforts to aid the protestors from their position of power, which was Twitter.

After the Dallas Police Department tweeted asking people to submit videos of "illegal activity" at protests to its iWatch Dallas app, K-pop fans organized on Twitter to flood it instead with fancams—quickly edited greatest hits of favorite performers dancing and preening, pieced together using basic software.[12] The app crashed within hours, and though it's never been confirmed as fact that the fancams caused this, the Dallas Police Department has yet to offer any other explanation. Soon after, the FBI tweeted asking for images of "individuals inciting violence" at protests, and K-pop fans were called into action again.

That wasn't the limit of their efforts. In group chats, various pop music fandoms organized to keep the internet's focus on Black Lives Matter by canceling all fandom-related hashtags. They repurposed news accounts with large followings that usually track chart positions or celebrity Instagram activity to instead disseminate information about the protests—reading material, bail fund links, shareable graphics. They realized that the platforms they had created to celebrate and amplify their favorite artists could be at any moment used for other things. The spontaneous uprising was covered by *The New York Times*, *The Washington Post*, and major TV broadcast networks and observed with bemused excitement by much of Twitter. People who had never taken any interest in K-pop fandom before started suggesting that K-pop fans be trusted to run the U.S. government, and complimented them for doing more tangible work than elected members of

Congress.[13] That the broader internet noticed what they were doing was not unusual—it was only unusual that they liked it. "Locals and kpop stans are known for not getting along very well," one BTS fan who participated in the effort told me at the time. "The fact that some people were praising us for the effort or even joining in was crazy to me."[14]

In general, K-pop fandoms' default status is "being noticed," to the irritation of many, and it is difficult at this point to look anywhere on social media without seeing their handiwork. A common tactic for promoting a new K-pop group is just wandering around comment sections and replies to viral tweets, dropping names: when BTS was first rising to popularity, its fandom—called ARMY—started commenting "any ARMYs here?" under seemingly random YouTube videos. Loona, a new girl group that debuted in 2018, was promoted similarly but with even more dedication, as the phrase "stan loona" took over Twitter. Fans—known as "Orbits"—replied to any viral tweet with the phrase and still do. (When President Trump contracted the coronavirus, he was of course informed that he should have stanned Loona.) As I'm writing, the phrase "stan loona" is tweeted about once every fifteen seconds.

The problem with all this is that "K-pop fandom" is a loose term that applies to millions of people. Everyone seems to know that there are a lot of K-pop fans, but that knowledge has not led to the reasonable conclusion that many types of people—with different political ideologies and different motivations for stirring things up—must therefore be K-pop fans. Soon after the Black Lives Matter protests, I spoke to the fandom researcher Lori Morimoto, whose work has been primarily on transcultural fandom—how border-crossing fandoms interact with the disparate gender, sexual, and political contexts of different countries—as well as fandom cross-fertilization that happens online. She laughed when she talked about the way K-pop fans had been recently framed as Gen Z heroes, saving the world from cops and Trump. The way that the media describes fans "tends to go from one extreme to the other," she said. "It's either hormonal oversexed teenagers to the polar opposite, *Oh, they're politically savvy! They're activists!* That doesn't capture the culture or the fandom any more than the derisive or derogatory take." Though, of course, many K-pop fans were participating sincerely in the Black Lives Matter movement, Morimoto felt it was somewhat overlooked that this was "an event that made particularly good use of skills that they happened to have, because they're cultivated within that fandom." It didn't mean that K-pop fans were suddenly the most politically active people in the world; it meant that K-pop fans were the best in the world at flooding social media with easily repeated messages. "There's nothing intrinsic about K-pop fandom that makes it somehow more socially aware," she said. "It had everything to do with the material contexts of how that fandom plays out."[15]

And though the tools K-pop fans have at their disposal are powerful, they're also limited. They can post, and they can boost posts. The fandom's skill set mostly allows it to amplify ideas, not to stifle them. Soon after the protests started, the stans took to hunting down racist hashtags, such as #WhiteLivesMatter or #AllLivesMatter, and filling them up with fancams as well, with the intention of derailing conversation for those who were attempting to use them sincerely. "All that does is make it trend," Zina, a writer who runs the blog *Stitch's Media Mix*, told me afterward, expressing frustration. "The hashtag is the message. You flood a hashtag, you make a hashtag trend, you terrorize your fellow fans. I couldn't stand seeing White Lives Matter trending in K-pop in the U.S."[16]

IN THE K-POP FORUM ON REDDIT IN THE SUMMER OF 2020, fans and observers discussed the effort to take down police apps with fancam videos and the fact that trolls on 4chan were planning a counterattack with "gore" clips (a term for shocking, usually violent videos that can be spammed at online enemies). They brushed off the threat.

If K-pop fans and 4chan trolls were going to be the new dueling forces of the internet, K-pop would win because it would have at least tacit support from the commercial platforms. "Twitter already favors the K-pop stans," one wrote. "Trust me, in the list of user abuses of the system, K-pop stans rank pretty high. Twitter loves them because they get to call it engagement."[17] This was followed by a short debate comparing 4chan and K-pop fans, solely on the metrics of who was more "numerous" and who more "zealous." The verdict: definitely K-pop fans on both counts, though "channers" do know more about how to use bots.

As I watched the fandom protest actions that summer, I felt a little like something had been let out of the box. Fans were having an important realization about themselves, and it wasn't clear what they would do with the information. Miranda Ruth Larsen, a K-pop researcher based at the University of Tokyo, told *MIT Technology Review* that, while the police-spamming actions were positive, she was concerned about online manipulation "being held up as the representative of what it means to like K-pop."[18] Meanwhile, several news outlets dubbed K-pop fans "the new Anonymous," referring to the diffuse, politically active, and culturally bizarre hacking collective that took shape on 4chan and related spaces in the early aughts, rising to the level of publicly pranking entities like PayPal, the Church of Scientology, and various local governments around the time of Occupy Wall Street. After a spate of arrests in the early 2010s, Anonymous *had* mostly disappeared. What was left of it had splintered over competing interests in activism and in straight-up trolling, as well as disagreements over the appropriateness of certain tactics and the demands of big egos. Amid the online hacktivist actions that sprang up to aid the 2020 resurgence of the Black Lives Matter movement, Anonymous had seemed to come back. The group reappeared after George Floyd was killed, threatening to leak confidential information from the Minneapolis Police Department. Journalists speculated that they could have been responsible for several related pranks—hijacking Chicago police scanners to play "Fuck tha Police" and "Chocolate Rain," taking down the Minneapolis Police Department's website with a DDoS attack—but some reporters were skeptical. It was unclear whether Anonymous was "back" with a meaningful reconstitution of its old participants or whether the spirit of Anonymous was being invoked by disparate copycats who were brought together by different shared affinities.

The borders of the group were blurry. In the first place, Anonymous was meant to be a movement that anybody could join. (In a 2014 *New Yorker* profile of the movement, the computer security researcher Mikko Hypponen said it was "not a group," but a "series of relationships.")[19] So when K-pop stans found themselves operating in a similar space, whatever had returned of

Anonymous, or whoever was taking up the mantle of Anonymous, welcomed them. "Anonymous stans ALL KPop allies!" the account @YourAnonNews posted after the Dallas police app went down.[20] Soon after, *The Independent* reported that some K-pop stan accounts were changing their profile names and photos and posting instead as members of Anonymous.[21]

Which group was really in control, or whether they were distinct groups at all, became harder to determine. "Anonymous is now weaponizing stan energy," one person wrote in the K-pop subreddit. But others disagreed, pointing out that some Anons sincerely considered themselves ARMY as well. "If you think about it, this is the only logical outcome, lmao," one person commented. I have to agree—this does seem like the most logical outcome of the last ten years of the internet. "If we don't understand K-pop fans, then we have a more difficult time understanding when fandom or fan culture start to permeate other aspects of our political cultures," Lori Morimoto told me. "If K-pop fans are activists, then it becomes more difficult to explain how Gamergate or doxing is related to fandom, but they are actually on a continuum. They're not unrelated things." The original Anonymous crumbled in part because its participants couldn't decide what tactics and traditions were appropriate to use. Maybe fans understand the power of social media better than everyone else does, or maybe it's exactly the opposite. They certainly don't consider themselves a malevolent force—and they usually aren't—but haven't they employed the same tactics as those online groups who do?

One Direction made me care about the internet. Time will tell if this was a blessing or the worst thing that ever happened to me. I'm still inspired by the political power fans seem to have created from thin air and are now prepared to use, and I'm still nervous about the fact that it has been so underexamined. There have been so many calls for empathy, inspection, and nuanced understanding on behalf of the angry men the internet has raised, but there have been far fewer for the fangirls whose beliefs are far more convoluted. They've been dismissed and despised, and now they're exalted, but they have yet to be taken seriously. Real scrutiny would reveal everything that the internet has made possible: unimpeded creativity, remarkable feats of will, the unexpected easing of loneliness, the goofy precursors to solidarity, but also devastating atomization and division, overstimulation realized as constant anxiety, emotion mutilated into absurdities, attention rendered an addiction, passion funneled into targeted harassment.

Fans have started using their networked power for good, bad, amoral, indecipherable reasons—the political climate of the last decade has tempted them to play with their power in new ways. As they get better at wielding it, it's anyone's guess what they might use it for. "2020 will be the year Twitter stans will be liked by people," one person wrote in the K-pop subreddit during a summer of protest.[22] Another corrected them politely. It would be more than that. It would be the year stan Twitter would be seen for what it was: "a source of unlimited *chaotic* energy."

Conclusion: 1Dead

WHEN I WAS TWENTY-FIVE, I WAS LONELY AGAIN. IT FELT clarifying, kind of like that game kids play in restaurants where they see who can hold their hand above a candle for the longest, at the closest distance. Usually, I would instigate that game and then lose immediately, but this time I was really winning.

I wouldn't do anything interesting. I would get a cheap manicure and then browse the used bookstore near my apartment for an hour or sit in front of the bagel shop with a Diet Coke and a cup of ice for most of an afternoon. Sometimes I would walk to a junk store on the other side of Brooklyn and look at old dishes and postcards, or I would take the train all the way to the top of Manhattan to visit a diner I'd liked during my first summer in New York. I don't know that I had anything useful to think about—mainly I was pushing into wounds from the breakup my friends were sick of hearing about and avoiding exposure to anyone who seemed happy—but it felt at least a little better than making conversation or watching television.

In the fall, I met a financial analyst I described as having goldfish eyes and cartoon hair. On our first date, I asked him to tell me a secret, and he told me that when he was sixteen, growing up in Kansas, he'd driven into the woods and been cursed by a witch who lived there. I thought this was incredible, and I reasoned I could date someone who worked in finance, so long as they were also cursed by a Kansan witch. But I actually couldn't. I broke up with him after two months, a few days before I was set to fly to California to see the release show for Harry Styles's second album and to find the shrine to his vomit on the freeway. I cried over it not because I was going to miss him, but because I'd have to go back to being a little freak, wandering around aimlessly and sneaking chicken salad sandwiches into buildings they shouldn't be in. I would have to go back to dealing with myself, which had been making me so tired. Once it was done, I regretted it, and wondered if I could take it back. Simultaneously, I was thrilled. I knew that I'd done it so that I wouldn't have to keep in touch via text while I was in California. I wanted to be totally free, and not have to try to explain my experience to anyone while it was happening. At 4:30 in the morning, getting into a car to go to the airport, I downloaded the new album, which had been released only hours before. I listened to it in the back seat, dropping in and out of sleep. But about halfway through, I opened my eyes.

"Don't call me baby again," Styles said, a bit petulantly, following the curious plucking of a ukulele and some hand-clapping. "It's hard for me to go home, be so lonely." The chorus was mostly that: "To be so lonely / To be so." Stupidly, the taxi became a getaway car and the darkness of early morning became electric. How important that Harry Styles and I were learning about love with such similar timing, I thought, and that we are the same age. "I'm just an arrogant son of a bitch," he said with the familiar cadence of someone who thinks that epiphanies will last. *There is a cello on this song,* I realized—how sweet! There was also something chant-y about it, in a soccer team way. I felt like I was jogging. It was one of the rare moments in which the shape of my life, normally hazy, took on a bright outline. There are so few things I love to do more than coughing up money for a cheap hotel, sleeping there alone, and waking up in the morning with a sight to see: a boy in pearls and high-waisted pants, for example, plus fifteen thousand people who have grounded themselves the same way I have, using someone else's gestures and vocal tics to mark time, to help them remember, and to return them over and over to the question of who they are.

• • •

BY THE END OF ONE DIRECTION, THE MEDIA'S TREATMENT OF the band's music and its fans had changed significantly. In part, this was because of a rise in the estimation of pop music among critics, and a new focus among content makers on women's websites for celebrating almost everything any girl did as "inspiring" and "empowering." Guilty pleasures were to be enjoyed, not insulted, and then in the next churn of the blogging cycle, it was rude to call them guilty pleasures at all. Pop music fans also worked hard to drive these cultural changes for their own reasons, particularly within boy band fandoms. After Tumblr's full-court press, "No Control" became a favorite among serious music writers, who started to look at the band's work in retrospect and uncover gems they had ignored. The indie rock star Mitski recorded a cover of "Fireproof," a song from the band's fourth album. Zayn Malik's solo album was reviewed by *Pitchfork*, then Harry Styles's was too. It is inappropriate now to make fun of girls for screaming or boy bands for existing or anybody for liking anything—this is what we asked for, but it doesn't feel like enough.

In the spring of 2017, Harry Styles appeared on the cover of *Rolling Stone*, interviewed by the music journalist and *Almost Famous* writer-director Cameron Crowe. It was just three months after the Women's March, the perfect time to discuss a pop star's entry into some version of feminism, and Styles delivered.

"Who's to say that young girls who like pop music—short for popular, right?—have worse musical taste than a 30-year-old hipster guy? That's not up to you to say," he told Crowe, addressing an undefined audience. "Young girls like the Beatles. You gonna tell me they're not serious? How can you say young girls don't get it? They're our future. Our future doctors, lawyers, mothers, presidents, they kind of keep the world going." He really went for it. "Teenage-girl fans—they don't lie. If they like you, they're *there.* They don't act 'too cool.' They like you, and they tell you. Which is *sick.*"[1] This was what they call a Big Deal online, and to this day there is hardly a piece of writing about Styles that doesn't mention it.

I'm happy that he said that, because I know it meant something important to a lot of people. But it's hard to celebrate the victories of fangirls the way I'd like to, because those victories are also being celebrated by the sort of people who will use them to make more money off of us. And they're being celebrated by well-meaning people in sort of embarrassing ways—as if liking a boy band is a radical political act, the same way wearing well-designed T-shirts with punchy slogans on them is a sincere expression of feminism, and the same way Pantone creating a shade of red called "Period" is empowering for anyone who menstruates. Not all women are "our future doctors, lawyers, mothers, presidents," I would love to tell Harry Styles. Not all women keep the world going! And it is not, in fact, okay to like whatever you want. Some stuff is genuinely bad, like Mark Zuckerberg or the Harry Styles song "Woman."

Many of the changes of the last few years are illusory in their generosity toward the people who have made pop music a foundation of their personal histories. As is often the case with "acceptance," what's really been agreed on is that women and girls are "important" enough where it makes good business sense that they be marketed to with greater specificity than they were before. This somehow winds up being as impersonal as it is invasive. I first started to notice it at the end of 2017, when Ticketmaster launched its Verified Fan product, a new technology designed to kill professional ticket scalping.[2] The idea was that the program could determine—in some opaque way—who is *really* a fan and therefore unlikely to resell the ticket they are buying to a concert. Some artists customize the system by adding a layer of "boosts," which are opportunities for fans to improve their position in a Ticketmaster queue by purchasing copies of the artist's album or other merchandise. Fans who don't have the extra money to spend on such things can perform less dignified tasks, such as watching a music video some absurd number of times. But when all is said and done, those mechanisms are frills. Really, Ticketmaster considers a "fan" any person who is not a piece of software.

Stan Twitter has also been turned into a product. It is famously annoying, and so many of its cultural contributions have slid under the radar, but its capacity for profit never has. Those with large enough followings are sometimes rewarded with access to the celebrities they love—they can boast about direct messages or handwritten notes or invitations to secret listening parties to further bolster their brands. In recent years, record labels have caught on to the possibility of making friends with these Twitter superstars, feeding them exclusive content that they can post without fear of copyright takedowns in exchange for promotion of industry-approved campaigns. I once met a Taylor Swift fan who had been paid to promote sponsored content from some of the brands Swift had endorsement deals with.[3] I spoke to a Lorde fan who was offered free tickets to an award show in exchange for tweeting branded promotional images, and who had started adding public relations skills to his résumé.[4] All of their work, done for free, was being repackaged into something productive.

Now brands can speak like fans, too. Whoever runs Ticketmaster's social media accounts takes care to make it sound as if the brand itself relates to the experiences of those with a crushing love for a boy band. "My best friend in high school had a 1D ship account on Tumblr," the company's official Twitter account shared on One Direction's tenth anniversary, "and when I got shipped with Niall I almost cried tears of joy."[5] This kind of thing makes me want to cry, too!

BECAUSE ONE DIRECTION IS DEAD, THE GIRLS ON TWITTER call them by the name "1Dead."

The tweets tend to be cold, clear-eyed—*I remember when I used to stan 1Dead, that was years ago, I was a child, haven't heard that name in years.* Or they'll be the opposite: "life ended with 1Dead, Twitter was pointless after 2015, each year is a series of dates that used to be important and now mean nothing." The nickname is both a sign of disrespect and a sign of unending love. It both hurts me and delights me to see it.

At its best, fandom is an inside joke that never ends. Years after some Tumblr user shared that bad second-person micro-fiction suggesting that Niall Horan had crawled into the ear of whoever was reading it, my sister came across a TikTok video of a woman my age with a gravelly voice, digitally shrinking her head down to mite size and dragging it into Niall Horan's ear canal. "Oh, how the tables have turned," she taunted him as she went. "Yes, sir. I am in there."[6] I can't tell you how many times I have watched this clip, always wondering why that ridiculous post affected her the same way that it did me. Why did she remember it for so long? Why am I touching my ear?

I wrote this book in part in defense of myself, a

fangirl, because I know that my experience is typical. The little indignities of being young and the big disappointments of not finding the love you want or of not becoming the person you'd hoped—these things are tempered by fandom, which is such an ugly, boring word. Fandom is an interruption; it's as simple as enjoying something for no reason, and it's as complicated as growing up. It should be celebrated for what it can provide in individual lives, but it should also be taken seriously for what it can do at scale—not because I like it or because being a girl is cool now, but because fans are connecting based on affinity and instinct and participating in hyperconnected networks that they built for one purpose but can use for many others. We need to know what fandom can do and what it can't, and we need to figure out who might try to manipulate it and why. Everything we need is right in front of us. We should talk about how we went online, driven by some sort of longing, and why we stayed there, pushing that want outward, over and over, until it couldn't be ignored.

A NOTE ON SOURCES

When deciding how to cite social media posts in this book, I referred to the approach used in *A Tumblr Book: Platform and Cultures*, edited by Allison McCracken, Alexander Cho, Louisa Stein, and Indira Neill Hoch, and published by University of Michigan Press in 2020. "As user-scholars of Tumblr," they write, "we are aware of the degree to which posts can be decontextualized and recirculated in harmful ways or can allow users to be easily targeted through search engines." While many social media posts have a natural expectation of publicness, Tumblr's structural insularity demands different consideration, as do posts made on any platform by people who do not have a large online following and would not expect to see their words reappearing in this context.

With this in mind, I attempted to contact every person whose social media posts I intended to quote significantly or describe in detail in the book. Most asked to be identified in these notes by their usernames only; if I could not get in contact with someone, I have opted not to identify them at all, with a few exceptions for users who are already well known in fandom circles. (The editors of *A Tumblr Book* also offered Tumblr users whose posts were quoted in their book the option to have their words "slightly altered to prevent them from being searchable," but I did not make this offer.) If a post was deleted after I'd seen it, I was sometimes able to use the Internet Archive's Wayback Machine to recover it. I note a few instances in which this was not possible, where I had to rely on my notes as the source for the original text.

Though not directly referenced, for context about subcultural and fandom studies, I read and benefited from Matt Hills's *Fan Cultures*, Katherine Larsen and Lynn S. Zubernis's *Fangasm: Supernatural Fangirls*, Rob Sheffield's *Dreaming the Beatles: The Love Story of One Band and the Whole World*, Gretchen McCulloch's *Because Internet: Understanding the New Rules of Language*, and Zoe Fraade-Blanar and Aaron M. Glazer's *Superfandom: How Our Obsessions Are Changing What We Buy and Who We Are*, as well as *Hop on Pop: The Politics and Pleasures of Popular Culture*, edited by Henry Jenkins, Tara McPherson, and Jane Shattuc; *Girl Wide Web: Girls, the Internet, and the Negotiation of Identity* and *Girl Wide Web 2.0: Revisiting Girls, the Internet, and the Negotiation of Identity*, edited by Sharon

R. Mazzarella; the second edition of *Fandom: Identities and Communities in a Mediated World*, edited by Jonathan Gray, Cornel Sandvoss, and C. Lee Harrington; and the second edition of *The Subcultures Reader*, edited by Ken Geldner.

NOTES

Introduction

1. The Twitter account @isasdfghjkls was deleted at some point after I saw this tweet and could not be accessed using the Internet Archive's Wayback Machine.
2. Anonymous, "your fav is problematic," Tumblr post, September 13, 2015.
3. Editors, "Let Them Eat Print!," *n+1* 15 (Winter 2013), https://nplusonemag.com/issue-15/the-intellectual-situation/let-them-eat-print/.
4. Moira Weigel, "The Internet of Women," *Logic*, April 1, 2018, https://logicmag.io/scale/the-internet-of-women/.
5. Kaitlyn Tiffany, "The Founder of Pinboard on Why Understanding Fandom Is Good for Business," *The Verge*, June 12, 2017, https://theverge.com/2017/6/12/15746916/pinboard-founder-maciej-ceglowski-interview-yahoo-delicious-fandom.
6. Maciej Cegłowski, "Fan Is a Tool-Using Animal," *Idle Words*, 2013, https://idlewords.com/talks/fan_is_a_tool_using_animal.htm.
7. Jamie Crossan, "One Direction's Harry Styles: 'We're Bigger Than the Beatles, Fame-wise,'" *New Musical Express*, February 9, 2014 (aggregation of quotations originally published in *Top of the Pops*), https://nme.com/news/music/one-direction-149-1239904.

8. Timothy Bella, "Lou Pearlman Was a Disgraced Mogul Who Defrauded Boy Bands. Then Came the $300 Million Ponzi Scheme," *The Washington Post*, March 3, 2019, https://washingtonpost.com/nation/2019/03/13/lou-pearlman-was-disgraced-mogul-who-defrauded-s-boy-bands-then-came-million-ponzi-scheme/.
9. Brooke Marine, "The Jonas Brothers Finally Explained Their Purity-Ring Origin Story," *W*, March 8, 2019, https://wmagazine.com/story/jonas-brother-purity-rings.
10. *One Direction: This Is Us*, directed by Morgan Spurlock (2013; Culver City, CA: TriStar Pictures).
11. OneDirectionVewo, "Niall Horan Calling Fans a 'Shower of Cunts,'" YouTube video, July 6, 2012, https://youtu.be/CCRLUGTiLqY.
12. Caroline Moss, "A Four Year-Old Tweet from One Direction Just Leapt Past Obama's Four More Years Tweet to Be the Second Most Popular Ever," *Business Insider Australia*, January 14, 2015, www.businessinsider.com.au/one-direction-tweet-2015-1.
13. Rebecca Davison, "Oh Baby! One Direction's Niall Horan Is Mobbed as He Attends Nephew's Christening in Ireland Where He Served as Godfather," *Daily Mail*, November 9, 2013, https://dailymail.co.uk/tvshowbiz/article-2496371/One-Directions-Niall-Horan-mobbed-attends-nephews-christening-Ireland.html.
14. Maëlys Wandelst (yourssincerelylarry), "Larry Hug," 2015, accessed via Sacha Judd's personal website, https://sachajudd.com/one-direction.
15. Maëlys Wandelst, email to the author, January 21, 2020.
16. Kaitlyn Tiffany, "Harry Styles Fans Are Trying to Beat the Billboard Charts with VPNS and Mass Coordination," *The Verge*, May 5, 2017, https://theverge.com/2017/5/5/15533760/harry-styles-streaming-data-billboard-tumblr-fan-effort.
17. "What Tumblr's Ban on 'Adult Content' Actually Did," Tossed Out, Electronic Frontier Foundation, last modified May 20, 2019, https://eff.org/tossedout/tumblr-ban-adult-content.

18. "Copyright policy," Twitter Rules and Policies, Twitter, https://help.twitter.com/en/rules-and-policies/copyright-policy; Katherine Trendacosta, "Unfiltered: How YouTube's Content ID Discourages Fair Use and Dictates What We See Online," Electronic Frontier Foundation, December 10, 2020, https://eff.org/wp/unfiltered-how-youtubes-content-id-discourages-fair-use-and-dictates-what-we-see-online.
19. Samantha Hunt, "There Is Only One Direction," *The Cut*, May 12, 2015, https://thecut.com/2015/05/there-is-only-one-direction.html.

1. Screaming

1. J. Mack Slaughter, Jr., and Lynn Roppolo, "'Screaming Your Lungs Out!' A Case of Boy Band-Induced Pneumothorax, Pneumomediastinum, and Pneumoretropharyngeum," *The Journal of Emergency Medicine* 53, no. 5 (October 2017): 762–64, https://doi.org/10.1016/j.jemermed.2017.08.006.
2. Abby Armada (@mygiantrobot), "That's worse than when I," Twitter, November 1, 2020, https://twitter.com/mygiantrobot/status/1322919976265748480.
3. J. Mack Slaughter, Jr., MD, email to the author, January 12, 2020.
4. Barbara Ehrenreich, Elizabeth Hess, and Gloria Jacobs, "Beatlemania: Girls Just Want to Have Fun," in *The Adoring Audience*, ed. Lisa A. Lewis (London: Routledge, 1992), 84–106.
5. Frederick Lewis, "Britons Succumb to 'Beatlemania,'" *The New York Times*, December 1, 1963, https://timesmachine.nytimes.com/timesmachine/1963/12/01/105229577.html.
6. Jim Farber, "Beatles' Historic Arrival in New York City 50 Years Ago Gave Big Apple Unforgettable Lift," *New York Daily News*, January 24, 2014, https://nydailynews.com/new-york/beatles-electrified-nyc-50-years-article-1.1590579; Robert Alden, "Wild-Eyed Mobs Pursue Beatles; Dozen Girls Injured Here in Fervent Demonstrations," *The New York Times*, February 13, 1964, https://timesmachine.nytimes.com/timesmachine/1964/02/13/97379540.pdf.

7. Paul Russell, memo from Capitol Records, December 23, 1963, images accessed via http://rarebeatles.com/photopg2/comstk.htm.
8. James Barron, "Historic Hysterics: Witnesses to a Really Big Show," *The New York Times*, February 7, 2014, https://nytimes.com/2014/02/08/nyregion/the-beatles-debut-on-ed-sullivan.html.
9. "What You Don't Know About the Beatles' U.S. Debut," NBC News, February 7, 2014, https://nbcnews.com/nightly-news/what-you-dont-know-about-beatles-u-s-debut-n24171.
10. David Dempsey, "Why the Girls Scream, Weep, Flip; The Path to Understanding Is Psychological, Anthropological, and a Whole Lot Besides," *The New York Times*, February 23, 1964, https://nytimes.com/1964/02/23/archives/why-the-girls-scream-weep-flip-the-path-to-understanding-is.html.
11. Theodor Adorno, "On the Fetish Character in Music and the Regression of Listening," 1938, in *The Culture Industry: Selected Essays on Mass Culture* (London: Routledge, 2001), quoted by Dempsey, "Why the Girls Scream."
12. Adorno, "On the Fetish Character in Music," 53.
13. Dempsey, "Why the Girls Scream."
14. Al Aronowitz, "Beatlemania in 1964: 'This Has Gotten Entirely Out of Control,'" *Saturday Evening Post*, March 1964, in *The Guardian*, January 29, 2014, https://theguardian.com/music/2014/jan/29/the-beatles.
15. Casey McNerthney, "Beatles' Stay at Edgewater Helped Mark Its Place in History," *Seattle P-I*, August 19, 2009, https://seattlepi.com/local/article/Beatles-stay-at-Edgewater-helped-mark-its-place-1305857.php; Bob Greene, "Hotel Stripped Its Bed and Now Must Lie in It," *Chicago Tribune*, August 18, 1993, https://chicagotribune.com/news/ct-xpm-1993-08-18-9308180075-story.html.
16. Jim Cushman, "A Beatle Slept with This: Pieces of the Mania," *Collectors Weekly*, March 11, 2011, https://collectorsweekly.com/articles/a-beatle-slept-with-this-pieces-of-the-mania/.

17. Anthony Burton, "Beatlemania Hits N.Y.: The Beatles Appear on 'The Ed Sullivan Show' in 1964," *New York Daily News*, February 10, 1964, https://nydailynews.com/entertainment/music/beatlemania-hits-new-york-beatles-ed-sullivan-article-1.2525425.
18. Alan Rinzler, "No Soul in Beatlesville," *The Nation*, 1964, published online April 6, 2009, https://thenation.com/article/archive/no-soul-beatlesville/.
19. Bernard Hollowood, "Beatlemaniac," *Punch*, reprinted in *The New York Times*, December 1, 1963, https://timesmachine.nytimes.com/timesmachine/1963/12/01/105229577.pdf.
20. Betty Friedan, *The Feminine Mystique* (New York: W. W. Norton, 1963), quoted in Ehrenreich et al., "Beatlemania."
21. Ehrenreich et al., "Beatlemania," 103.
22. Maureen Cleave, "Paul All Alone: Running Hard to Catch Up with the Music," *London Evening Standard*, September 1, 1966.
23. Allison McCracken, interview with the author, November 8, 2019.
24. Allison McCracken, *Real Men Don't Sing: Crooning in American Culture* (Durham, NC: Duke University Press, 2015), 201.
25. Allison McCracken, email to the author, June 1, 2021.
26. McCracken notes that this collection has shifted ownership and is now part of the University of California at Santa Barbara's Performing Arts Collection.
27. McCracken, interview with the author, November 8, 2019.
28. McCracken, *Real Men Don't Sing*, 201.
29. Ehrenreich et al., "Beatlemania," 98.
30. George E. Pitts, "TV's 'American Bandstand' a Noisy Menagerie!," *The Pittsburgh Courier*, July 12, 1958, accessed via Newspapers.com.
31. Jon Caramanica, "Send in the Heartthrobs, Cue the Shrieks," *The New York Times*, September 1, 2010, https://nytimes.com/2010/09/02/arts/music/02bieber.html.
32. James C. McKinley, Jr., "Bieber Fever Comes to Macy's," *The New York Times*, June 18, 2012, https://artsbeat.blogs.nytimes.com/2012/06/18/bieber-fever-comes-to-macys.

33. Jon Carmanica, "Riding the Boy Band Wave While It Lasts," *The New York Times*, November 14, 2012, https://nytimes.com/2012/11/15/arts/music/one-direction-rides-boy-band-wave-with-take-me-home.html.
34. Jon Carmanica, "Heading Wherever, Together," *The New York Times*, November 27, 2013, https://nytimes.com/2013/11/28/arts/music/one-direction-releases-a-new-album-midnight-memories.html.
35. Daniela Marino, interview with the author, October 29, 2019.
36. Freya Whitfield, interview with the author, September 22, 2019.
37. Jacob Gaspar, interview with the author, October 1, 2019.
38. "How to Kick the Beatle Habit," *Life*, August 28, 1964.
39. Cheryl Tuso, letter to the editor, *Life*, October 9, 1964.
40. Ehrenreich et al., "Beatlemania."

2. Deep-Frying

1. Zan Romanoff, "One Direction's Female Fans Love to Dress Like Harry Styles," *Racked*, May 16, 2017, https://racked.com/2017/5/16/15609830/one-direction-cosplay.
2. Obsession_inc, "Affirmational fandom vs. Transformational fandom," Dreamwidth post, June 1, 2009, https://obsession-inc.dreamwidth.org/82589.html.
3. "DeepFriedMemes Goodbye Message," Google Doc linked in Reddit post, October 10, 2020, https://docs.google.com/document/d/1yEQg3TRB7w8cHcI3ss5fn8m-VsuVVSGq640DN6Dzdoo/view.
4. "Friend: i don't like 1D Because there not bad boy," archived by bad1dimagines, Tumblr post, July 7, 2016, https://bad1dimagines.tumblr.com/post/147064657448.
5. Theodor Adorno, "On the Fetish Character in Music and the Regression of Listening," 1938, in *The Culture Industry: Selected Essays on Mass Culture* (London: Routledge, 2001), 29–60.
6. ChutJeDors, email to the author, May 31, 2021.
7. "Beatles RPF," RPF Fandom, Fanlore, last modified October 28, 2019, https://fanlore.org/wiki/Beatles_RPF.

8. Llamaonfire, "Just my kind of sickness," Archive of Our Own, January 10, 2014, https://archiveofourown.org/works/1128159.
9. Llamaonfire, "Beatle baby," Archive of Our Own, March 27, 2014, https://archiveofourown.org/works/1158721.
10. *Your Quality John/Paul-Library*, Tumblr, https://thejplibrary.tumblr.com/.
11. ChutJeDors, "5 Thomas Lane," Archive of Our Own, January 1, 2021, https://archiveofourown.org/works/13818678.
12. "Imagine: you and Harry are on a date and you're playing chubby bunny," archived by bad1dimagines, Tumblr, March 18, 2017, https://bad1dimagines.tumblr.com/post/158552923878.
13. "Imagine: Zayn just moved to your neighborhood," archived by bad1dimagines, Tumblr, October 17, 2019, https://bad1dimagines.tumblr.com/post/188405787103/i-wonder-if-theyre-staring-at-you-bc-youre-with.
14. bad1dimagines, "Dark Harry" tag, Tumblr, last updated October 30, 2019, https://bad1dimagines.tumblr.com/tagged/dark-harry.
15. Jessica Misener, "Why Justin Bieber Keeps Dying in Fan Fiction," *BuzzFeed*, October 10, 2012, https://buzzfeed.com/jessicamisener/the-many-deaths-of-justin-bieber.
16. "Imagine: Harry nibbling at your ear," archived by bad1dimagines, Tumblr, September 17, 2018, https://bad1dimagines.tumblr.com/post/178196944263.
17. "Imagine: the outfit you wear to jump in front of niall's car," archived by bad1dimagines, Tumblr, March 14, 2016, https://bad1dimagines.tumblr.com/post/141070376788/please.
18. "Imagine: niall horan crawling inside your ear," archived by bad1dimagines, Tumblr, July 13, 2015, https://bad1dimagines.tumblr.com/post/123997770038.

3. Shrines

1. harryx, "Harry on the puke sign," Tumblr, April 21, 2017, https://harryx.tumblr.com/post/159843358974/harry-on-the-puke-sign.

2. Rebecca Davison, "One Di-RETCH-tion: Fans Erect a Shrine in Honour of Harry Styles' Vomit on Los Angeles Freeway," *Daily Mail*, October 15, 2014, https://dailymail.co.uk/tvshowbiz/article-2793668/a-shrine-erected-honour-harry-styles-vomit.html.
3. Christie D'Zurilla, "Harry Styles Drops $4 Million on House near Beverly Hills," *Los Angeles Times*, March 18, 2014, https://latimes.com/entertainment/la-xpm-2014-mar-18-la-et-mg-harry-styles-buys-house-beverly-hills-post-office-photos-20140318-story.html.
4. Nancy K. Baym, *Playing to the Crowd: Musicians, Audiences, and the Intimate Work of Connection* (New York: New York University Press, 2018), 95.
5. Ibid., 96.
6. Jesse Jarnow, *Heads: A Biography of Psychedelic America* (Philadelphia, PA: Da Capo, 2015), 97.
7. Baym, *Playing to the Crowd*, 96.
8. Howard Rheingold, *The Virtual Community* (Cambridge, MA: MIT Press, 1993), 30–39.
9. Ibid., 30.
10. Ibid., 37.
11. OoCities, GeoCities archive, http://oocities.org/#gsc.tab=0.
12. Ethan Kaplan, "Shutting Down My Life's Work," *Medium*, May 21, 2014, https://ethankaplan.com/shutting-down-my-lifes-work-c358320e7689.
13. Tresa Redburn and Mitch Schneider, "Countdown Begins for David Bowie's 'Bowienet' Internet Service," Mitch Schneider Organization, August 28, 1998, http://msopr.com/press-releases/countdown-begins-for-david-bowies-bowienet-internet-service-as-hes-set-to-launch-historic-internet-service-provider/.
14. Hiroshi Ono and Madeline Zavodny, "Gender and the Internet," *Social Science Quarterly* 84, no. 1 (March 2003): 111–21, https://doi.org/10.1111/1540-6237.t01-1-8401007.
15. "Rules of the Internet," Encyclopedia Dramatica, January 10, 2007, archived by Wayback Machine, http://web.archive

.org/web/20070110035128/http://encyclopediadramatica.com/index.php/Rules_Of_The_Internet.

16. Siân Brooke, "'There Are No Girls on the Internet': Gender Performances in Animal Advice Memes," *First Monday* 24, no. 10 (October 2019), https://doi.org/10.5210/fm.v24i10.9593.
17. Nancy Kaplan and Eva Farrell, "Weavers of Webs: A Portrait of Young Women on the Net," *The Arachnet Electronic Journal on Visual Culture* 2, no. 3 (1994).
18. Pamela Takayoshi, "No Boys Allowed: The World Wide Web as a Clubhouse for Girls," *Computers and Composition* 16, no. 1 (1999): 89–106, https://doi.org/10.1016/S8755-4615(99)80007-3.
19. John B. Horrigan, "New Users: What They Do Online, What They Don't, and Implications for the 'Net's Future," Pew Internet and American Life Project, September 2000, https://pewinternet.org/wp-content/uploads/sites/9/media/Files/Reports/2000/New_User_Report.pdf.
20. Deborah Fallows, "How Women and Men Use the Internet," Pew Research Center, December 28, 2005, https://pewresearch.org/internet/2005/12/28/how-women-and-men-use-the-internet.
21. "Internet/Broadband Fact Sheet," Pew Research Center, last modified April 7, 2021, https://pewresearch.org/internet/fact-sheet/internet-broadband/.
22. Julia Carpenter, "Meme Librarian Is a Real Job—and It's the Best One on the Internet," *The Washington Post*, December 21, 2015, https://washingtonpost.com/news/the-intersect/wp/2015/12/21/tumblrs-meme-librarian-has-the-best-job-on-the-internet/.
23. Alexander Cho, "Sensuous Participation: Queer Youth of Color, Affect, and Social Media" (Ph.D. diss., University of Texas at Austin, 2015), 201.
24. Ibid., 20.
25. Kaitlyn Tiffany, "The Story of the Internet, as Told by Know Your Meme," *The Verge*, March 6, 2018, https://theverge

.com/2018/3/6/17044344/know-your-meme-10-year-anniversary-brad-kim-interview.

26. Anonymous, "I like this blog a lot because sometimes when people ask about a specific thing," Tumblr post responded to by bad1dimagines, November 9, 2019, https://bad1dimagines.tumblr.com/post/188935607618/i-like-this-blog-a-lot-because-sometimes-when.
27. bad1dimagines, Tumblr message to the author, June 1, 2021.
28. Abigail De Kosnik, *Rogue Archives: Digital Cultural Memory and Media Fandom* (Cambridge, MA: MIT Press, 2016), 4.
29. Ibid., 3.
30. bad1dimagines, "i'm not even posting this as a joke," Tumblr, March 12, 2016, https://bad1dimagines.tumblr.com/post/140919782608/im-not-even-posting-this-as-a-joke-like-i.
31. Stewart Brand, "Escaping the Digital Dark Age," *Library Journal* 124, no. 2 (February 1, 1999), quoted in De Kosnik, *Rogue Archives*, 46.
32. Francesca Bacardi, "Harry Styles Knew He'd Made It When His Vomit Ended Up on eBay," *Page Six*, June 2, 2017, https://pagesix.com/2017/06/02/harry-styles-knew-he-made-it-when-his-vomit-ended-up-on-ebay/.
33. Gabrielle Kopera, email to the author, February 10, 2020.

4. Trending

1. Steven J. Horowitz, "One Direction & the Wanted: The Billboard Cover Story," *Billboard*, March 27, 2012, https://billboard.com/articles/news/499360/one-direction-the-wanted-the-billboard-cover-story.
2. Caspar Llewellyn Smith, "One Direction: The Fab Five Take America," *The Guardian*, March 15, 2012, https://theguardian.com/music/2012/mar/15/one-direction-fab-five-america.
3. 5 News, "Are One Direction Bigger Than the Beatles?," YouTube video, February 11, 2014, https://youtu.be/JvyxaOWQaiE.
4. Matt Stopera and Dave Stopera, "23 of the Craziest and

Scariest Things One Direction Fans Have Ever Done," *BuzzFeed*, November 7, 2019, https://buzzfeed.com/mjs538/what-a-time-it-was.

5. @Dat10inchYo, Twitter account, last updated April 12, 2014, https://twitter.com/dat10inchyo.
6. Anonymous, "The boys blood types- Liam: AB. Louis: O. Niall: A. Harry & Zayn: B," Twitter, April 4, 2015.
7. Darcy DiNucci, "Fragmented Future," *Print*, January 1999, 32, 221–22, http://darcyd.com/fragmented_future.pdf.
8. Tim O'Reilly, "What Is Web 2.0," *O'Reilly* (blog), September 30, 2005, https://oreilly.com/pub/a/web2/archive/what-is-web-20.html.
9. Jean Burgess and Nancy K. Baym, *Twitter: A Biography* (New York: New York University Press, 2020), 36–69.
10. Susannah Fox, Kathryn Zickuhr, and Aaron Smith, "Twitter and Status Updating, Fall 2009," Pew Research Center, October 21, 2009, https://pewresearch.org/internet/2009/10/21/twitter-and-status-updating-fall-2009/.
11. John Herrman and Katie Notopoulos, "Weird Twitter: The Oral History," *BuzzFeed*, April 5, 2013, https://buzzfeednews.com/article/jwherrman/weird-twitter-the-oral-history; Leon Chang (@leyawn), "SOMEONE PUMP MY STOMACH ITS FULL OF EVIL," Twitter, June 26, 2009, https://twitter.com/leyawn/status/2349522508; @dril, "it is with a heavy heart that i must announce that the celebs are at it again," Twitter, September 24, 2014, https://twitter.com/dril/status/514845232509501440.
12. Martha Stewart (@MarthaStewart), "just got home, let out the dogs, within minutes they cornered,attacked and killed an opossum," Twitter, November 11, 2009, https://twitter.com/MarthaStewart/status/5638126088.
13. Britney Spears (@britneyspears), "Does anyone think global warming is a good thing? I love Lady Gaga," Twitter, February 10, 2011, https://twitter.com/britneyspears/status/35767743634481152.
14. Choire Sicha, "What Were Black People Talking About on

Twitter Last Night?," *The Awl*, November 11, 2009, https://medium.com/the-awl/what-were-black-people-talking-about-on-twitter-last-night-4408ca0ba3d6.

15. Farhad Manjoo, "How Black People Use Twitter," *Slate*, August 10, 2010, https://slate.com/technology/2010/08/how-black-people-use-twitter.html.
16. Zach Hull, "Stan Stories: Meet the Commander of Rihanna's Navy," *Paper*, June 6, 2019, https://papermag.com/stan-stories-rihanna-2638715945.html.
17. "Interview: Young Experts on How to Create a Legion of Followers from Tumblr to Twitter," *Brandwatch*, September 5, 2016, https://brandwatch.com/blog/react-interview-young-experts-on-how-to-create-a-legion-of-followers-from-tumblr-to-twitter/.
18. Brian Ries, "Justin Bieber and His Crazy Twitter Fans," *The Daily Beast*, September 9, 2010, https://thedailybeast.com/justin-bieber-and-his-crazy-twitter-fans.
19. Leena Rao, "Beyonce Pregnancy News at MTV VMAs Births New Twitter Record of 8,868 Tweets Per Second," *TechCrunch*, August 29, 2011, https://techcrunch.com/2011/08/29/beyonce-pregnancy-news-at-the-mtv-vmas-births-new-twitter-record-with-8868-tweets-per-second/.
20. Simon Owens, "The Secrets of Lady Gaga's Social Media Success," *The Next Web*, March 15, 2011, https://thenextweb.com/news/the-secrets-of-lady-gagas-social-media-success.
21. Lacey Rose, "Lady Gaga, Twitter Queen," *Forbes*, August 23, 2010, https://forbes.com/sites/laceyrose/2010/08/23/lady-gaga-twitter-queen/.
22. Lady Gaga, "An Inaugural Message from Tween Gaga," YouTube video, August 22, 2010, https://youtu.be/nyf4LGQdbB8.
23. Emily Yahr, "One Direction, Justin Bieber Fans in Epic Twitter Battles over MTV EMAs Voting," *The Washington Post*, October 28, 2014, https://washingtonpost.com/news/arts-and-entertainment/wp/2014/10/28/justin-bieber-one-direction-fans-in-epic-twitter-battle-over-mtv-emas-voting/.
24. This tweet seems to have been deleted. The quote and description are from a transcribed version in the author's notes.

25. *Billboard* staff, "Fan Army Face-Off: And the Winner Is . . . ," *Billboard*, August 18, 2014, https://billboard.com/articles/news/6221800/fan-army-face-off-winner.
26. Lewis Wiltshire, "2013: The Year on Twitter," Twitter blog, Twitter, December 11, 2013, https://blog.twitter.com/en_gb/a/en-gb/2013/2013-the-year-on-twitter.html.
27. Nicole Kelsey Santero, "'Nobody Can #DragMeDown': An Analysis of the One Direction Fandom's Ability to Influence and Dominate Worldwide Twitter Trends" (master's thesis, University of Nevada, Las Vegas, 2016).
28. Anonymous, "if taylor swift murders me DO NOT PROSECUTE HER," Twitter, November 24, 2019.
29. Anonymous, "he's so sexy break my back like a glow stick daddy," Twitter, November 25, 2019.
30. Target (@Target), "We have no choice but to stan," Twitter, January 16, 2020, https://twitter.com/target/status/1217856741897129985.
31. Brad Esposito, "Lady Gaga Fans Are Pretending to Be Soccer Moms on Twitter to Con Radio Stations," *BuzzFeed*, September 5, 2016, https://buzzfeed.com/bradesposito/soccer-moms-unite-for-gaga.
32. Andrew Martin, "#CuttingForBieber: Most Disturbing Hashtag of All Time?," *Complex Magazine*, January 7, 2013, https://complex.com/music/2013/01/cuttingforbieber-most-disturbing-hashtag-of-all-time.
33. Fernando Alfonso III, "#SkinFor1D: 4chan Hoax Asks Teens to Strip for One Direction," *The Daily Dot*, May 28, 2014, https://dailydot.com/unclick/one-direction-4chan-prank/.
34. Jonathan Heaf, "This One Direction Interview Got Us Death Threats," *GQ*, August 23, 2015, https://gq-magazine.co.uk/article/one-direction-gq-covers-interview.
35. "The Most Terrifying Responses to Our One Direction Covers," *GQ*, February 25, 2014, https://gq-magazine.co.uk/article/one-direction-gq-covers-most-terrifying-responses.
36. Angelina Chapin, "The Wrath of Beyoncé's Beyhive: How Fans Have Lost the Plot," *The Guardian*, April 30, 2016, https://theguardian.com/music/2016/apr/30/beyonce

-beyhive-fans-rachel-roy-lemonade. Roy denied the rumors and addressed the online harassment, tweeting: "I respect love, marriages, families and strength. What shouldn't be tolerated by anyone, no matter what, is bullying, of any kind."

37. Joe Coscarelli, "How One Tweet About Nicki Minaj Spiraled into Internet Chaos," *The New York Times*, July 10, 2018, https://nytimes.com/2018/07/10/arts/music/nicki-minaj-wanna-thompson-twitter-stans.html.
38. Laura Bradley, "Taylor Swift Remains Silent as Fans Doxx and Harass Music Critic over 'Folklore' Review," *The Daily Beast*, July 30, 2020, https://thedailybeast.com/taylor-swift-remains-silent-as-fans-doxx-and-harass-music-critic-over-folkore-review.
39. Katie Dey (@katie_dey), "my ass is fatter than taylor's at least," Twitter, July 24, 2020. This post was deleted after I saw it, but it is preserved in news coverage.
40. Katie Dey (@katie_dey), "i knew my fat ass would ruin my life someday didnt think itd go down like this tho," Twitter, July 24, 2020, https://twitter.com/katie_dey/status/1286867100737236992.
41. Michael Trice and Liza Potts, "Building Dark Patterns into Platforms: How GamerGate Perturbed Twitter's User Experience," *Present Tense: A Journal of Rhetoric in Society* 6, no. 3 (January 2018), https://presenttensejournal.org/volume-6/building-dark-patterns-into-platforms-how-gamergate-perturbed-twitters-user-experience/.
42. 1D Predictions (@1DPsychic), "This is the 6th Christmas without One Direction," Twitter, December 23, 2020, https://twitter.com/1DPsychic/status/1341813495785017345.
43. 1D Predictions (@1DPsychic), "Niall Horan will be the first to go bald," Twitter, January 13, 2021, https://twitter.com/1DPsychic/status/1349438620646699008.
44. 1D Predictions (@1DPsychic), "Louis Tomlinson will show us his wisdom teeth removal video," Twitter, March 1, 2021, https://web.archive.org/web/20210302003222/https://twitter.com/1DPsychic/status/1366539633027391488.
45. @fuckwesanderson, "help so my cousin got upset after read-

ing a fan fiction where harry styles dies and now she's been peeling potatoes for 3 hours," Twitter, February 3, 2017, https://twitter.com/fuckwesanderson/status/827487005885952000.

46. Lily Redman (@finelinelily), "Yesterday was like a breath of fresh air after literally one of the worst years of everyone's life," Twitter, July 24, 2020, https://twitter.com/finelinelily/status/1286665153258414081.

5. Trash

1. Morgan Rodriguez (@morganrodrigz), "what's up guys one direction ruined my life stop celebrating 10 years grow up if they didn't ruin you, you did it wrong," Twitter, July 23, 2020, https://twitter.com/morganrodrigz/status/1286164440250028032.
2. @bailiebonitaa, "the only time I get seratonin is when I watch videos about a stupid boyband that isn't even together anymore," Twitter, February 19, 2020, https://twitter.com/bailiebonitaaa/status/1230220030010445826.
3. Alexander Cho, "Sensuous Participation: Queer Youth of Color, Affect, and Social Media" (Ph.D. diss., University of Texas at Austin, 2015), 60.
4. Megan McNeeley, interview with the author, October 24, 2019.
5. Chiara Mueller, interview with the author, October 30, 2019.
6. Ashlynne Arnett, interview with the author, November 14, 2019.
7. Jacob Gaspar, interview with the author, October 1, 2019.
8. Daniel Cavicchi, *Tramps Like Us: Music and Meaning Among Springsteen Fans* (Oxford: Oxford University Press, 1998), 45–46.
9. Ibid., 43.
10. Ibid., 59.
11. Daniel Cavicchi, "Fandom Before 'Fan': Shaping the History of Enthusiastic Audiences," *Reception: Texts, Readers, Audiences, History* 6 (2014): 52–72, https://doi.org/10.5325/reception.6.1.0052.

12. Lilian Min, "The Strange Story of How Internet Superfans Reclaimed the Insult 'Trash,'" *Splinter*, May 19, 2016, https://splinternews.com/the-strange-story-of-how-internet-superfans-reclaimed-t-1793856895.
13. Henry Jenkins, interview with the author, November 5, 2019.
14. Dave Marsh, *Glory Days: Bruce Springsteen in the 1980s* (New York: Pantheon, 1987), 439.
15. Ibid., 16.
16. @LegitTayUpdates has been suspended from Twitter.
17. "Taking a Stan: An Interview with LegitTayUpdates," *Jacobin*, April 8, 2019, https://jacobinmag.com/2019/04/israel-defense-forces-taylor-swift-fan.
18. Abby Armada, interview with the author, November 15, 2019.
19. Cavicchi, *Tramps Like Us*, 157.
20. Janice Radway, *Reading the Romance: Women, Patriarchy, and Popular Literature* (Durham: University of North Carolina Press, 1984), 102.
21. Ibid., 109.
22. Ibid., 103–104.
23. Laura Vroomen, "This Woman's Work: Kate Bush, Female Fans, and Practices of Distinction" (Ph.D. diss., University of Warwick, 2002).
24. Angela Gibbs, interview with the author, October 11, 2019.
25. Liz Harvatine, interview with the author, September 25, 2019.
26. Lily Puckett, "I Think This Harry Styles Song Is About Abortion," *The Hairpin*, May 15, 2017, https://medium.com/the-hairpin/i-think-this-harry-styles-song-is-about-abortion-9f63e1ba9eb5.
27. Daniel Cavicchi, interview with the author, November 5, 2019.

6. Promo

1. Kaitlyn Tiffany, "Harry Styles Fans Are Trying to Beat the Billboard Charts with VPNS and Mass Coordination," *The*

Verge, May 5, 2017, https://theverge.com/2017/5/5/15533760/harry-styles-streaming-data-billboard-tumblr-fan-effort.

2. Stephen Duncombe, *Notes from Underground: Zines and the Politics of Alternative Culture* (Cleveland, OH: Microcosm, 1997), 102.
3. Maggie Malach, "Directioners Are Trying to Buy One Direction," *PopCrush*, April 3, 2015, https://popcrush.com/directioners-are-trying-to-buy-one-direction/.
4. Anna Franceschi, "Since this fandom is a black hole nowadays with no light at the end of the tunnel, I want to make a wish," Tumblr, May 11, 2015.
5. Anonymous, "1DHQ is like that lazy partner you were paired up with for a school project so you have to do the whole thing yourself," Tumblr, May 13, 2015.
6. Anonymous, "THE GAME PLAN: PROJECT NO CONTROL," Tumblr, May 16, 2015.
7. 1dstreetteam, "No Control iTunes Sponsorships!," Tumblr, May 16, 2015, https://1dstreetteam.tumblr.com/post/119130096269/no-control-itunes-sponsorships.
8. 1dstreetteam, "WE NEED SPONSORS FOR NO CONTROL!," Tumblr, May 17, 2015, https://1dstreetteam.tumblr.com/post/119200745774/we-need-sponsors-for-no-control.
9. Denny's Blog, "Denny's how you feel about No Control?" Tumblr, May 14, 2015, https://blog.dennys.com/post/118909537588/dennys-how-you-feel-about-no-control.
10. *The Late Late Show with James Corden*, "One Direction & James Talk 'No Control,'" YouTube video, May 15, 2015, https://youtu.be/a7nw4DQuI40.
11. "How My 'Random Idea' Led to a One Direction Single, Nearly," BBC News, May 13, 2015, https://bbc.com/news/newsbeat-32719530.
12. Katie Buenneke, "One Direction Is Now a DIY Band," *LA Weekly*, May 18, 2015, https://laweekly.com/one-direction-is-now-a-diy-band/.
13. beccasafan, Tumblr message to the author, June 5, 2021.

14. Anonymous, "It's finally time for Home Sponsorships!," Tumblr, April 24, 2016.
15. Kat Hazzard (@Kitty_16), "Also - I'm never going to end my one-woman campaign to get @onedirection and @benwinston to give us the finished(?) and buried music video for 'Infinity,'" Twitter, November 13, 2020, https://twitter.com/Kitty_16/status/1327343057855946754.
16. @voguecigrry, "JUST HAND IT OVER. WHATEVER IT IS, EVEN IF IT'S A 3 SECOND CLIP OF NIALL EXHALING," Twitter, November 13, 2020, https://twitter.com/voguecigrry/status/1327363427598098432.
17. @VictoriaPalms_, "ben have u seen the fancams this fandom makes? we dont care if its not edited chile we're shitty editing connoisseurs," Twitter, November 13, 2020, https://twitter.com/VictoriaPalms_/status/1327363262560817152.
18. Tiffany, "Harry Styles Fans Are Trying to Beat the Billboard Charts."
19. Ibid.
20. Sarah Thornton, *Club Cultures: Music, Media and Subcultural Capital* (New York: John Wiley and Sons, 1995), 137.
21. Olivia Diaz, interview with the author, August 13, 2020.
22. Olivia Diaz, "The Harry Styles Photo Dropper: A Campus Mystery," *The Review*, October 24, 2019, https://uvureview.com/valley-life/artsculture/the-harry-styles-photo-dropper/.
23. Anonymous "Harry Fairy," email to the author, August 16, 2020.
24. Anonymous "Harry Fairy," interview with the author, August 16, 2020.

7. Secrets

1. Ashley Hull, interview with the author, October 2, 2019.
2. Ashley Hull, email to the author, May 31, 2021.
3. "The Harry+Louis Treatise: Introduction," Tumblr, April 24, 2014, accessed via the Wayback Machine.
4. "The Harry+Louis Treatise: They are really in love," Tumblr, April 24, 2014, accessed via the Wayback Machine.

5. Anonymous, "In my opinion- Elevator is just a glorified dog sitter," Tumblr, February 28, 2018.
6. "Larrie," Fanlore, last modified September 22, 2019, https://fanlore.org/wiki/Larrie.
7. Mina Hughes, interview with the author, October 7, 2019.
8. Abby Armada, interview with the author, November 15, 2019.
9. Skye, interview with the author, October 9, 2019.
10. Skye, Tumblr message to the author, May 30, 2021.
11. Em, interview with the author, May 11, 2020.
12. Lisa, email to the author, September 21, 2019.
13. When I wrote to fact-check this book, I asked this blogger how she would like to be identified and told her that I would use a pseudonym if she did not state a preference. When she wrote back, she expressed concern about readers doxing her. She did not respond to my question about how to refer to her, but I've chosen the pseudonym Lisa to protect her identity.
14. Lisa, "FAQ - pinned," Tumblr, August 30, 2020.
15. Lisa, "i have no interest in engaging with antis," Tumblr, May 10, 2020.
16. Henry Jenkins, "An Archive Not of Their Own: Fan Fiction & Controversy in China," *Confessions of an Aca-Fan*, March 24, 2020, http://henryjenkins.org/blog/2020/3/24/an-archive-not-of-their-own-fan-fiction-controversy-in-china.
17. Xing Li, "This will be longest announcement in FanFiction.Net's 4 year history," Fanfiction.net, September 12, 2002, accessed via the Wayback Machine, https://web.archive.org/web/20020929011210/http://www.fanfiction.net:80/.
18. "Strikethrough and Boldthrough," Fanlore, last modified May 11, 2020, https://fanlore.org/wiki/Strikethrough_and_Boldthrough.
19. Anna Martin, "Writing the Star: Stardom, Fandom, and Real Person Fanfiction" (Ph.D. diss., Trinity College, 2014), 61.
20. Ibid., 70.
21. Em, interview with the author, May 11, 2020.

22. Louis Tomlinson (@louis_tomlinson), "Always in my heart @Harry_Styles," Twitter, October 2, 2011, https://twitter.com/louis_tomlinson/status/120620074301267968.
23. "The Harry+Louis Treatise: Public narratives," Tumblr, April 24, 2014, accessed via the Wayback Machine.
24. Hannah McCann and Clare Southerton, "Repetitions of Desire: Queering the One Direction Fangirl," *Girlhood Studies* 12, no. 1 (Spring 2019).
25. Angela Gibbs, interview with the author, October 11, 2019.
26. Duncan Cooper, "Zayn Malik's Next Direction," *The Fader*, November 17, 2015, https://thefader.com/2015/11/17/zayn-malik-fader-cover-story-interview-solo-album-one-direction.
27. "The Harry+Louis Treatise: Tattoos," Tumblr, April 24, 2014, accessed via the Wayback Machine.
28. Louis Tomlinson (@Louis_Tomlinson), "Hows this , Larry is the biggest load of bullshit I've ever heard," Twitter, September 16, 2012, https://twitter.com/louis_tomlinson/status/247381724760264704.
29. "The Harry+Louis Treatise: Denials and management," Tumblr, April 24, 2014, accessed via the Wayback Machine.
30. *Crazy About One Direction*, directed by Daisy Asquith (2013; London: Channel 4).
31. Liam Payne (@LiamPayne), "Not really sure what's going on right now I just hope everyone's ok xxx," Twitter, August 16, 2013, https://twitter.com/liampayne/status/368276090747645952.
32. Alexander Abad-Santos, "The Internet Is Mourning 42 Suicidal, Potentially Non-Existent One Direction Fans," *The Atlantic*, August 16, 2013, https://theatlantic.com/culture/archive/2013/08/internet-mourning-42-suicidal-one-direction-fans-might-not-even-exist/312076/.
33. Gavia Baker-Whitelaw, "Suicide Rumors Spread After Documentary About One Direction Fandom," *The Daily Dot*, August 16, 2013, https://dailydot.com/parsec/fandom/suicide-rumors-one-direction-riplarryshippers-documentary/.
34. Daisy Asquith, "Crazy About One Direction: Whose Shame

Is It Anyway?" in *Seeing Fans*, ed. Paul Booth and Lucy Bennett (London: Bloomsbury Academic, 2016), 79–88.

35. Harry Styles (@Harry_Styles), "We don't need no piece of paper from the city hall," Twitter, September 29, 2013, https://twitter.com/Harry_Styles/status/384267513388744705.
36. Em, interview with the author, May 11, 2020.

8. Proof

1. Mina Hughes, interview with the author, October 7, 2019.
2. Kelly Conaboy, "Michael Strahan Forces Louis Tomlinson to Admit Impending Fatherhood," *Gawker*, August 4, 2015, http://defamer.gawker.com/michael-strahan-forces-louis-tomlinson-to-admit-impendi-1721982739.
3. Rachel Zarrell, "Stylist Is Pregnant with Louis Tomlinson's Baby, Her Ex-Stepdad Confirms," *BuzzFeed News*, July 15, 2015, https://buzzfeednews.com/article/rachelzarrell/ex-stepdad-of-briana-jungwirth-confirms-shes-pregnant-with-l.
4. Anonymous, "BABYGATE IN PICTURES PART 2. - FORESHADOWING BABYGATE," Tumblr, April 15, 2016.
5. Sex at Oxbridge, interview with the author. Details were confirmed with screenshots, and they had previously been described on Tumblr: Sex at Oxbridge, "People bringing up that Buzzfeed BG article which basically stole everything I wrote," Tumblr, August 8, 2019, https://sexatoxbridge.tumblr.com/post/186865953928/sexatoxbridge-sexatoxbridge-people-bringing.
6. Sex at Oxbridge, "Please educate yourself," Tumblr, September 3, 2016. This post was deleted after I saw it, but was excerpted on another Tumblr.
7. Sex at Oxbridge, "Is Louis Tomlinson's Bizarre Behavior Actually Just Him Mocking Simon Cowell?," email newsletter, June 3, 2016, https://us4.campaign-archive.com/?u=a7fddf71a60dcd3a599d22f6c&id=e68c985fa4.
8. Sex at Oxbridge, email to the author, June 2, 2021.
9. Lisa, "3: The Immaculate Conception," Tumblr, April 19,

2020. This post was deleted after I read it, but was preserved through reblogs on other accounts.

10. Anonymous, "protect briana jungwirth," Tumblr, July 14, 2015.
11. Anonymous, "Not to give that attention seeker what she wants," Tumblr, July 14, 2015. This post was deleted after I read it, but was preserved through reblogs on other accounts.
12. Lisa, "14: The Makeover," Tumblr, April 19, 2020. This post was deleted after I read it, but was preserved through reblogs on other accounts.
13. Lisa, "11: Paparazzi, Tabloids, and Babies - Oh My!," Tumblr post, April 19, 2020. This post was deleted after I read it, but was preserved through reblogs on other accounts.
14. Lisa, "11: Paparazzi, Tabloids, and Babies."
15. Anonymous, "Briana The Exception™" Tumblr, February 20, 2016. This post was deleted after I read it, but it was preserved through reblogs on other accounts.
16. Ellie Woodward, "There's a Wild Conspiracy Theory That Louis Tomlinson's Baby Is Fake," *BuzzFeed*, April 7, 2016, https://buzzfeed.com/elliewoodward/theres-a-conspiracy-theory-that-louis-tomlinsons-baby-is-fak.
17. Megan Collins, interview with the author, October 30, 2019.
18. Kaitlyn Tiffany, "How a Fake Baby Is Born," *The Atlantic*, July 13, 2020, https://theatlantic.com/technology/archive/2020/07/fake-pregnancy-celebrity-theories-benedict-cumberbacth-babygate/614089/.
19. Angela Gibbs, interview with the author, October 11, 2019.
20. Richard Lawson, interview with the author, September 8, 2020.
21. This post was deleted after I read it, and I relied on my notes.
22. Weirdetta, "The problem with babygate," Tumblr, April 17, 2020.
23. Anna Martin, "Writing the Star: Stardom, Fandom, and Real Person Fanfiction" (Ph.D. diss., Trinity College, 2014).
24. Mary, Tumblr messages to the author, May 11, 2020.

25. Lisa, "1: Introduction," Tumblr, April 19, 2020. This post was deleted after I read it, but was preserved through reblogs on other accounts.
26. Anonymous, "I can't believe they're trying to pull off a Zigi baby," Tumblr, April 29, 2020.
27. Anonymous, "I think they end these babygate like this," Tumblr, May 20, 2020.
28. @celebrity_reality__, "If zayn confirms it in his social media dont worry," Instagram, April 30, 2020, https://instagram.com/p/B_n81uKFmUTTrY_6snpA3FCuolFX9zkJVsMEV0o/.

9. Belonging

1. Niall Horan (@NiallOfficial), "Cmon Ireland ! This is your day to make another great decision," Twitter, May 25, 2018, https://twitter.com/NiallOfficial/status/999944836160655361.
2. Naomi Fry, "The Trouble with Elon Musk and Grimes," *The New Yorker*, May 10, 2018, https://newyorker.com/culture/annals-of-appearances/the-trouble-with-elon-musk-and-grimes.
3. "One Direction's Harry Planning to Restore Niall's Barack Obama Waxwork," Capital FM, December 15, 2011, https://capitalfm.com/artists/one-direction/news/niall-barack-obama-waxwork/.
4. Megan C. Hills, "One Direction Were Kicked Out of a Trump Hotel for a Selfish Reason," *Marie Claire*, June 20, 2018, https://marieclaire.co.uk/neaws/celebrity-news/one-direction-trump-hotel-603502.
5. Niall Horan (@NiallOfficial), "@realDonaldTrump Wish you would use common sense before you open your mouth," Twitter, April 26, 2020, https://twitter.com/niallofficial/status/1254379636324290560.
6. Niall Horan (@NiallOfficial), "THUGS ?? these people are protesting against the fact that one of YOUR animalistic white policemen kneeled on George's windpipe and forced him to stop breathing and killed him??," Twitter, May 29,

2020, https://twitter.com/niallofficial/status/1266319868636389377.

7. Niall Horan (@NiallOfficial), "I wish I could vote in this election," Twitter, October 28, 2020, https://twitter.com/NiallOfficial/status/1321409661334151168; Harry Styles (@Harry_Styles), "If I could vote in America, I'd vote with kindness," Twitter, October 27, 2020, https://twitter.com/harry_styles/status/1321174540223795201.
8. Allyson Gross, "To Wave a Flag: Identification, #BlackLivesMatter, and Populism in Harry Styles Fandom," *Transformative Works and Cultures* 32 (2020), https://doi.org/10.3983/twc.2020.1765.
9. Gabrielle Foster, interview with the author, May 3, 2020.
10. @sorrybythway, "@Harry_Styles use your fucking platform," Twitter, November 1, 2017, https://twitter.com/sorrybythway/status/925859725635411968.
11. Anonymous, "I love harry he's my safest place but I feel so disconnected," Twitter, November 1, 2017.
12. Anonymous, "You flower, you white feministe," Twitter, November 1, 2017.
13. Harry Styles (@harrystyles), "Love," Instagram, November 2, 2017, https://instagram.com/p/Ba_3ik2DUXH/.
14. Chris Thomas, "Harry Styles: 'If You Are Black, White, Gay, Straight, Transgender . . . I Support You,'" *Out*, November 6, 2017, https://out.com/music/2017/11/06/harry-styles-if-you-are-black-white-gay-straight-transgender-i-support-you.
15. Taylor Weatherby, "Liam Payne Is Not Homophobic, and Here's His Twitter Rant to Prove It," *Billboard*, August 19, 2015, https://billboard.com/articles/news/6670349/liam-payne-homophobic-accusation-twitter-response.
16. Tyler Scruggs, interview with the author, October 21, 2019.
17. Kat Lewis, email exchange with the author, October 28, 2020.
18. Bri Mattia, "Rainbow Direction and Fan-Based Citizenship Performance," *Journal of Transformative Works* 28 (2018), https://doi.org/10.3983/twc.2018.1414.
19. Christian Guiltenane, "Liam Payne Talks Homophobia Ac-

cusations and Gay 1D Fan Fiction," *Attitude*, issue 262, October 2015, https://attitude.co.uk/article/liam-payne-talks-homophobia-accusations-and-gay-1d-fan-fiction-in-attitude-archive-interview/14635/.

20. Ezz Mbamalu, interview with the author, November 1, 2019.
21. Ezz Mbamalu (@Nipsstagram), "BROWN SKIN AND LEMON OVER ICE!!!!! THE BLACKS HAVE FINALLY WON!," Twitter, December 6, 2019, https://twitter.com/Nipsstagram/status/1202820299315666944.
22. @angeIsofcoIour, "harries of colour this one is going in the history books," Twitter, December 6, 2019, https://twitter.com/angeIsofcoIour/status/1202822520585388033.
23. Elul Adoga, interview with the author, November 19, 2019.
24. The Black Harries Matter Twitter account (@blckharries) has since been suspended. I was unable to contact Gabrielle Foster to learn why, because our conversations took place over Twitter messages.
25. Rob Sheffield, "The Eternal Sunshine of Harry Styles," *Rolling Stone*, August 26, 2019, https://rollingstone.com/music/music-features/harry-styles-cover-interview-album-871568/.
26. Kaitlyn Tiffany, "Why K-Pop Fans Are No Longer Posting About K-Pop," *The Atlantic*, June 6, 2020, https://theatlantic.com/technology/archive/2020/06/twitter-k-pop-protest-black-lives-matter/612742/.
27. Teo Bugbee, "Structure! Sabotage! Salvation! K-Pop Has It All," *SSENSE*, July 16, 2020, https://ssense.com/en-us/editorial/culture/structure-sabotage-salvation-k-pop-has-it-all.
28. Jessica Pruett, interview with the author, November 1, 2019.
29. 1dgaymagines, Tumblr, https://1dgaymagines.tumblr.com.

10. Power

1. Kaitlyn Tiffany, "The People Who Really, Really Love Mark Zuckerberg," *The Atlantic*, October 22, 2019, https://theatlantic.com/technology/archive/2019/10/the-biggest-fans-of-mark-zuckerberg-and-facebook/600490/.

2. Kaitlyn Tiffany, "The Creepy Trump Meme Taking Over Twitter," *The Atlantic*, October 7, 2020, https://theatlantic.com/technology/archive/2020/10/trump-coronavirus-hex-stan-twitter/616589/.
3. Stuart Hall and Tony Jefferson, *Resistance Through Rituals: Youth Subcultures in Post-War Britain*, 2nd ed. (New York: Routledge, 2006), 7.
4. Ibid., 36–37.
5. Angela McRobbie and Jenny Garber, "Girls and Subcultures," in *Resistance Through Rituals: Youth Subcultures in Post-War Britain*, 2nd ed., edited by Stuart Hall and Tony Jefferson (New York: Routledge, 2006), 420.
6. Ibid., 424.
7. Ibid., 441.
8. Ibid., 442.
9. Jenny Garber, "Girls and Subcultures," in *Feminism and Youth Culture, Youth Questions* (London: Palgrave Macmillan, 1991), https://doi.org/10.1007/978-1-349-21168-5_1.
10. Mary Celeste Kearney, "Productive Spaces: Girls' Bedrooms as Sites of Cultural Production," *Journal of Children and Media* 1, no. 2 (2007): 126–41, https://doi.org/10.1080/17482790701339126.
11. Ibid.
12. Kaitlyn Tiffany, "Why K-Pop Fans Are No Longer Posting About K-Pop," *The Atlantic*, June 6, 2020, https://theatlantic.com/technology/archive/2020/06/twitter-k-pop-protest-black-lives-matter/612742/.
13. Lori Morimoto (@acafanmom), "Seriously, people. Seriously - fan studies is a fucking thing," Twitter, June 21, 2020, https://twitter.com/acafanmom/status/1274745051441246208.
14. Tiffany, "Why K-Pop Fans Are No Longer Posting About K-Pop."
15. Lori Morimoto, interview with the author, September 17, 2020.
16. Zina, interview with the author, September 19, 2020.

17. r/kpop, Reddit, https://www.reddit.com/r/kpop/. This thread was deleted after I read it, and I relied on my notes.
18. Abby Olheiser, "TikTok Teens and K-Pop Stans Don't Belong to the 'Resistance,'" *MIT Technology Review*, June 23, 2020, https://technologyreview.com/2020/06/23/1004336/tiktok-teens-kpop-stans-trump-resistance-its-complicated/.
19. David Kushner, "The Masked Avengers," *The New Yorker*, September 1, 2014, https://newyorker.com/magazine/2014/09/08/masked-avengers.
20. @youranonnews, "Anonymous stans ALL KPop allies!," Twitter, June 3, 2020, https://twitter.com/youranonnews/status/1268150512421154816.
21. Andrew Griffin, "Anonymous Activists and K-Pop Fans Enjoy Unexpected Allegiance as They Join Black Lives Matter Protests," *The Independent*, June 3, 2020, https://independent.co.uk/life-style/gadgets-and-tech/news/anonymous-k-pop-black-lives-matter-george-floyd-protests-a9547401.html.
22. r/kpop, Reddit, https://www.reddit.com/r/kpop/. This thread was deleted after I read it, and I relied on my notes.

Conclusion: 1Dead

1. Cameron Crowe, "Harry Styles' New Direction," *Rolling Stone*, April 18, 2017, https://rollingstone.com/feature/harry-styles-new-direction-119432/.
2. Kaitlyn Tiffany, "How Ticketmaster's Verified Fan Program Toys with the Passions of Fandom," *The Verge*, February 7, 2018, https://theverge.com/2018/2/7/16923616/ticketmaster-verified-fan-tumblr-reddit-taylor-swift-harry-styles.
3. Kaitlyn Tiffany, "How to Succeed in Business by Being a Taylor Swift Fan," *Vox*, November 7, 2018, https://vox.com/the-goods/2018/11/7/18068564/taylor-swift-update-account-twitter-fandom-profit.
4. Kaitlyn Tiffany, "Running a Celebrity News Account Is No Joke," *The Verge*, June 15, 2017, https://theverge.com/2017/6/15/15796580/celebrity-fan-account-lorde-news-day-in-the-life-process.

5. Ticketmaster (@Tickemaster), "My best friend in high school had a 1D ship account on Tumblr," Twitter, July 23, 2020, https://twitter.com/Ticketmaster/status/1286380350764126208.
6. @emellydt, "I STILL CANNOT GET OVER THIS FEATURE," TikTok video, July 1, 2020, https://tiktok.com/@emellydt/video/6844635091969314054.

ACKNOWLEDGMENTS

One Direction—I love you! Thank you for all that you've done for me without really trying.

Thank you to my agent, Laura Usselman, who got me and this idea immediately. (Our first conversation was as thrilling as the best first date you can imagine—I remember what I wore, but not what I ate.) Thank you to Jackson Howard for taking a "chonce" on a book about a boy band that *doesn't exist anymore*, and for so kindly punching a first draft of a first book into the shape of something I didn't want to disown.

Thank you to my editors at *The Verge* and *Vox* and *The Atlantic*—especially Chris Plante, the last great blogger, and Julia Rubin, the world's humblest visionary. Thank you to Amelia Holowaty-Krales, my favorite photographer! Thank you to my parents for their unconditional stan behavior, to my sisters for calling me a "fake fan" whenever I missed a meme, and to all the brilliant friends who help me think through everything, without whom I would be very lonely and very stupid: Katie, Stephanie, Tamar, Lizzie, Ashley, James, and Sam, my New York heroes. Thank you to Nathan for watching *parts* of the One Direction documentary and for being so tall and composed in a crisis.

Finally, thank you to all the One Direction fans who spoke to me for this book. It's an honor simply to be mutuals.